< OUTDOOR >

Photographer's Handbook

<OUTDOOR> Photographer's Handbook

Barry and Cathy Beck

STACKPOLE
BOOKS

Published by
STACKPOLE BOOKS
5067 Ritter Road
Mechanicsburg, PA 17055
www.stackpolebooks.com

Printed in China

First edition

10 9 8 7 6 5 4 3 2 1

Photographs by Barry and Cathy Beck
Cover design by Tracy Patterson

Library of Congress Cataloging-in-Publication Data

Beck, Barry.
Outdoor photographer's handbook / Barry and Cathy Beck.— 1st ed.
p. cm.
Includes index.
ISBN 0-8117-3120-0 (alk. paper)
1. Outdoor photography—Handbooks, manuals, etc. I. Beck, Cathy.
II. Title.
TR659.5.B43 2004
778.7'1—dc22

2003025411

< CONTENTS >

	Introduction	vii
Chapter 1	*Film Cameras*	1
Chapter 2	*Digital Cameras*	17
Chapter 3	*Light and Composition*	27
Chapter 4	*Flash*	41
Chapter 5	*Your Camera Bag*	47
Chapter 6	*Having Fun with Your Camera*	53
Chapter 7	*Taking Better Fishing Photos*	71
	Tips	85
	Index	89

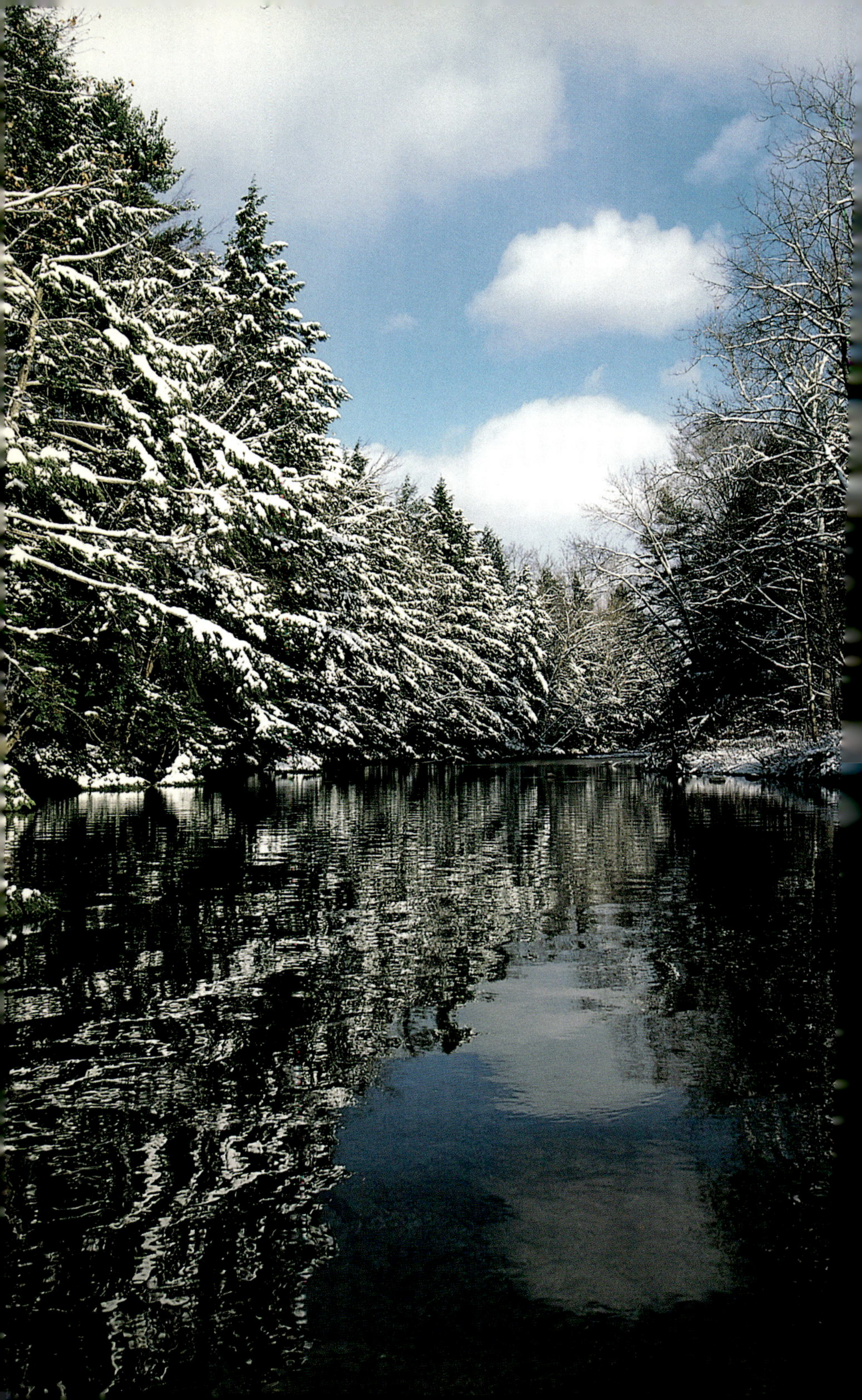

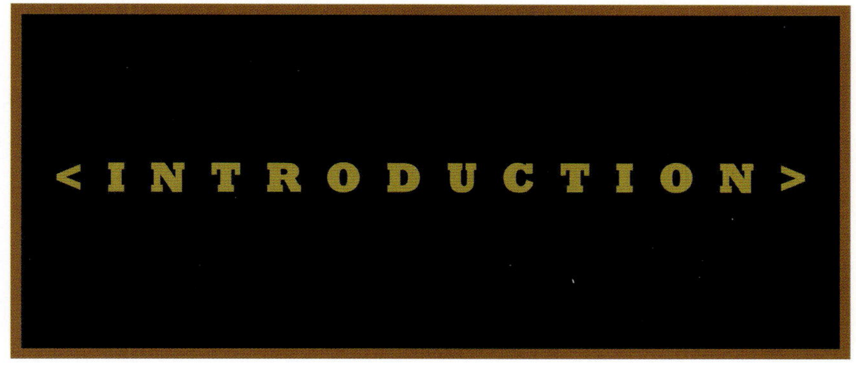

< I N T R O D U C T I O N >

Making pictures is a way of life for us. We spend a good part of our year traveling for Frontiers International, one of the world's largest sporting travel agencies. Our responsibilities range from hosting fly-fishing trips around the world in both fresh and salt water to leading African photo safaris. Part of each trip, regardless of its destination, is to photograph the lodges we visit, our clients having fun, and scenes Frontiers can use in its brochures and travel ads. In addition to the Frontiers' connection, we run our own stock photography business selling book and magazine publishers, calendar companies, and other commercial clients a wide selection of images of outdoor subjects, including fly fishing, wildlife, horses, cats, dogs, wildflowers, insects, and people.

As professionals who spend much of our lives working and playing outdoors, we appreciate the natural world and want to capture its beauty on film. The possibilities are endless: snow-capped volcanoes, fog-shrouded misty mornings, flower-covered vistas, a rainbow after a storm, a newborn zebra's first steps, or a baby calf on the farm next to us. And then there are friends and

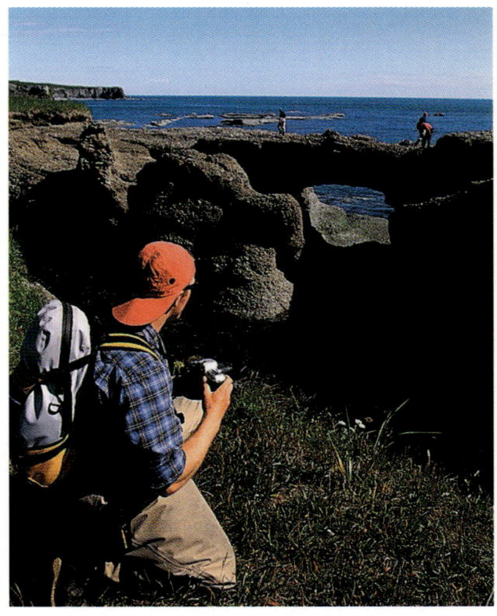

A photo opportunity on the coast of Alaska.

Left: *A spectacular winter day shows the reflection of the snow on Fishing Creek.*

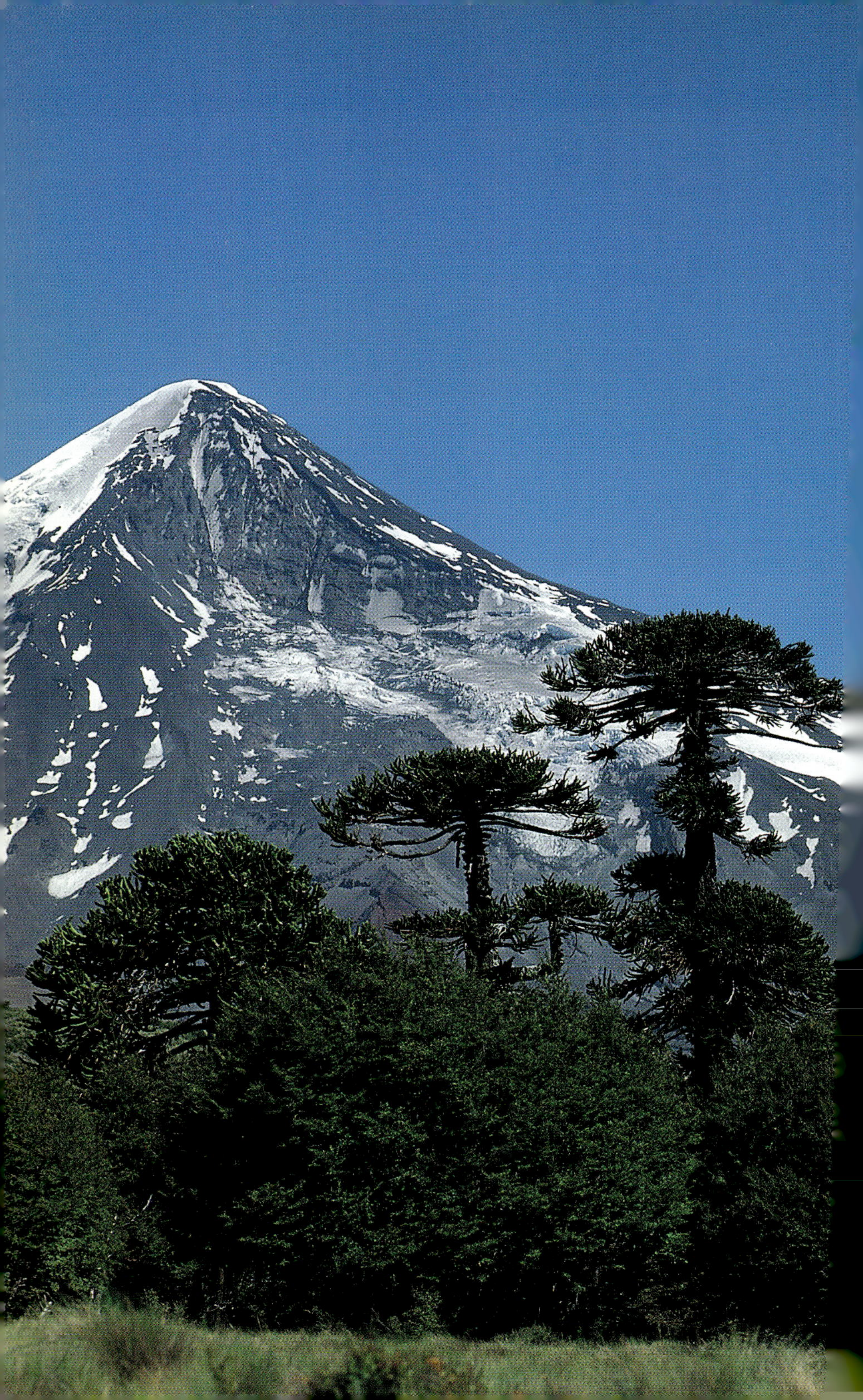

family, birthday parties, picnics, and graduations. Photographs record those special moments, and today's technology has given us an impressive selection of cameras to choose from, starting with incredibly easy to use point-and-shoot cameras to highly technical systems—and everything in between. Today we have the choice of film or digital with memory cards and scanners and photo editing software programs that allow us the creative freedom to work in our computer darkrooms to create our own images.

The idea for this book came from friends and clients who, once back from trips, would call to tell us how disappointed they were with their photos. We would hear stories of washed-out prints or images that were too dark and almost always about how fuzzy a lot of their pictures were. We heard of all the missed opportunities and how, if they had the chance to do it over again, they would shoot more film. There was often the story about the big fish—the fish looks great but the angler blinked at the very moment the shutter clicked, and it only clicked once, so now he's got a photograph of him and his big fish . . . with his eyes closed.

And the bad pictures are just part of the story. There are the travelers who show up without film or film that is outdated. There are cameras with dead batteries and no fresh ones. "I just used it last summer and the battery was good. . . ." Or the time that a good friend brought along one roll of film for a two-week trip in southern Argentina. He told us he had never in his life shot more than one roll of film on a trip. It turned out to be the trip of a lifetime and he ended up buying photographs from us.

If you sometimes find yourself in one of these situations, then this guide is for you. We want to encourage you to take more and better pictures. We promise to keep our suggestions clear and simple. We want to help you take photographs you can be proud to show. Photography should and can be fun.

Special thanks to our editors, Judith Schnell and Amy Lerner at Stackpole Books, for their patience and guidance, and for understanding that photographers are happiest in the field making pictures rather then sitting in front of their computers trying to write about them. Thanks also go to Ron Taniwaki at Nikon for his friendship and technical assistance, Terry Panasuk at F-11 in Bozeman, Montana, for always taking good care of our lab needs, and outdoor photographer Denver Bryan for all his inspiration over the years.

Lanin Volcano with monkey puzzle trees in the foreground that date to the time of Christ.

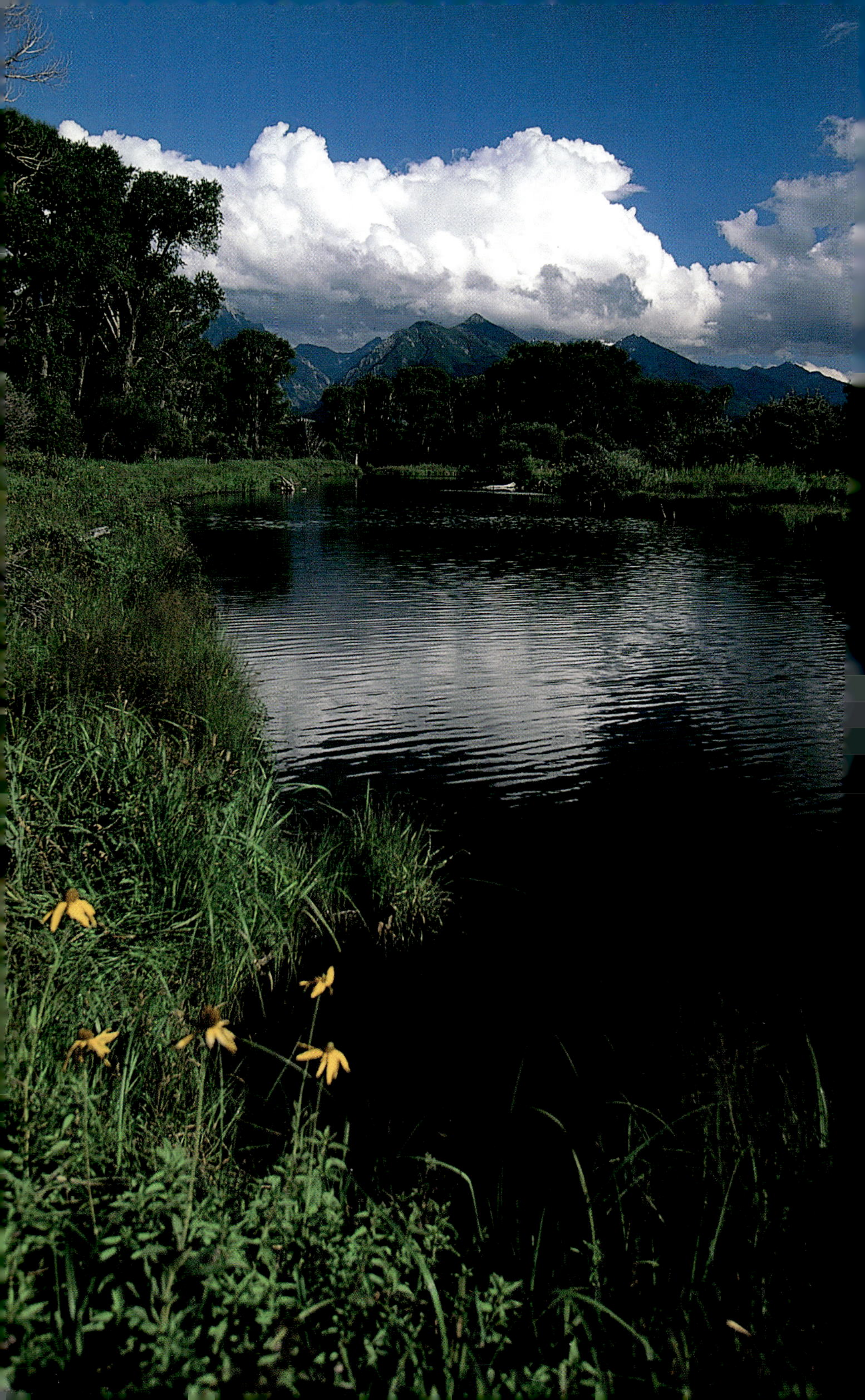

< CHAPTER 1 >

Film Cameras

When it comes to selecting a camera, there are so many choices you can quickly get overwhelmed shopping for one. Your camera should include the features you need to accomplish your photographic goals. The controls should be easy to use, and the price should fit your budget. Like a good glove, your camera should feel comfortable in your hand. A quick look in any photo magazine or camera shop and you'll find everything from point-and-shoot models, SLRs (single-lens reflex), and medium- and large-format cameras. Film camera formats are based on the size of the film frame, which varies from the smaller APS (advanced photo systems) and 35mm, to the 11 x 14-inch film sheets used by professionals.

POINT-AND-SHOOT CAMERAS

Of all the options, the small, efficient 35mm point-and-shoot cameras are the most popular. These cameras are easy to use, with most having a built-in zoom lens and permanently attached flash, auto focusing, and automatic exposure. Getting a picture is as easy as looking through the viewfinder, composing the shot, and pressing the shutter button. These cameras are generally small enough

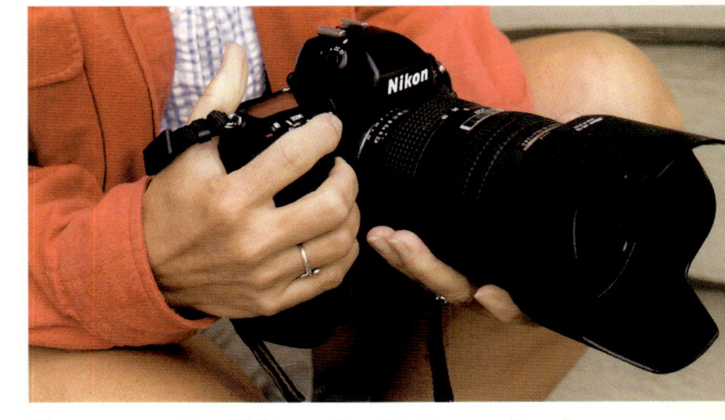

Your camera should fit comfortably in your hand.

***Left:** The Gallatin Range is reflected on DePuys Spring Creek in the Paradise Valley of Montana.*

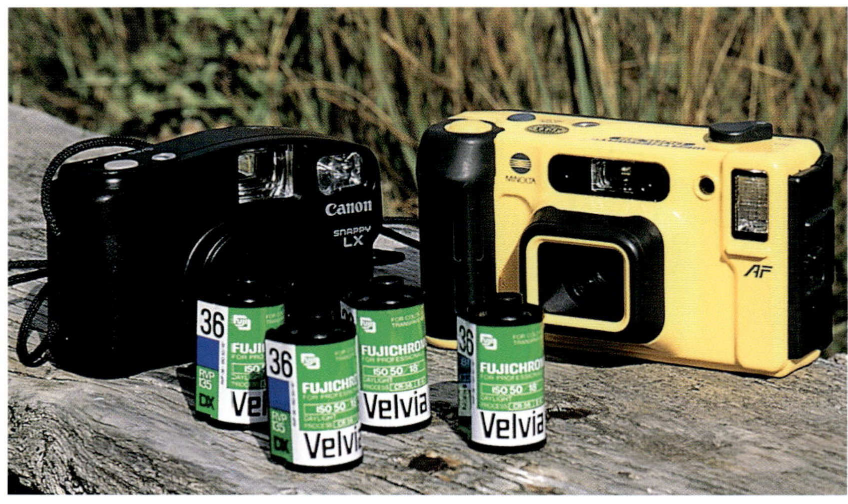

Of all the options, a small, efficient 35mm point-and-shoot camera is the most popular.

to fit in a coat pocket, and submersible models are available for underwater photography. One downfall of the point-and-shoot camera, however, is that you view the image through a second lens and not the lens that actually takes the picture, so your framing may not be entirely accurate. Keep in mind, too, that the cheaper models have low-quality lenses, which can produce images that may not be up to your standards. If you stay with one of the better models, you will be happy with the results. Serious photographers often downplay the point-and-shoot cameras as mere toys, but the good ones can be a lot of fun and no hassle, and you'll get good pictures with them.

Get acquainted with your camera controls. Most manufacturers now include a Quick Start set of directions with a new camera to quickly get you shooting. The Quick Start version will help you load the batteries and film and set the automatic program, letting the camera make all of your exposure decisions for you. Down the road you will want to explore all of your camera's options and become completely familiar with the owner's manual. The average instruction manual can be one hundred fifty pages of information! Take it one step at a time and have fun.

SLR CAMERAS

Today's choice for photographers who want to take their photography to the next level is the SLR. With an

SLR you look through the actual lens, so what you see is what you get—at least as far as framing is concerned. One advantage of the SLR camera is the ability to change lenses. Lenses range from the super wide and fish-eye to the normal ranges to the longer and super telephoto. Another advantage is having the option of controlling exposure: You can have total control of your exposures or, if you like, you can rely on the camera to automatically decide the exposure. Most of the better SLRs offer four options: an automatic program where the camera makes all of the decisions for you, a shutter priority program where you select the shutter speed and the camera picks the corresponding f-stop, an aperture priority mode where you choose the f-stop and the camera picks the corresponding shutter speed, and finally a manual mode where you make all of the decisions.

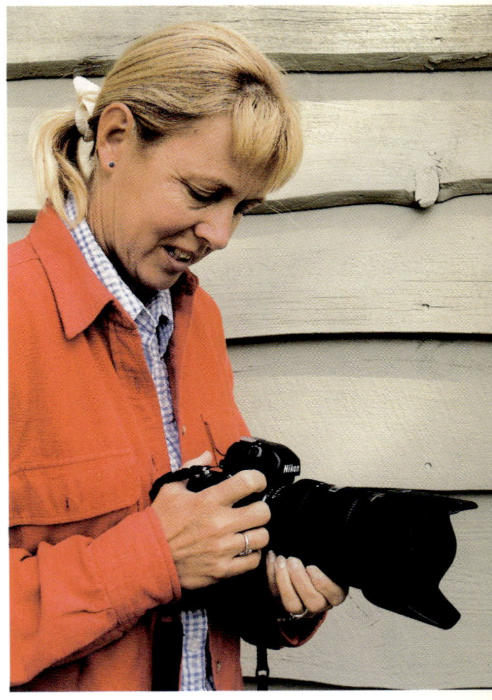

The Nikon F-100 is a good choice if you are looking for an SLR.

Meters

Metering is the way the light meter in your camera measures light. The intensity or brightness of light and tone is reflected from your subject through the lens to your camera's meter and measured to create the proper exposure value. Metering modes vary from one camera to the next, but on our Nikon SLRs we rely on three modes. The first is 3D color matrix, the second is center weighted, and the third is spot metering.

Matrix metering is almost always our first choice, especially when we are using the automatic program on the camera. In other words, we let the camera make our exposure decisions. This is especially useful when our subjects are on the move. Matrix metering can save the day when it comes to measuring brightness, contrast, and color in complex lighting situations. A microcomputer built into the camera reads the different

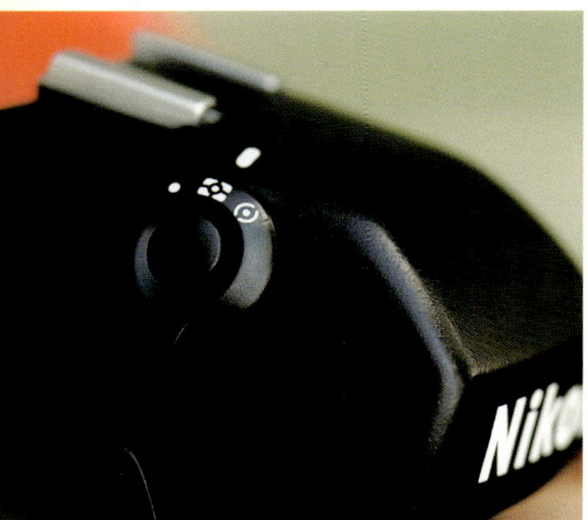

Metering modes on a Nikon SLR include spot, matrix, and center weighted.

areas of the image and then calculates the varying light levels to determine an exposure based on brightness and contrast.

Center-weighted metering works best when we want to base an exposure on a specific area of the image. In center-weighted metering, approximately 75 percent of the meter's sensitivity is concentrated on an 8mm to 15mm diameter circle within the center of the camera's viewfinder, making it best suited for portraits or other situations where the main subject is the primary factor for the exposure.

Spot metering puts nearly 100 percent of the meter's sensitivity on a 4mm diameter area within the selected focus area. Instead of reading the overall brightness, the spot meter concentrates on 1 percent of the entire area. This setting is very effective in difficult lighting situations where there is a lot of contrast and you're targeting a specific detail and is useful for highly selective exposure control.

Focus

Almost all SLRs offer a choice of either auto or manual focus. If you're in the market for a new camera, we would recommend a model that offers both. We have found that we rely on auto focus for almost all of our shooting—it's quick and tack sharp and it's especially useful in low-light situations. At the same time, having the manual option is useful when you want a critical area in a stationary image to be in focus, the eye in a portrait for instance, and when you want to create off-center compositions without using spot metering.

The horizon is curved in this photo of a bonefish taken with a wide-angle lens.

LENSES

Your film camera is technically a light box that holds the film. It's the lens and your composition that really make the image. Camera lenses come in different focal lengths, and this focal length will have a dramatic effect on the image. Most of the better point-and-shoot cameras have a zoom lens rather than a lens with a fixed focal length. This zoom lens normally falls somewhere between 28mm and 80mm. This is a great range to work with. At 28mm the lens is a fairly wide angle and at 80mm it's a short telephoto. In between you have the 35mm and 50mm ranges, which are the all-time favorites of many photographers.

One of the advantages of most SLRs is being able to change lenses. You can use the super-wide-angle lenses that start at 6mm and go up to 20mm or the wide angles, 24mm,

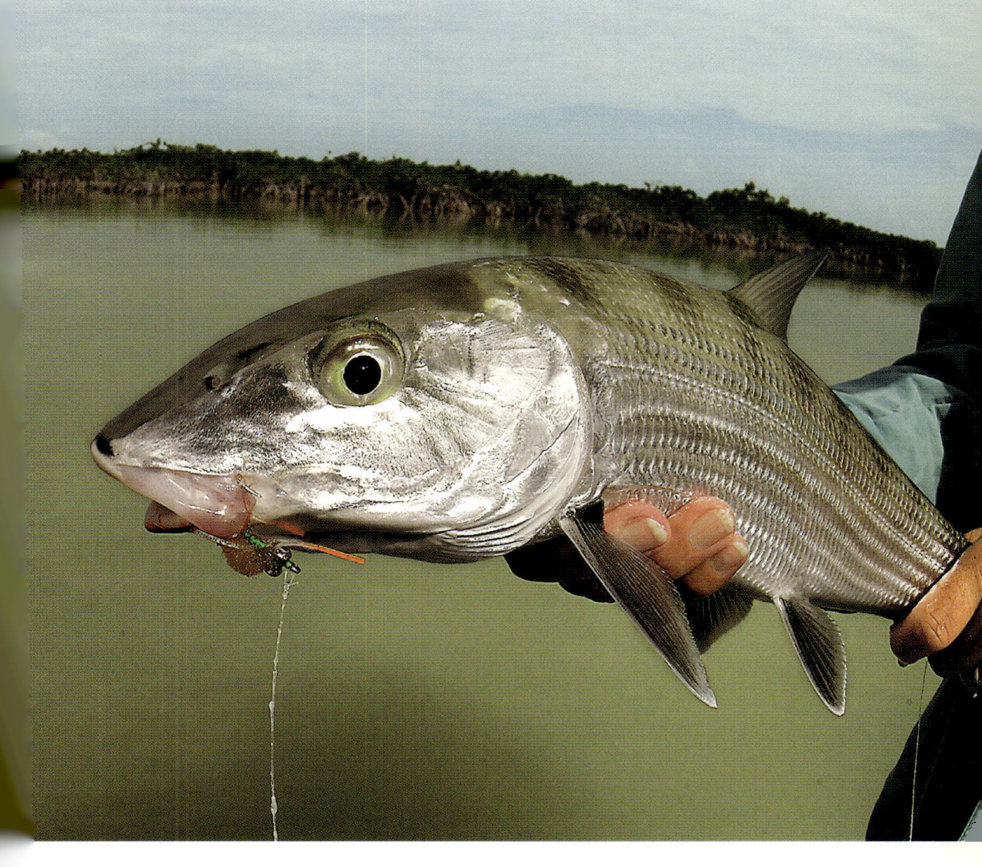

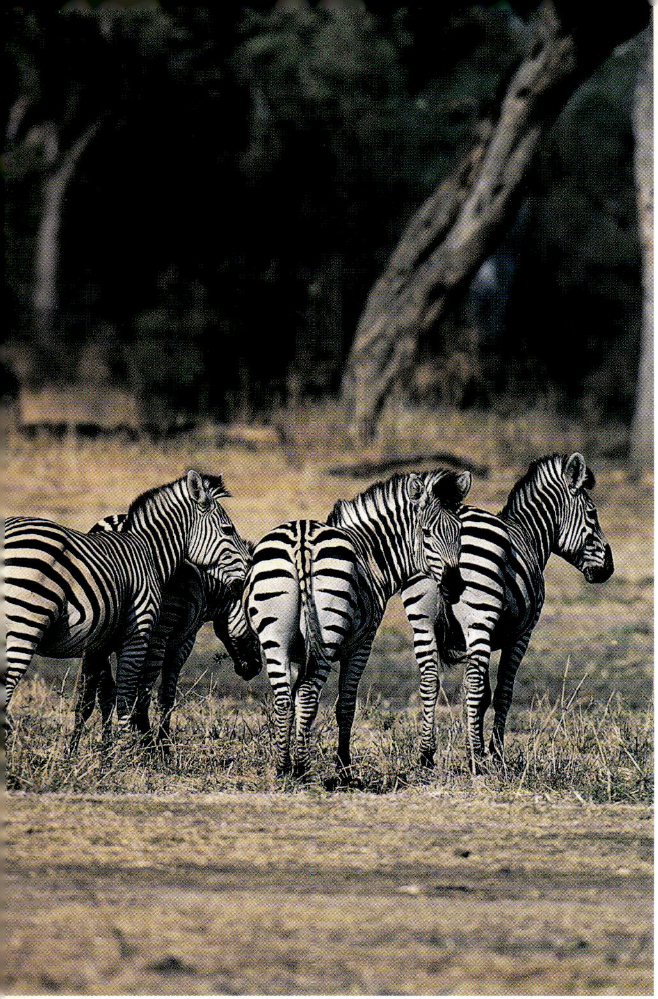

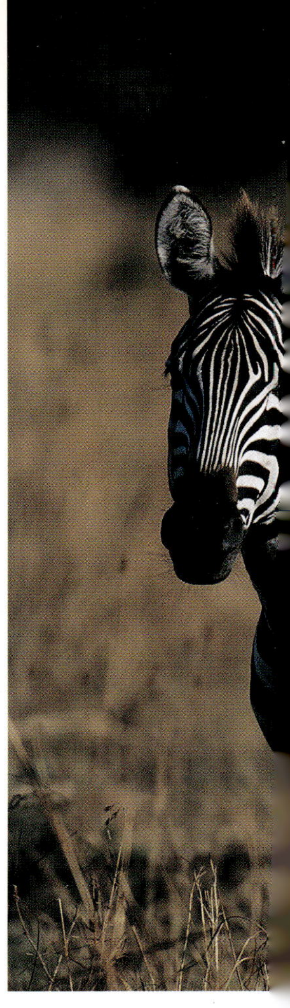

28mm, and 35mm. Wide-angle lenses allow you to capture more of a scene, and we rely on them for most of our landscape work as well as in situations that are tight and leave little room to back up or move around. You can be creative with a super-wide-angle lens, but the wider the lens, the more distortion becomes a problem. Distortion can make objects at the edge of the picture appear bent or bowed and horizons can become curved, and yet at times, there is a certain appeal to the off-the-wall look. Our favorite wide-angle lens is a Nikon zoom 17mm to 35mm.

The 50mm lens is what many photographers consider their normal or standard lens. Many camera stores offering SLR packages with a camera body and lens often include a 50mm lens. Although some would argue the fact, most photographers agree that

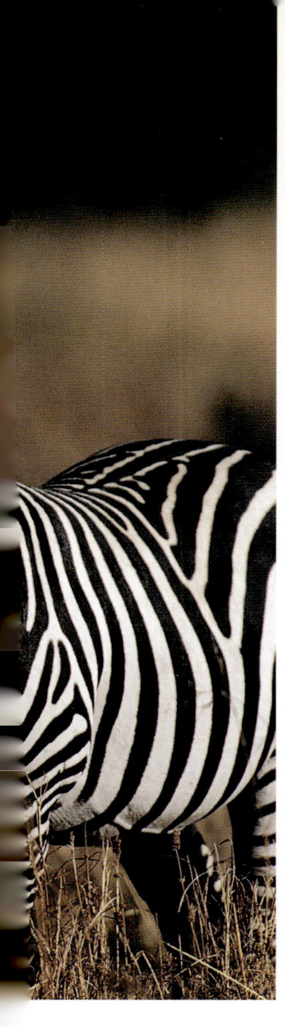

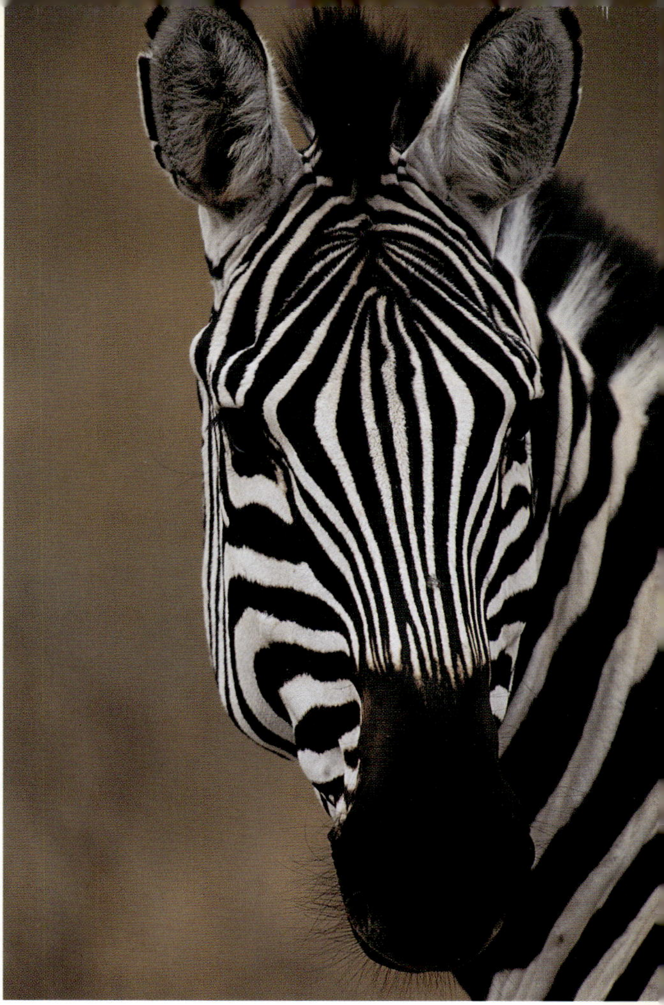

The zebras on the left were shot with an 80-200mm telephoto lens, the one in the middle with a 300mm telephoto lens, and the closeup on the right with a 500mm telephoto lens.

the 50mm lens provides approximately the same angle of view as the human eye.

From 60mm to 105mm is the range of focal length for the short telephoto lenses. Excellent for portrait work, the longer the focal length, the less depth of field. Most manufacturers offer a versatile zoom lens in the 80mm to 200mm category. Today's zoom lenses are sharper than ever, so don't be afraid to consider one. They give you more flexibility and freedom to compose than you get with a fixed focal length lens.

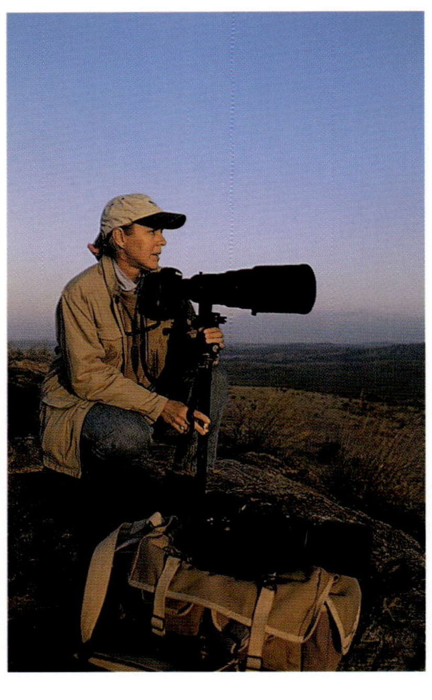

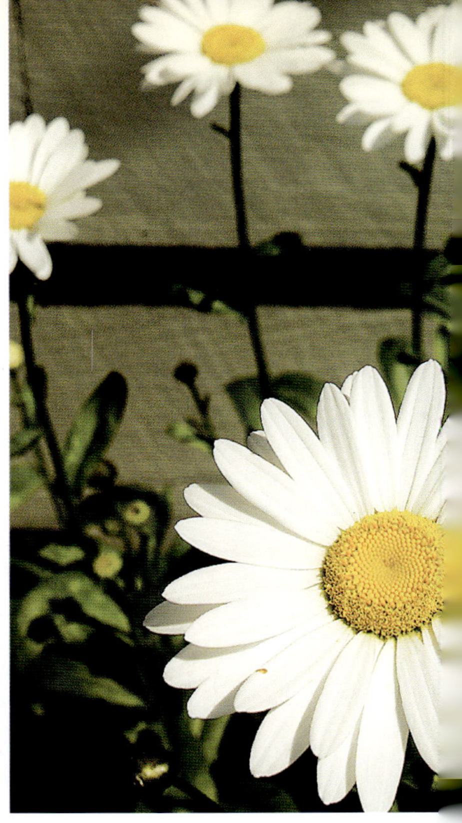

The super-telephoto lenses of 300mm and longer can be pricey, but if you're into shooting wildlife images they are the only way to go. Another option for Cannon and Nikon users is the new image stabilizer lens. We have been using a Nikon 80mm to 400mm with terrific results.

Macro lenses are designed for close focusing work. Your zoom lens may have a close focusing or macro mode, but it probably renders your subject at one third the life size. This will work fine for certain applications, but if you want to reproduce the subject at life size you'll need to consider a true macro lens. Nikon offers both a 60mm macro and a 105mm macro. Both are razor sharp, not only with macro subjects but with subjects at any distance.

Recommendation

We're often asked if we had to shoot with only one lens, what would it be? To be honest, we like to have the variety. However, if we were forced to live with just one lens it would be a 28mm to 70mm. We can cover a lot of ground with this zoom, and we rely on it for a lot of our work. This is an exceptionally sharp lens and we prefer it to a fixed focal length—with

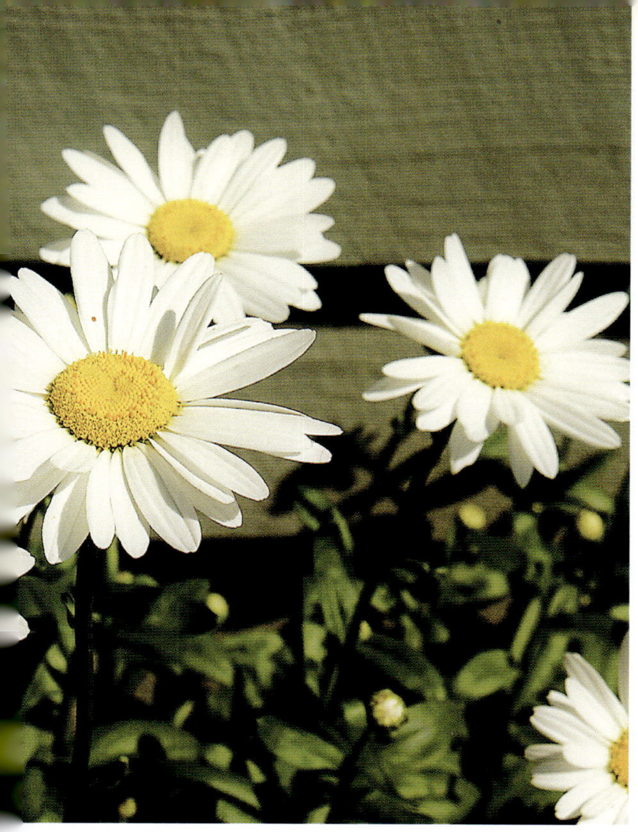

Far left: *A long lens like a 500mm can help you get close with your wildlife photography.*

Left: *Daisies taken with a macro lens.*

Below: *Macro photography allows you to get close to your image.*

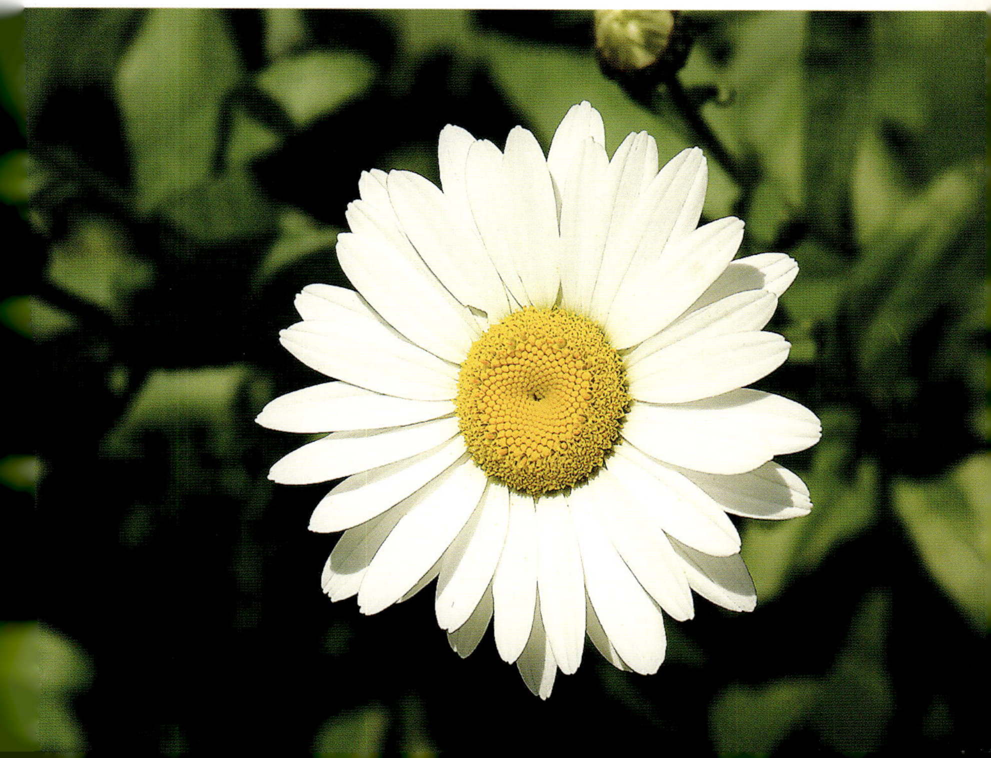

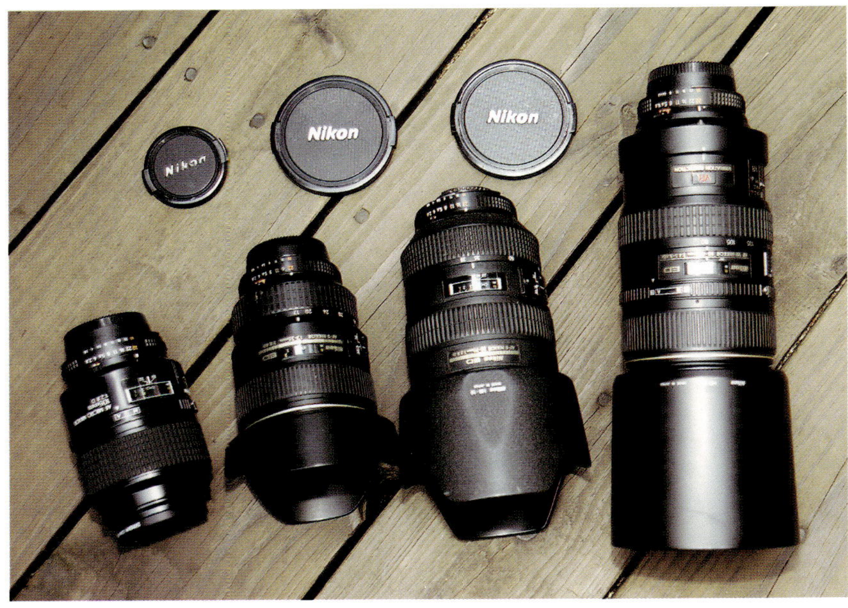

Recommended lenses include a 17 to 35mm, 28 to 70mm, 80 to 400mm, and 105mm macro.

the exception of a macro. If you look into our camera bag, you will find four Nikon lenses: a 17 to 35mm, a 28 to 70mm, an 80 to 400mm, and a 105mm macro.

HOW A FILM CAMERA WORKS

Exposure is the process of allowing light to pass through a fixed-size hole and then onto the film for a controlled amount of time. The amount of light that will pass through the hole during a given amount of time is determined by an f-stop. The smaller the f-stop number the wider the aperture (hole), and the larger the f-stop number the smaller the aperture. How long the light passes through the aperture is determined by the shutter speed. The slower the shutter speed, the more light will reach the film. Automatic point-and-shoot cameras make all the aperture and shutter speed decisions, and this makes life simple, but there are times and situations where having control over the aperture or shutter speed

Right: *A shallow depth of field, like f/4, will keep the subject in sharp focus but blur the background.*

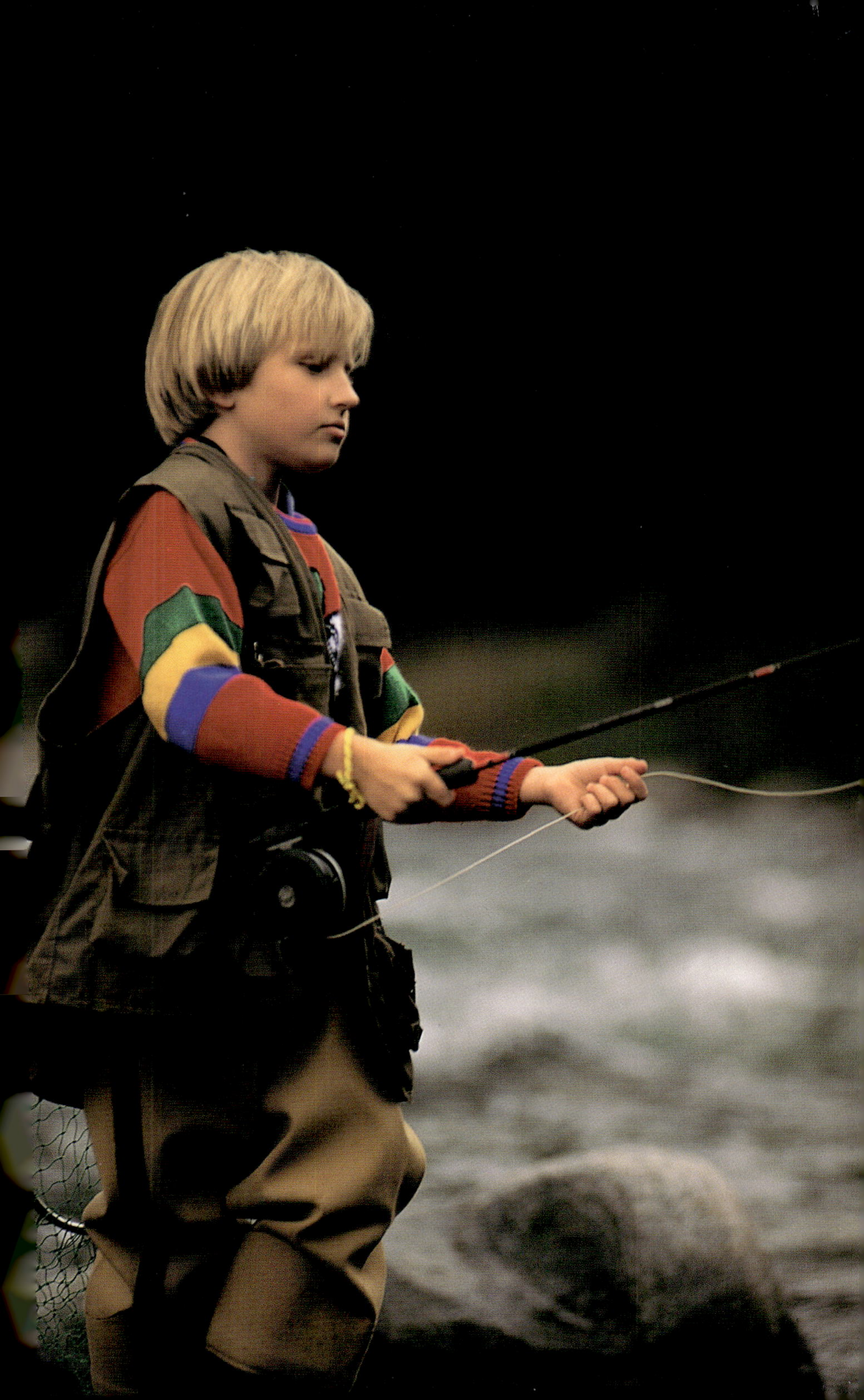

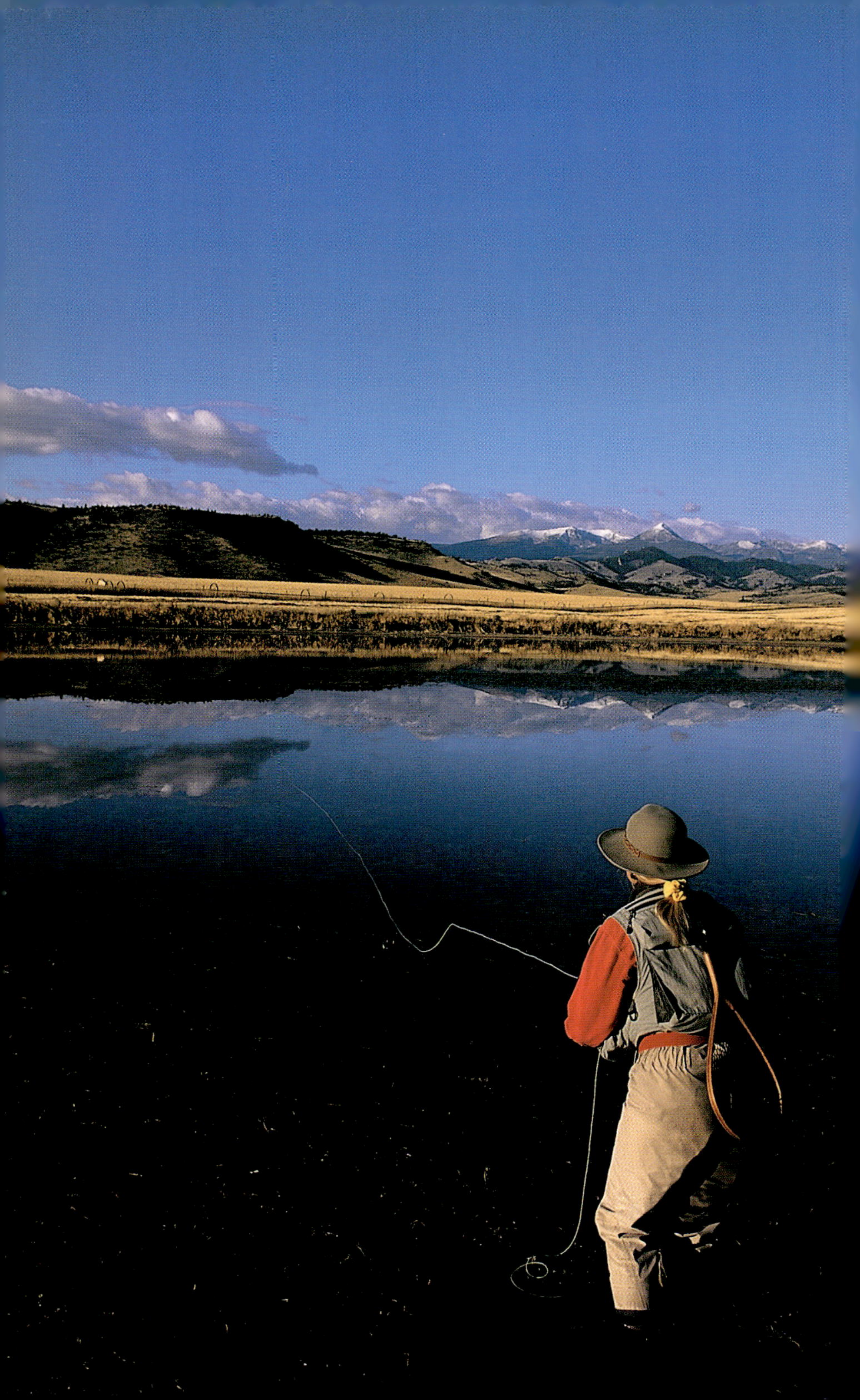

can give you a new sense of creativity. Advanced 35mm systems give you the options for making that choice.

The aperture not only controls the amount of light passing through the lens, but also controls the depth of field, which in turn affects how sharp and how much of the image is in focus. The aperture is manually controlled by either the aperture ring on the lens or a command dial on the camera body. Lenses have a range of stops or numbers that may include all or some of the following stops: f/1.4, f/2, f/2.8, f/4, f/5.6, f/8, f/11, f/16, and f/22. The larger the number, the larger the opening and the more light that is allowed in. As the number increases, the depth of field also increases. Depth of field is the area or zone in front of and behind your subject or focus point that is or is not in focus.

The shutter is a mechanism built into the camera body that opens up, thus uncovering the film, when you press the shutter button. The shutter speed determines how long the light passes through the aperture and strikes the film. This shutter speed also affects any blur or motion on your image. The longer the shutter stays open, the more effect it has on your photograph. Faster shutter speeds freeze motion and generally give you a sharper image. The most common shutter speeds include the following, from slow to fast: 1 second, 1/2, 1/4, 1/8, 1/15, 1/30, 1/60, 1/125, 1/250, 1/500, and 1/1000 of a second.

FILM AND FILM SPEED

The two most popular films are color print film (color negative) and color slide film (color transparency). There are pluses and minuses to each. We do almost all our shooting with slide film because magazine and book editors prefer color slides and we need them for slide shows and presentations. This will change somewhat as digital becomes more widely accepted. You can make prints from slide film, but it can be expensive. On the other hand, color slide film is less forgiving than color print film, so your exposure needs to be right on for a well-exposed image. Color print film allows you more room for exposure errors and is easier and less costly to make prints. If you're thinking of submitting your images for publication you'll need to work with slide film.

An easy way to tell slide film from print film is to remember that slide film is referred to as chrome while color print film is referred to as color. If you see a box of Fuji Chrome ISO 100, you're looking at slide film, but if the box is labeled Fuji Color ISO 100, it's color print film.

A larger f-stop, like f/16, puts both the angler and the background in sharp focus.

Film speed is the film's sensitivity to light and is part of the exposure equation. Slower films give us sharper, grain-free images while faster films show more grain in the final image and in general are not as sharp as slower films. Fast films do, however, allow us to shoot at faster shutter speeds to freeze motion and allow us to better handle low-light situations. How much light it takes on the film to produce an image is indicated by an ISO rating. The higher the ISO, the more sensitive it is to light. ISO 50 and 100 are on the slow side, but they are the choice of many professional outdoor photographers. An ISO speed of 200 is the middle of the road, while 400 is considered a fast film.

Most professional outdoor photographers shoot with a professional grade film. Professional films give better color saturation and skin colors because they are sold only when they have reached their optimum level of potential for color rendition and film speed. But you'll pay more for them, and they need to be refrigerated or kept in a cool place. Professional films may give you an edge with an art director or magazine editor if your images are intended for commercial or editorial work, but for prints and slides of family and friends, consumer film works fine.

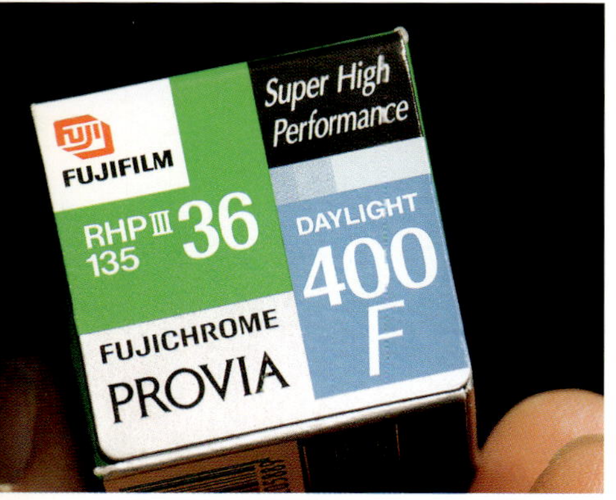

The ISO rating is marked on the end of the box (shown here is Provia 400f ISO).

We do most of our work with four different films, of which three are professional and one is consumer. Fuji Velvia at ISO 50, Fuji Provia at ISO 100, and Kodak Ektachrome 100VS are our three choices for most of our magazine work and commercial prints. Fuji Sensia at ISO 100 is a popular consumer film that is the equivalent of Provia 100 and is always in our camera bag. It's affordable, easy to find in any department or camera store, and gives excellent results. Stay away from film sales of outdated film regardless of manufacturer. Outdated film can lose its level of color accuracy, and you may be very disappointed with the results.

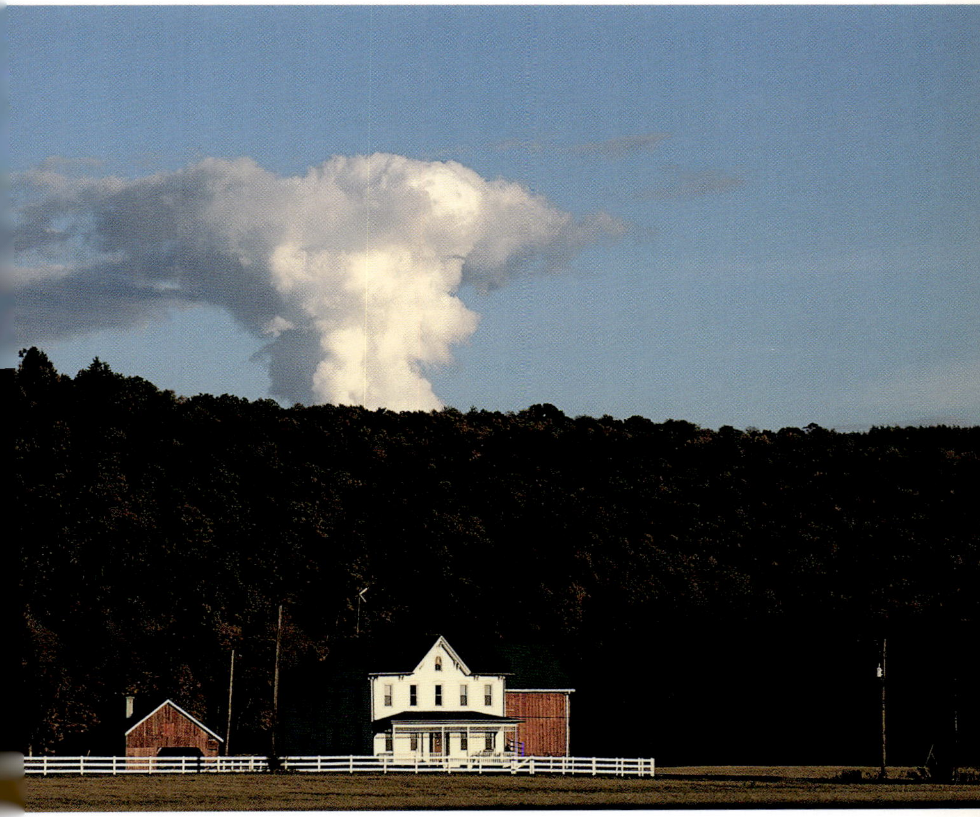

Clouds often help illustrate the scene below, as in this photo of a Pennsylvania farm backdropped by clouds from a nuclear power plant.

A reason for poor slides or prints may be the film processor. A good photo lab may be a little more expensive than some of the one-hour photo labs but is worth the extra money. If you go to the effort of shooting your film and getting shots that can't be repeated, or shots of a lifetime, the last thing you need is a film lab that does a poor job of processing your film. It happens more than you would think. We live in Pennsylvania, but after many years of experimenting with different labs, we send our film to Bozeman, Montana. We have worked with F-11 Photo Lab for over ten years and have complete confidence in their work. Our exposed film always goes to the lab by FedEx or UPS. We use three-day select delivery unless we need the images back sooner. Find a lab that's reliable and easy to work with.

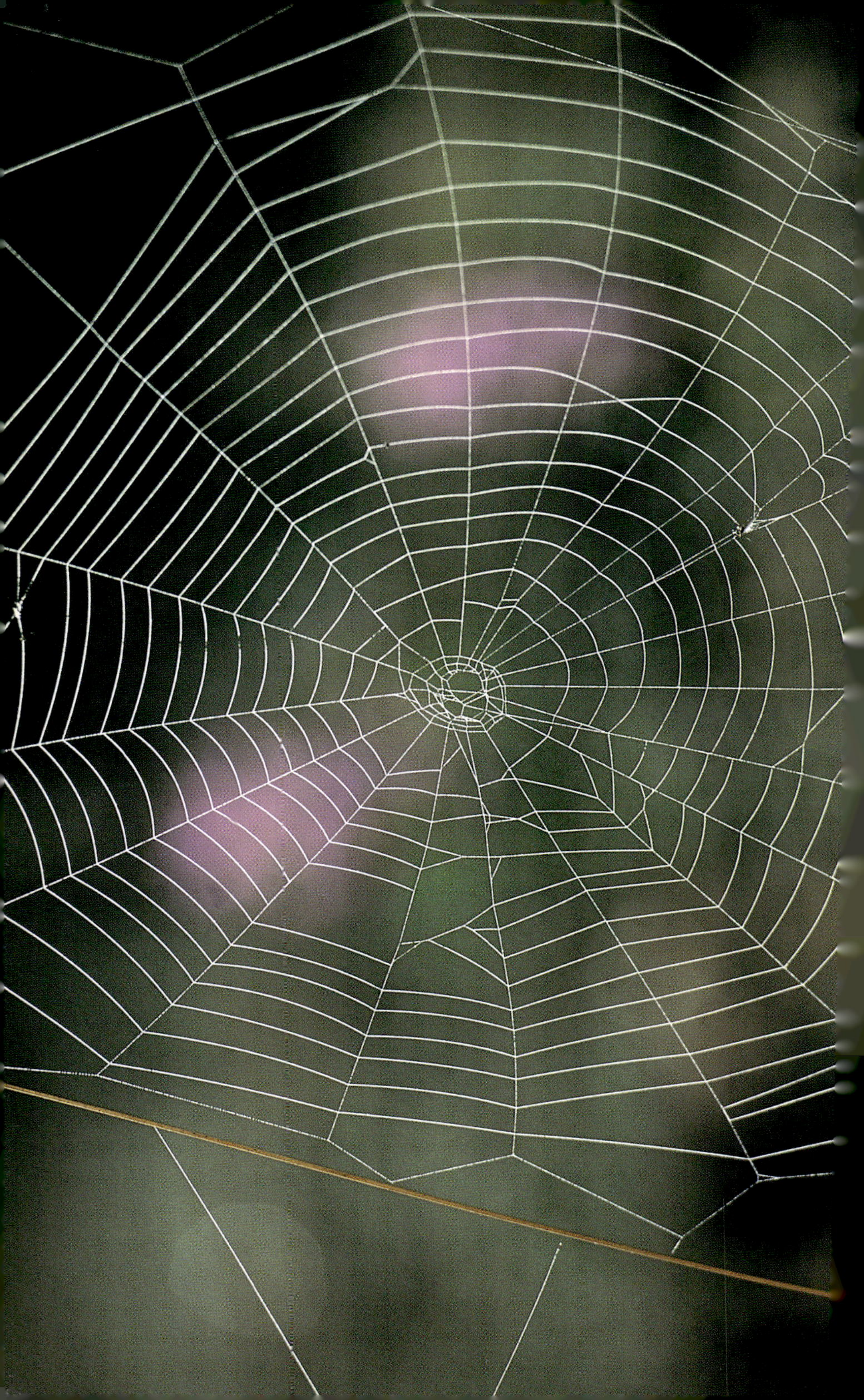

< CHAPTER 2 >

Digital Cameras

It was not all that long ago that we thought digital photography was the future. Well the future has arrived and digital is here, and what a revelation it is. Although there are film users who will not consider digital, digital will soon dominate the world of photography. That's not to say that film is a thing of the past. Film companies are still spending money on product development. So rest assured that film will be around for a long time and we will continue to shoot film, but digital is becoming a large part of our business.

It's important to remember that digital imaging is photography. We still need the basic ingredients of light and composition to make a good image; shutter speeds and apertures are still important, as is fill flash. One advantage digital offers is being able to preview your images on your camera monitor as you take them. If, when you view the shots, you don't like what you have just photographed, you simply delete and reshoot. A memory card replaces film and stores your pictures and can be reused over and over again. And, if you have a PC and a printer, you may never need a film lab again.

HOW A DIGITAL CAMERA WORKS

From the outside, many digital cameras look and operate like film cameras. If you are familiar with a film camera, you won't be too perplexed by the workings of a digital camera.

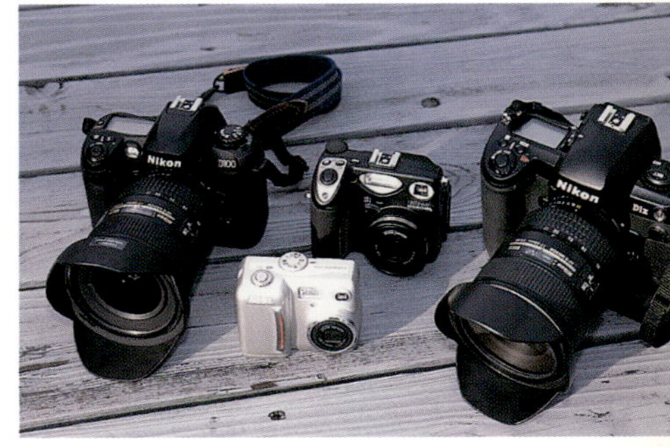

Digital cameras come in all shapes and sizes.

Left: *A spider's web makes an intricate pattern for this creative image.*

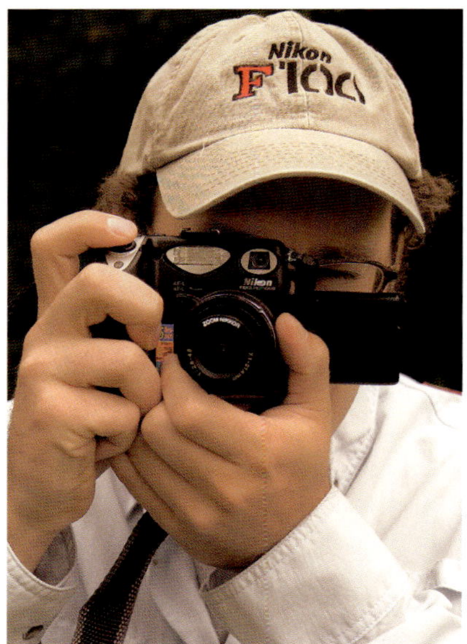

From the outside, many digital cameras look and operate like film cameras.

Fascinated is more like it. When we take a picture with a film camera, we capture light onto a piece of film. The captured light is composed of various colors of the spectrum that react to millions of microscopic silver halide crystals and with other chemicals to translate the colors onto the film. A digital camera differs from a film camera by what's inside. Digital cameras capture light, but on a light-sensitive computer chip called a CCD or charge-coupled device. When the shutter is depressed, the CCD is exposed to light. The light is measured electronically on the CCD and then sent to the internal memory or buffer of the camera. The CCD is composed of millions of color elements that are called pixels, short for picture elements. When light hits a CCD, each pixel on the CCD turns that light into an electrical charge. From there a processor transforms the charges into digital information. At this point we have a photographic image that is stored on a memory card in the camera. The stored images can be downloaded into your PC, and from there you can display, file, print, delete, or email them to your friends.

Like film cameras, digital cameras

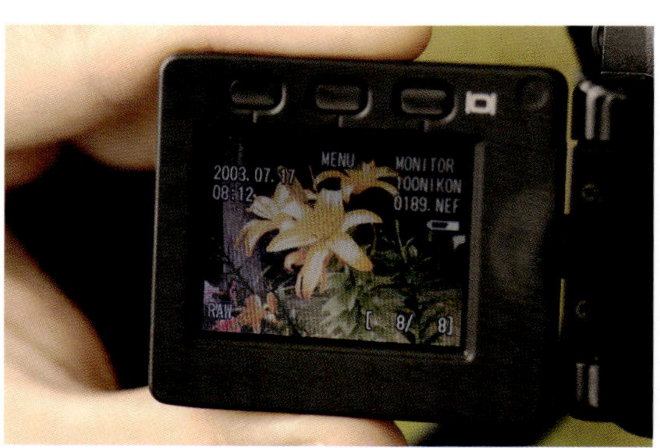

One of the great advantages of digital photography is being able to preview the image you have just taken. Good images can be saved, and bad ones can be deleted.

Right: *An image good enough to keep can be saved to a CD, DVD, Zip disk, or an external hard drive.*

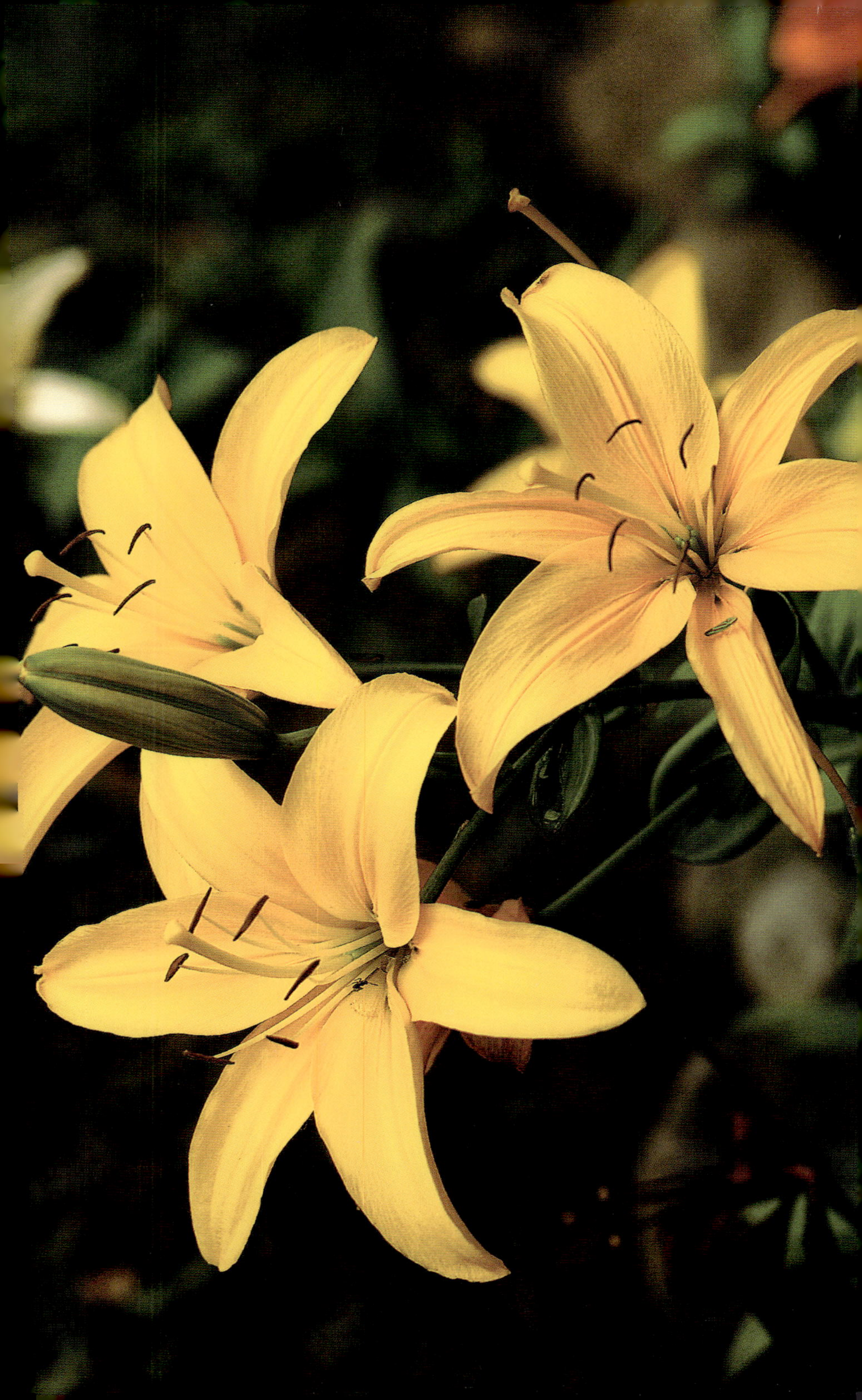

come in all sizes and price ranges. However, not all digital cameras are equal. Take resolution, for example. A digital image is measured in pixels. The number of pixels that are on the image area of the CCD determines the resolution of the image. A megapixel is one million pixels, and the more pixels your image has, the sharper and more detailed it will be. You need to decide how you want to use a digital camera before you buy one. If you're interested in just emailing images to friends or producing prints for a photo album, then a camera with a low resolution of under three megapixels will work just fine. But if you're planning on printing 8 x 10 or larger prints, then you will want to consider a camera of three or more megapixels. These higher-resolution cameras fall into a price range of between $400 and $1000. They offer better metering modes and other options that allow you to be more creative with your photography.

When you buy a digital camera, you'll receive a manual that may look like a small encyclopedia with enough information to scare the daylights out of most of us. You may even get a CD with instructions. Look first at the small fold-out Quick Start instructions to get you started. You'll learn how to charge the batteries and then how to load them (easy to do), how to insert the memory card and

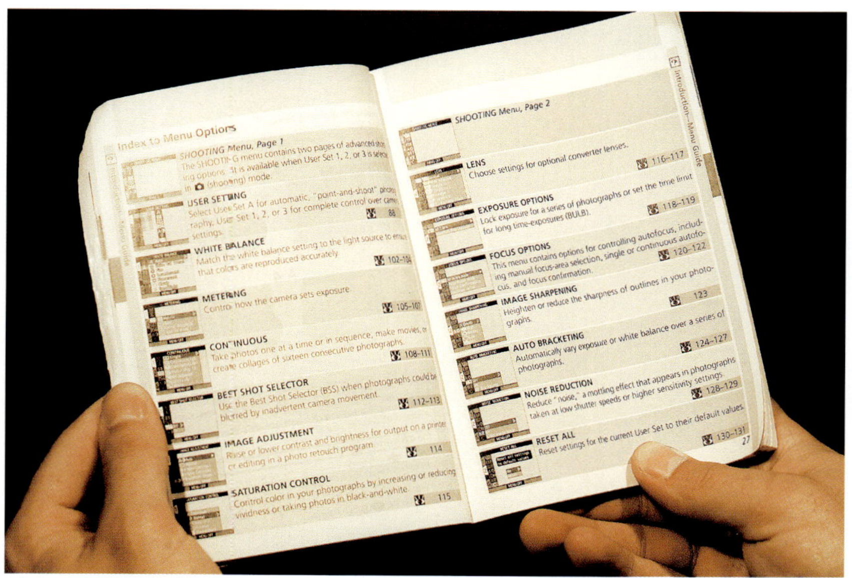

You camera's manual is full of information. Starting with a Quick Start program will get you off and running.

how to remove it. From there you'll find out how to turn on the camera, focus and frame your image, and shoot—there, you've done it. Now you can view the image on the camera monitor. If you don't like what you see, no problem—press the delete button and it's gone.

Your digital camera will have a menu that will appear on the camera LCD screen. Sometimes the menu will have more than one page. The menu gives the many options of your camera controls. There is a resolution setting that lets you change the size of the picture you're taking and perhaps a choice in metering options. Image quality will affect how much of your image is compressed. High compression allows for more image room on your memory card.

Formatting allows you to clean out your memory card. White balance adjusts the color contrast for the light you are shooting in. Most cameras have an automatic setting for the white balance, so it's not something that you immediately need to be concerned about. Exposure bracketing is a nice feature that tells the camera to automatically take three shots; the first one is one stop over, the second is right on, and the third is one stop under. This is one way of always making sure that you have the right exposure. The menu is your road map into the functions and features

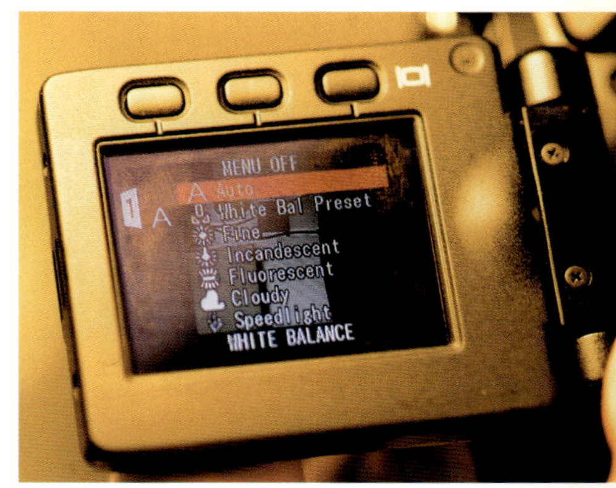

Your digital camera will have a menu that appears on the LCD screen.

of the camera. Once you get comfortable with the basics you'll want to explore all the wonderful options your digital camera can offer, but to get started, keep it simple and let the camera do the thinking for you.

MEMORY CARDS

Memory cards can be called digital film—with one big advantage: The card can be erased and used over and over again. Memory cards are about two inches square and come in different brands. The two most popular are Smart Media and Compact Flash. The card capacity is measured in bytes. The more bytes it has, the more digital images the card can hold. MB stands for megabyte, which means a million bytes. A gigabyte is a thousand megabytes. To give you an idea of storage capacity, we can use a one gig card and shoot in a Nikon

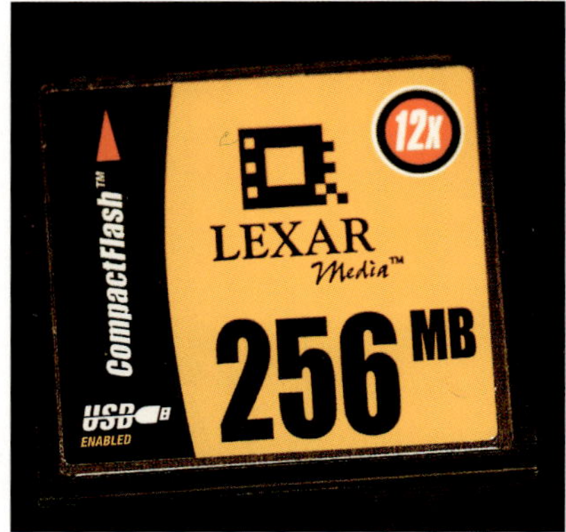

Left: Memory cards can be called digital film, but unlike film, they are reusable.

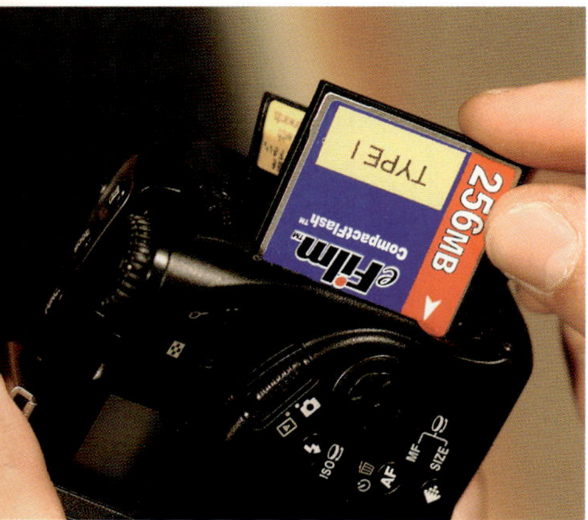

Inserting a memory card is easy.

Raw program in our D1X camera. The gig card will record 126 images before we need to download it. That's a lot of images. Once we download the card we simply reformat it and it's ready to use again.

Memory cards are great for traveling. They take up almost no space, are extremely durable, and when going through airport security, X-ray screening has no effect on the card.

SOFTWARE

You do not have to have a computer to use a digital camera. There are photo labs and places like pharmacies, Kmart, and Wal-mart that will accept memory cards and print your images for you. With the right camera you can connect to your televison and view your images. A computer and a printer do, however, give you the option of previewing, editing, and printing your images. In a sense you have your own digital darkroom.

Nikon View is a simple software program for Nikon users to transfer images from the camera to the computer. Within the program is Nikon Browser, which easily lets us view and organize thumbnail-size images to a selected folder. Nikon View allows us to work with larger individual images, while Nikon Editor takes us into a program well suited for cropping and editing images. All digital camera companies will offer similar basic software programs.

Once you're comfortable with the basic programs that come with your camera, you may want to consider more advanced software programs like Adobe Elements or Adobe Photoshop, or one of the many others. These programs offer endless opportunities in editing, cropping, resizing, and adding text. Available too are special borders and calendar and greeting card programs. We can correct, sharpen, adjust contrasts, give an image a watercolor look, or make it look like an artist's sketch. We can also print out our own contact sheets of images we've saved or create a printed page of smaller thumbnail prints within a specified folder for a quick reference sheet. The opportunities are endless!

FILE FORMATS

A file format is the way digital information is stored both on the memory card and in the computer. Some file formats allow you to compress images into less space; in other words, you can put more pictures on a card or on your hard drive. Other formats give you better picture quality. Use the menu to set your camera for different file formats. The most popular format is JPEG, which is an efficient way to store photos in a file without sacrificing card or disk space. It's also the most popular format for emailing your images to friends.

If you're interested in producing high-quality prints, then you may want to consider a TIFF format. TIFF is a noncompressed digital file offering the most image data. If you're planning to edit your images more than once, TIFF is recommended. You will not get as many images on a card if you shoot in TIFF, but you will get a professional-looking print.

There are other file formats, GIF, BMP, PDF, and so on, depending on the software program you're using. You can change an image from one format to another in your image editing program.

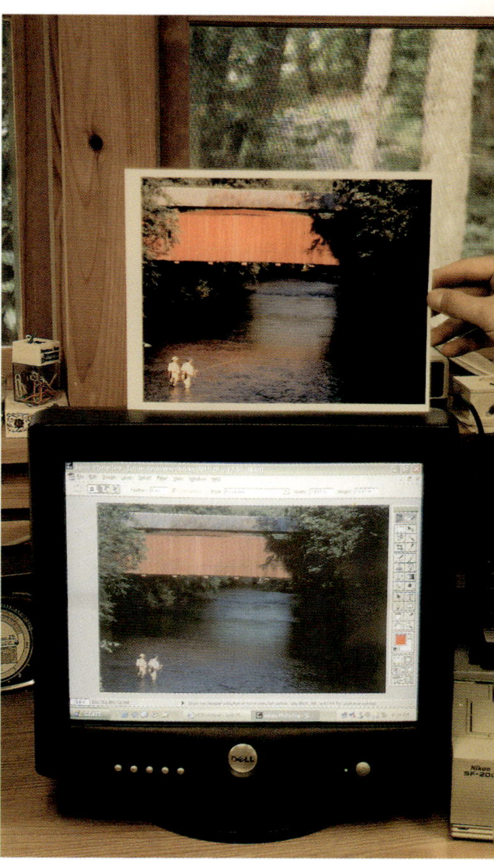

With a good photo editing program, your computer can provide your own personal darkroom.

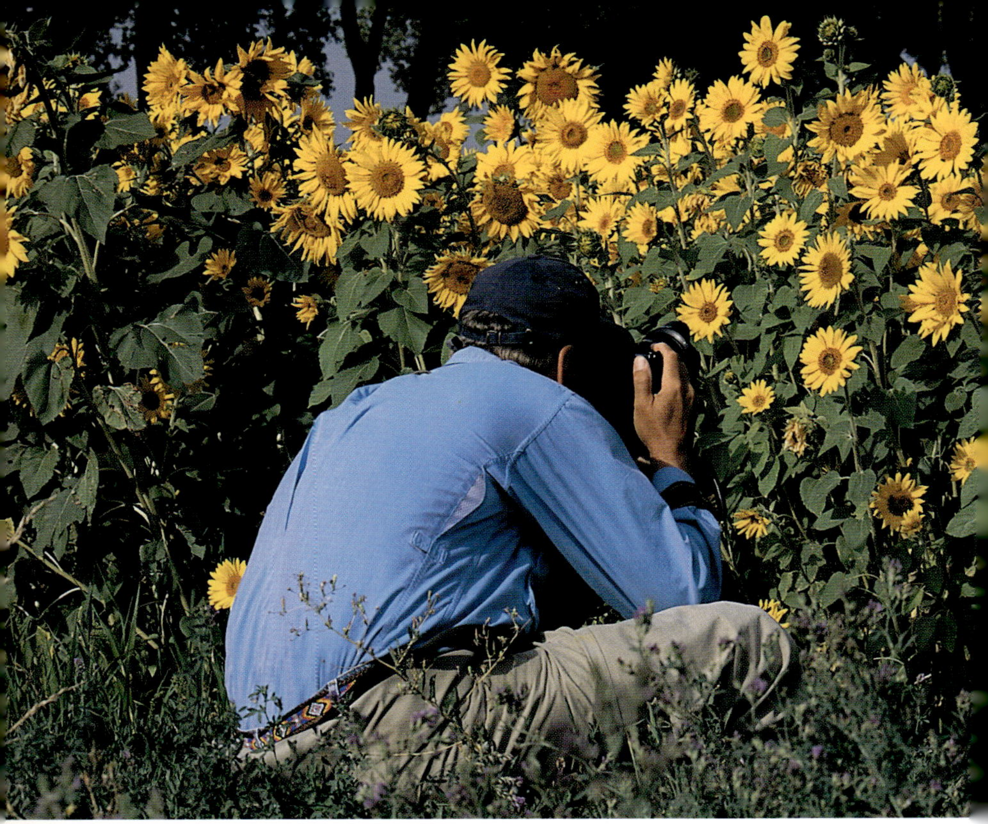

STORING IMAGES FOR THE LONG TERM

The hard drive in your computer represents a fixed storage space where you can temporarily store images. Because of the amount of space required, hard drives can bog down if there are too many images being stored, and you always run the risk of losing them if something goes wrong. You may not want to keep your images there permanently, but the hard drive is where you want the images while you're working with them. For permanent storage, consider burning your images on a CD. Depending on the file size you're using, the CD can store a lot of images. Because CDs are cheap, we keep a set with the images in our office where they are close at hand and store a duplicate in a safe-deposit box. If we suffered from theft or fire we would have the backup. In addition to CDs, you can use zip disks, DVDs, or even additional external hard drives, which sit on or beside your computer and provide extra storage space. These external hard drives can be stacked and will run smoothly with your computer operating programs when properly installed.

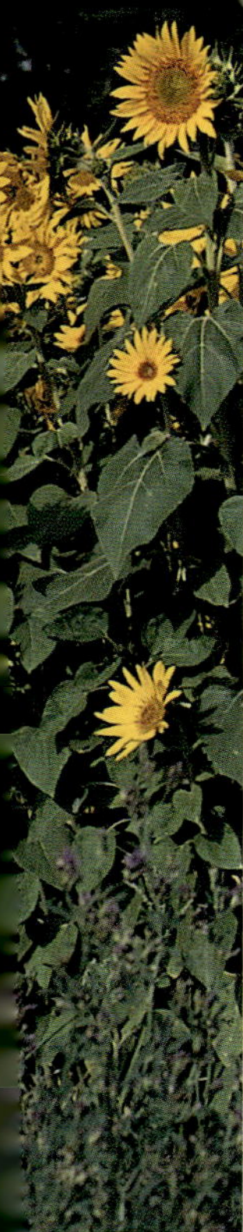

Play with different angles and experiment for more creative images.

PRINTING YOUR IMAGES

There are a lot of choices if you want to print your images. Inkjet and laser printers are the most popular, but they vary in speed, price, and print resolution. For sharp, crisp prints, you'll want high resolution, which is measured in dpi or dots per square inch. The higher the dpi, the sharper the prints. Printing on good photo paper will enhance the quality of your prints. Plain paper absorbs the ink and the dots tend to bleed together, and over time the color will fade. We use glossy photo-quality paper, which allows the ink to dry with less dispersion and gives a professional-looking print that will last.

WINDOWS OR MACINTOSH

Selecting the right computer operating system is a personal choice. Both Windows and Macintosh work well for digital photography. We use Windows XP, which is a great program geared to handle any image application. The Macintosh equivalent is OS X and does the same functions as Windows XP. We know all too well that in today's world models and programs are being upgraded constantly.

If you use your computer for editing images, the size of your monitor can make a big difference. While a smaller fifteen-inch screen will get you by, a larger nineteen- or twenty-one-inch screen will let you see your images more accurately, and you'll experience less eye fatigue and see a lot more detail as you edit and critique your images.

There are lots of good choices when it comes to digital cameras. We've used Nikon cameras for years. We carry a Cool Pix 5000 with us on all of our travels. It serves us well as a simple point-and-shoot and backup camera. At five megapixels, it produces extra sharp prints as large as 16 x 20 inches. The Nikon D100 with interchangeable lenses is a good choice for both the professional and the advanced amateur. The D1X and the D1H are high–end professional cameras that have become the standard for sports and news photographers.

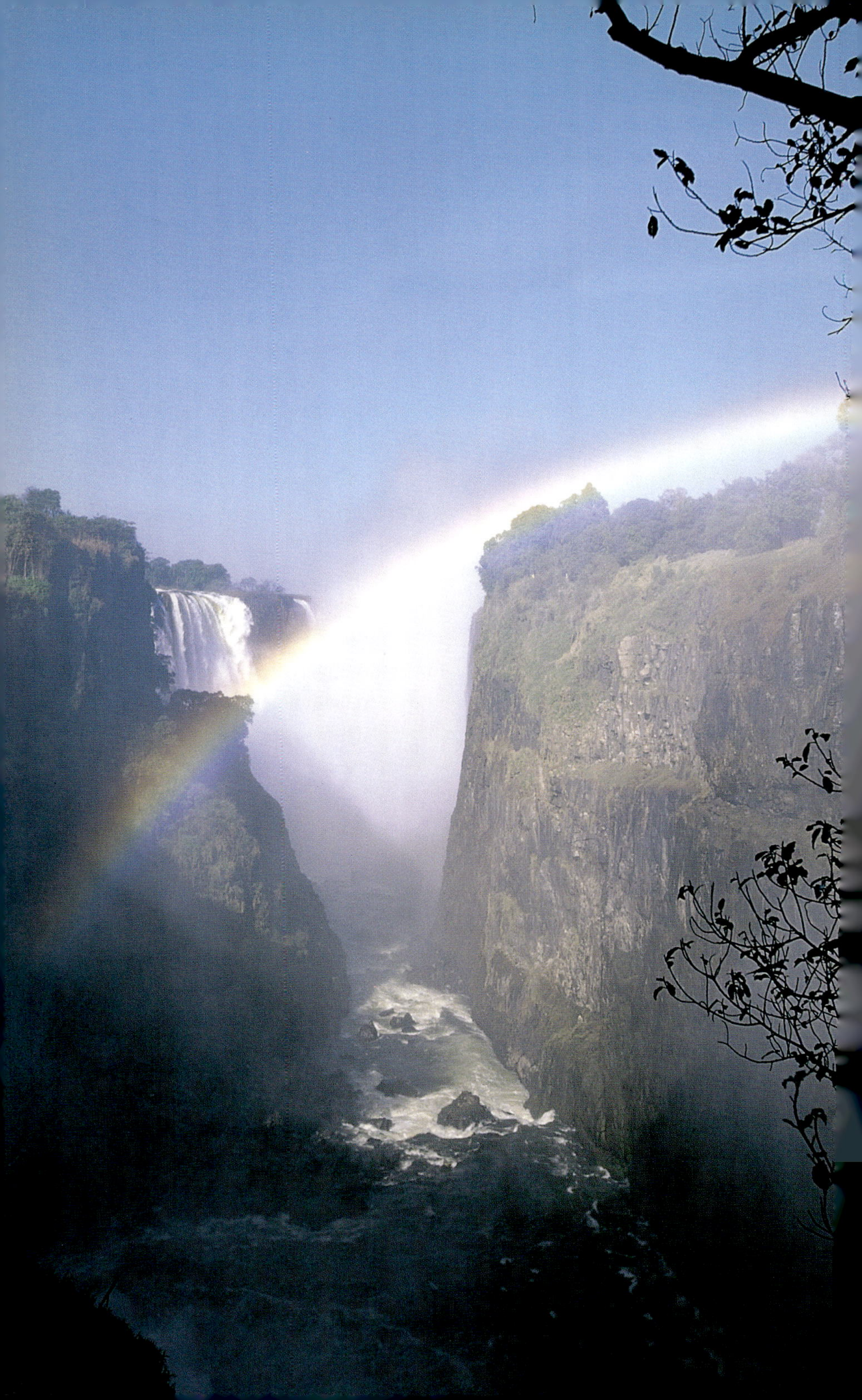

< CHAPTER 3 >

Light and Composition

Light makes the photograph. Without it the image simply would not exist. But it's more than just light that makes a great image. It's the type of light. For instance, gray skies are simply that: gray and unexciting, lacking any dramatic color or definition. They leave us with a flat-looking image. If we learn to recognize the quality of good light and then how to use it to our advantage, we'll be much better photographers.

SUNLIGHT AND WEATHER

The height of the sun has a tremendous impact on our photography. The higher and more intense the sun, the more contrast there is between bright and shadowy areas. This can be a real challenge for a light meter because high-contrast scenes are extremely difficult to properly meter, and we will generally lose some of the detail of the image. Therefore, we try not to shoot with a high midday sun unless there is no alternative.

The warmth of an early-morning or late-day sun has always been our favorite light to work with. Often described as magical, this kind of light can produce some great photo opportunities. Early-morning and late-afternoon light is warmer be-

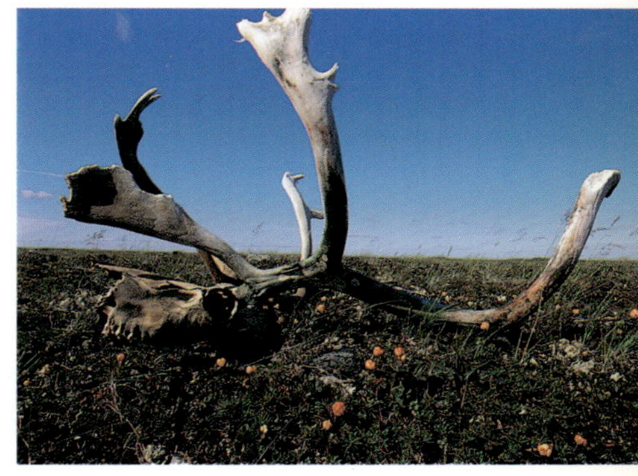

A low-profile shot that shows the remains of a tundra caribou tells the story of a harsh land, yet the tundra berries add a sense of color and new birth.

***Left:** Victoria Falls in Africa is one of the most photographed waterfalls in the world. The rainbow is enhanced with a polarizing filter.*

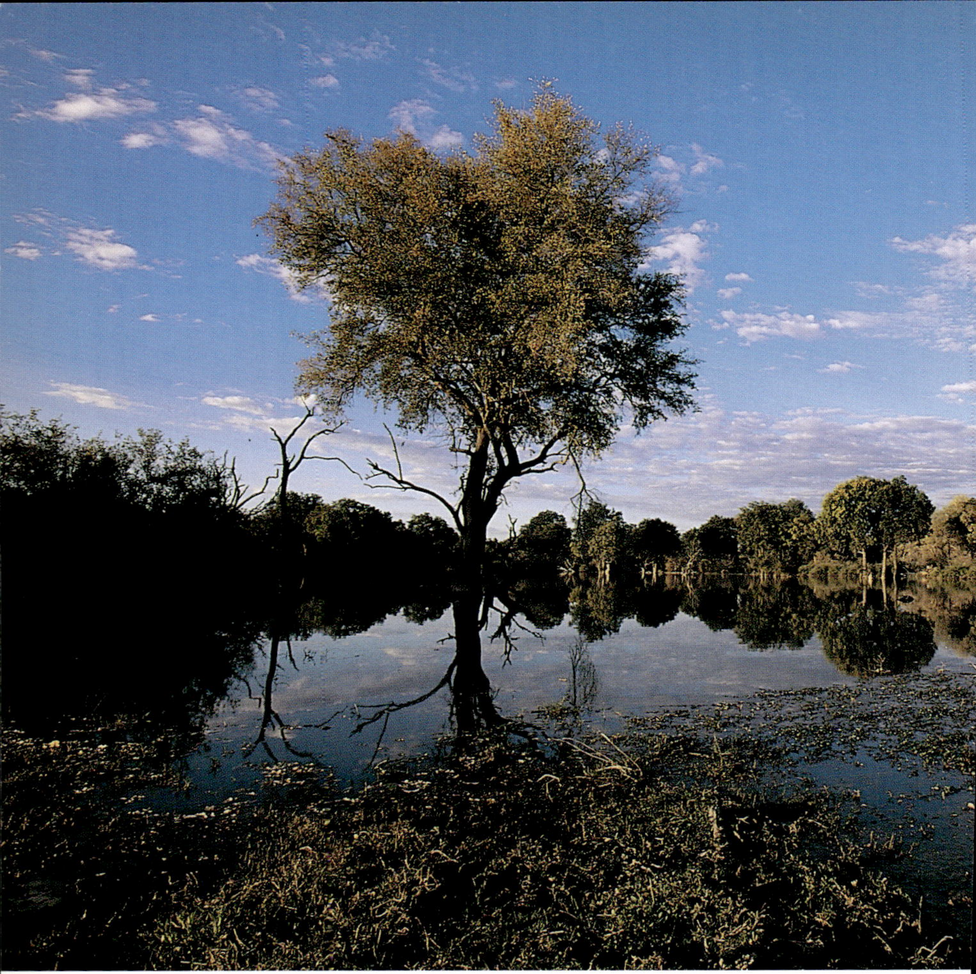

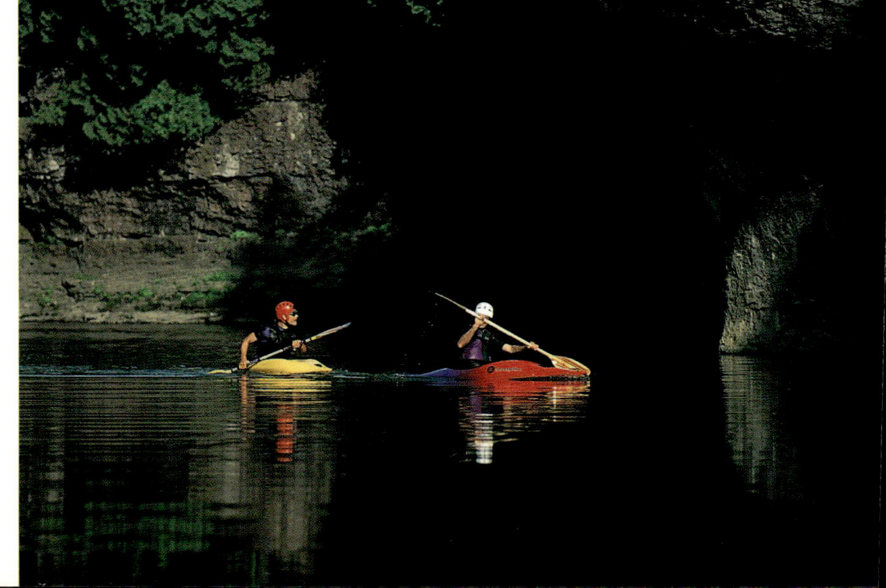

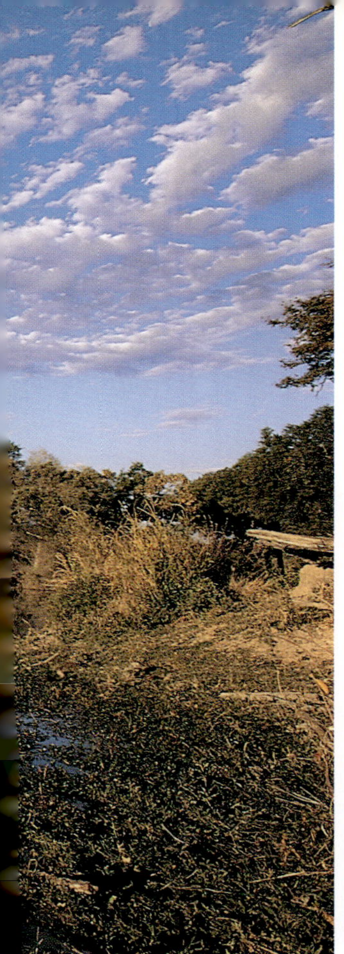

Left: *Early-morning light illuminates South Africa's Okawango Delta.*

Below left: *Soft afternoon light illuminates kayakers on Canada's Grand River.*

Below: *Side light plays an interesting effect.*

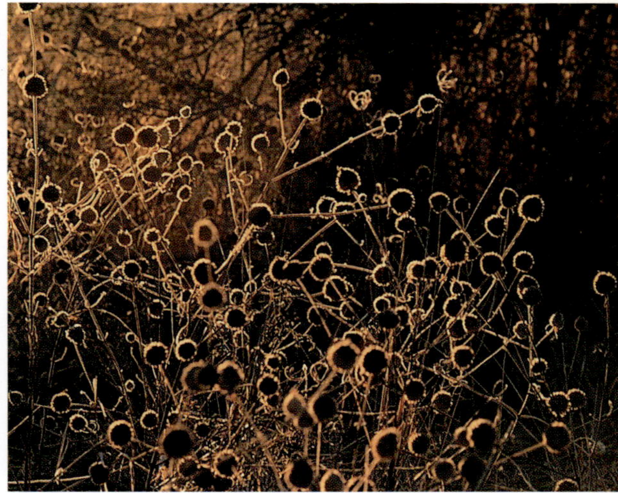

cause during this period less white light can penetrate the thicker layer of the earth's atmosphere. As the sun rises higher in the sky its warmth disappears as more white light comes in. Low light also produces long artistic shadows that enhance landscape photography.

The direction of the sun is key. A basic rule of photography is to keep the sun behind you when you are shooting. This is good advice, but there are times when we've found it works against us. Portraits are a good example. If our subject is looking straight into the sun, he or she will end up squinting. On the other hand, if we shoot directly into the sun, we'll end up with flare and more often than not a blown-out image. We try to position our subject so we can use side lighting to produce shadows that give greater depth to our image. Move around and look at the different angles of light on your subject and choose what looks best.

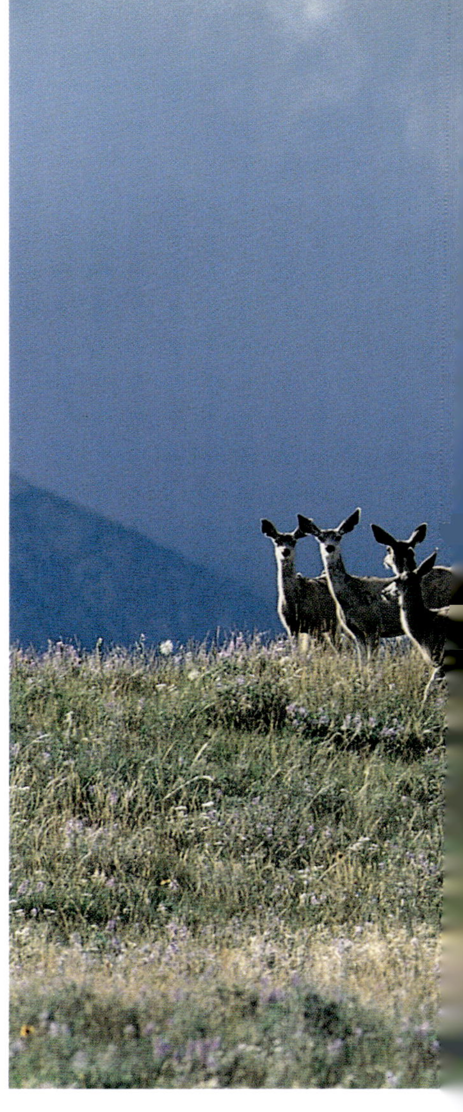

A herd of mule deer stands at attention on a Wyoming hillside enhanced by the magic light that often follows a storm.

We can't tell you how many times we have taken a picture from a certain angle thinking that looked good through the viewfinder only to move around a little more exploring different angles and then find the perfect shot.

Weather and light will change throughout the day, and we need to be prepared to react to the opportunities it presents. There have been times when traveling with friends that someone will comment on how nice the light is or draw attention to a certain landscape because of the way the light is falling. At that moment, if you've got the light and can find the composition, you need to take the picture. That magical light may only last for a brief moment, and if you don't respond, it's gone.

Rain can chase away the best of us, yet it can also create some wonderful moods and light. Rain cleans the air and can intensify natural colors. This is especially true in the fall when foliage is at its peak. There can be some really dramatic light that comes just before and after a thundershower. We were working in the Crazy Mountains of Montana a few years back and found ourselves in the middle of an intense summer storm. Moments after the storm passed a herd of mule deer stood on a hillside looking down at us. At that moment a ray of sunshine fell on the herd while the background of dark storm clouds kept building. That scene and light only lasted for a minute, but we managed to get four frames before the light and the deer were gone. This magical light created a great image.

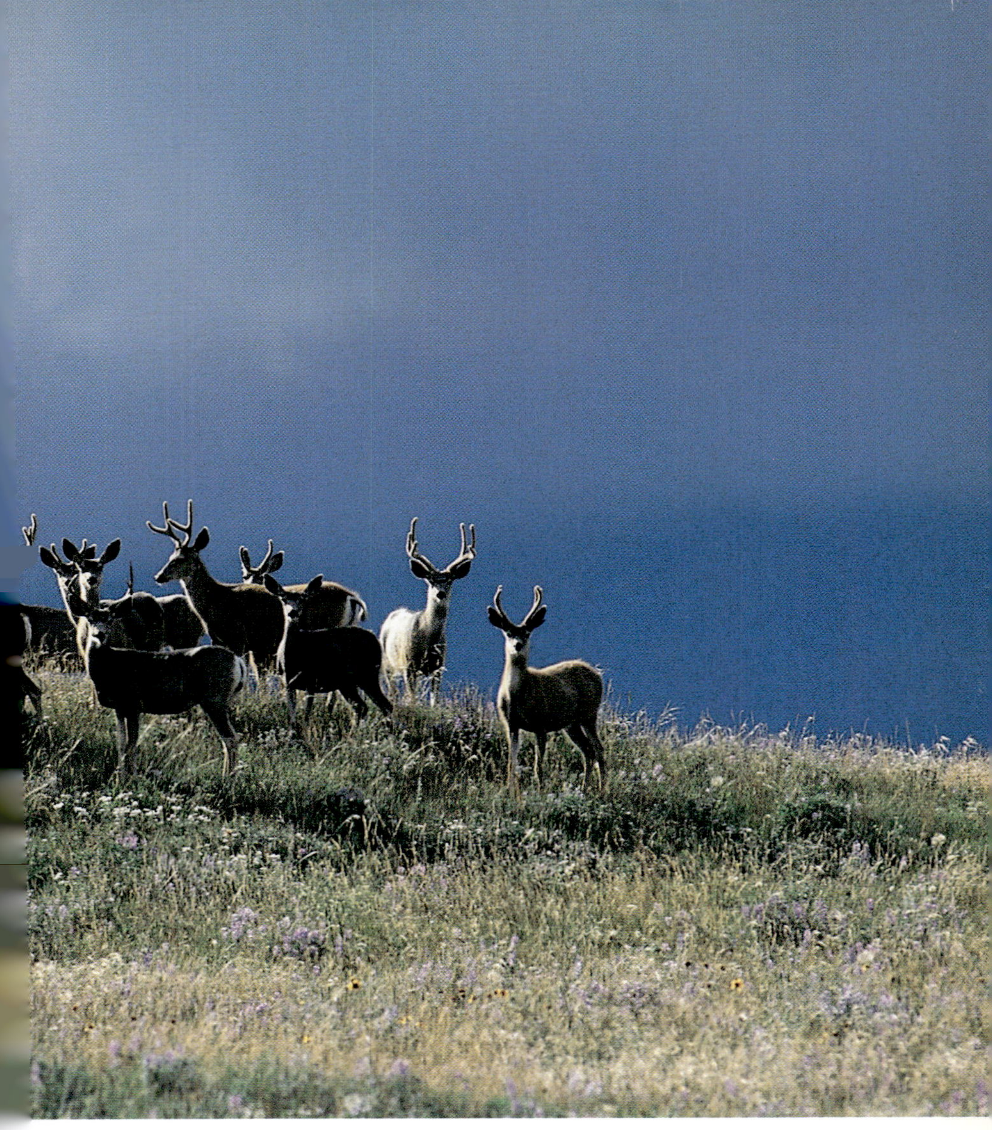

Rainbows are another side benefit of storms that you will want to take advantage of. They never last long, so you need to move quickly and compose your image. A polarizing filter is a must if you want to capture the colors. To see the effect of polarization, try looking at a rainbow without polarized sunglasses and then looking again through the polarized sunglasses.

Rain and even high humidity can cause problems with cameras, but don't let precipitation keep you from shooting. Carry a couple large plastic garbage bags to cover your equipment in bad weather. Even a plastic shower cap (free from hotel rooms)

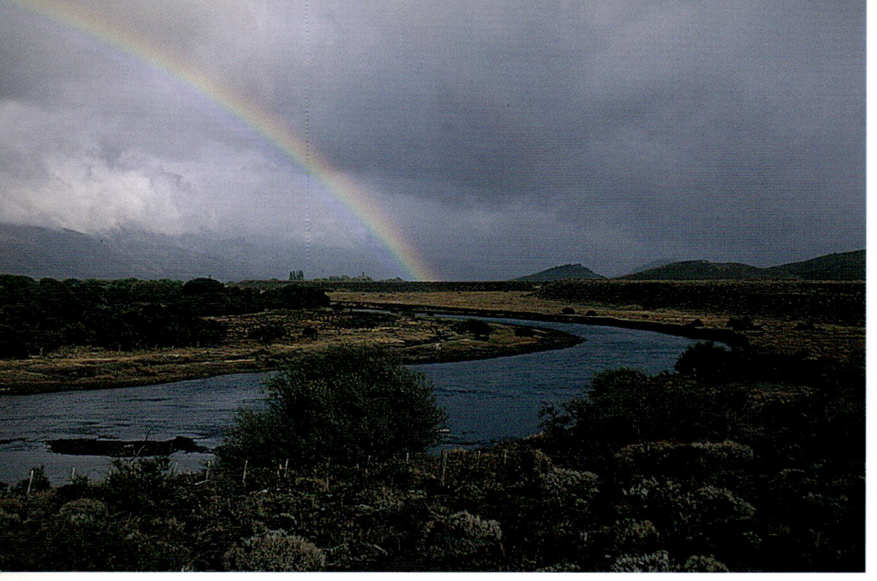

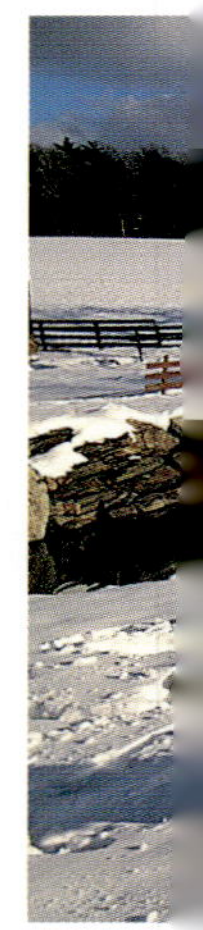

can help protect a camera body and a short lens. You can't shoot through the cap but it can be wrapped around the equipment to help keep things dry. You can even mount an umbrella on the leg of your tripod or use a space blanket to lay over the camera when it's on the tripod.

If your camera does get wet, immediately wipe it off with any absorbent cloth, even a paper towel. Keep an eye on your lenses and filters and remove any water that you find. We always keep some cloths cut from cotton tee shirts in our gear bag. These are free of lint, absorb water quickly, and when they start to look bad we simply throw them away. We don't use them on our lenses, we use special lens cloths for that, but they work well for everywhere else. It's very important to keep your equipment dry. Allowing water to penetrate your camera gear usually means very high repair costs or possibly ruined equipment.

Snow with its brilliance and reflective qualities can really fool a camera meter. The brightness causes the meter to underexpose and results in images that will come back from the lab dark and underexposed. When shooting in snow, use something in the scene that is a neutral color to check your meter, but make sure whatever you use is in the same light

Early morning was the perfect time to capture the mist on the Madison River in Yellowstone National Park.

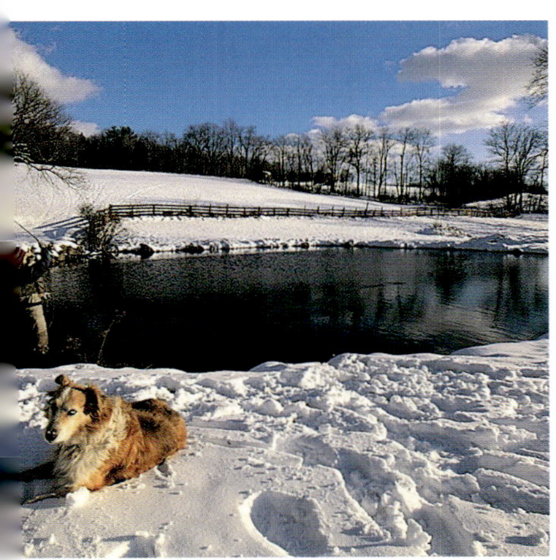

Snow can fool your camera's meter. Barry overexposed one stop to get a correct exposure of Polly and Cathy.

Far left: *A rainbow falls over the Rio Malleo in the Patagonia region of Argentina.*

as your subject. We generally overexpose snow by one or two stops to compensate, but we always bracket just to make sure that we get the shot. The type of film you use can also have a dramatic effect on how your images turn out. Some of our favorite films, like warm Fuji Velvia, may not give the best whites in this situation, so we may switch to the cooler colors of Provia or Sensia to bring out whiter whites. Try not to use a flash when it's snowing. The light from the flash will bounce off

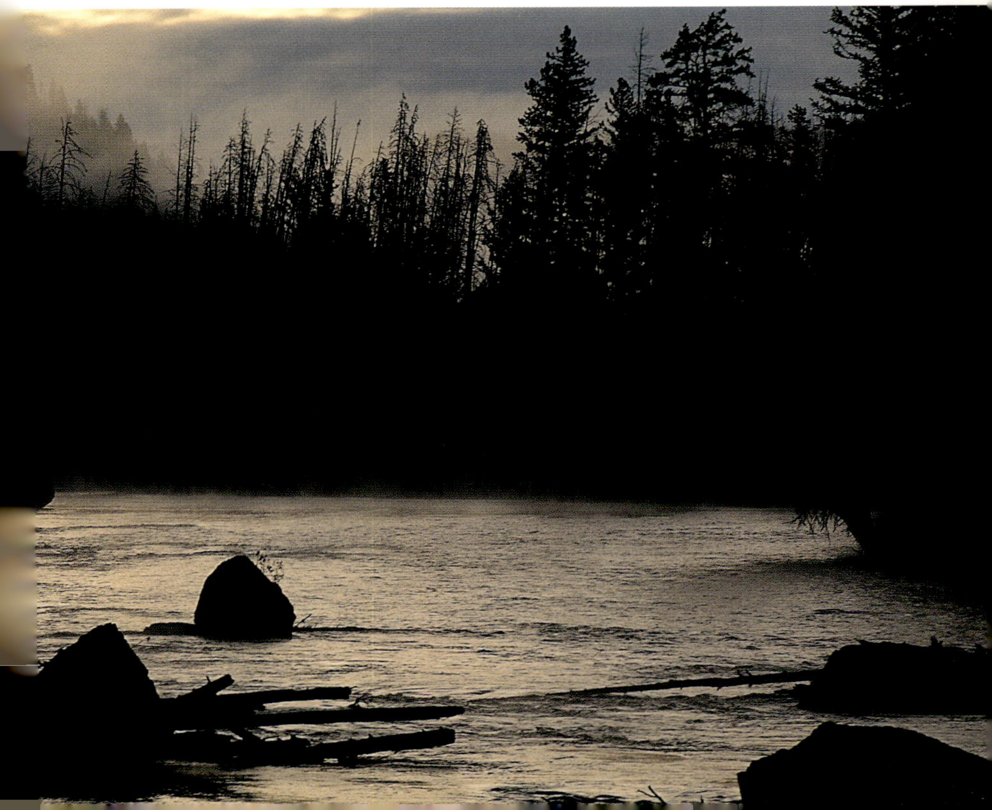

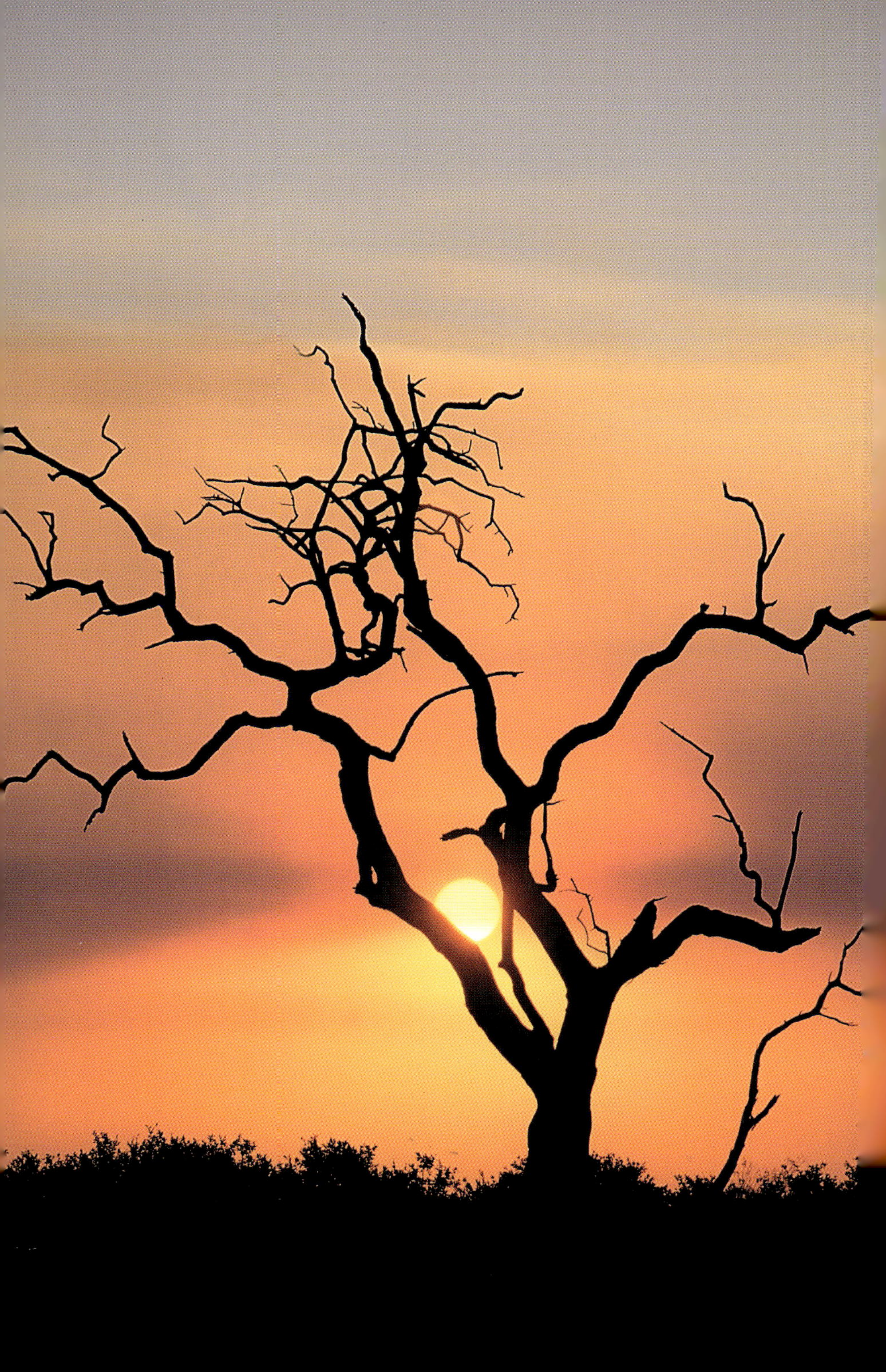

the nearest flakes, and it won't illuminate anything else.

Fog and mist can create mystical moods and present us with some very rewarding photo opportunities. When the early-morning sun starts to burn off the fog or mist, it's fun to be creative with your camera. This is one of the few times you can shoot into the sun for dramatic backlit effects. To catch this light you may have to get up early and be on location, but the results will be worth it.

Clouds play an essential role in landscape photography. We are always on the lookout for those perfect cloud formations that can help illustrate the scene below. A bright blue cloudless sky often lacks personality. Dramatic skies are eye-catchers, but a sky with some bright cloud cover can create the perfect light of the day for evenly lit portraits or still life compositions, eliminating harsh shadows and the need for subjects to squint. This is also great light for photographing fish and animals.

Low light photography can be fun and creative. Far too many photographers put their cameras away thinking that the light is gone, but that simply is not often the case. A good time to take photographs is that brief period of reflected light that can come just after the sun has set. If you're around water, there can be wonderful reflections of color from the afterglow of the sunset. When we encounter this kind of light, we always try to put something in the frame, like a canoe or fisherman on the water, to add to the composition. It's best if you can anticipate the event and be ready with your camera mounted on a tripod and an idea of what you want to shoot. There is a misconception that you need fast film for this kind of photography. Actually a slower speed film of 100 ISO or less will give you better clarity and color saturation. It's true that you will need a slow shutter speed, but that's easily accomplished with a tripod.

Silhouettes are easy to take and easy to meter for. We get good results when we manually meter off of the sky, but you should get great shots, too, if you set your camera on automatic because this is a straight-on kind of shot and easy for your camera meter to read. When you compose your image it's important for you to isolate the subject. Some of our favorite subjects to silhouette are mountains and dead trees or trees that have lost their leaves. Add a sunset or sunrise to a silhouetted tree and you've got a very interesting shot. Look for the unusual gothic-looking

An African sunset provides spectacular light at the end of the day, one of our favorite times to photograph.

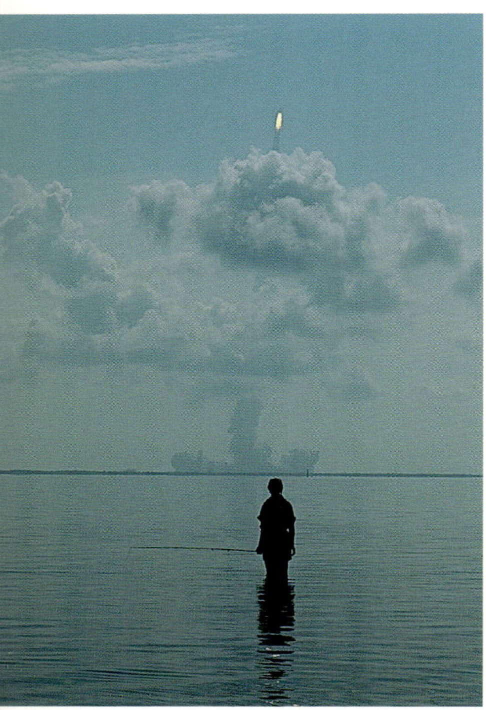

Cathy is silhouetted againt Mosquito Lagoon and a space shuttle launch.

trunks and limbs. You do have to be careful when shooting into the light to watch for lens flare that comes from stray light falling on the lens. If the sun is still in the frame even at the last moment before it sets it can cause flare. Be sure to use a lens hood and move about, changing angles until the flare disappears.

COMPOSITION

The second most important element in making a good photograph is composition. Knowing what to include and what to cut out makes the difference between a snapshot or a really eye-catching photograph. What we see or how we see through our camera viewfinder is the answer to successful composition.

When composing an image, start by taking a serious look through the viewfinder and ask yourself just what it is that makes this image. Play on those answers. For instance, if the subject or focal point is set in a landscape, would it look best in a vertical or horizontal format? We often think that framing our photographs horizontally is the only way to go. You might be surprised at the results you get by simply trying both vertical and horizontal formats.

The rule of thirds is a guideline used by artists and photographers. The center of your picture is not usually the best place for the focal point or main subject to be positioned. The center is not a resting place for the eye. Try off-center placement to create and compose a well-balanced image. Imagine that your viewfinder has a set of grid lines that resemble a game of tic-tac-toe. As you view a scene, place your subject at one of the intersecting points and see how much more interesting the image becomes.

Pay attention to horizons. They should be straight or level and not

The Tobacco Root Mountains of Montana are reflected in a roadside spring pond.

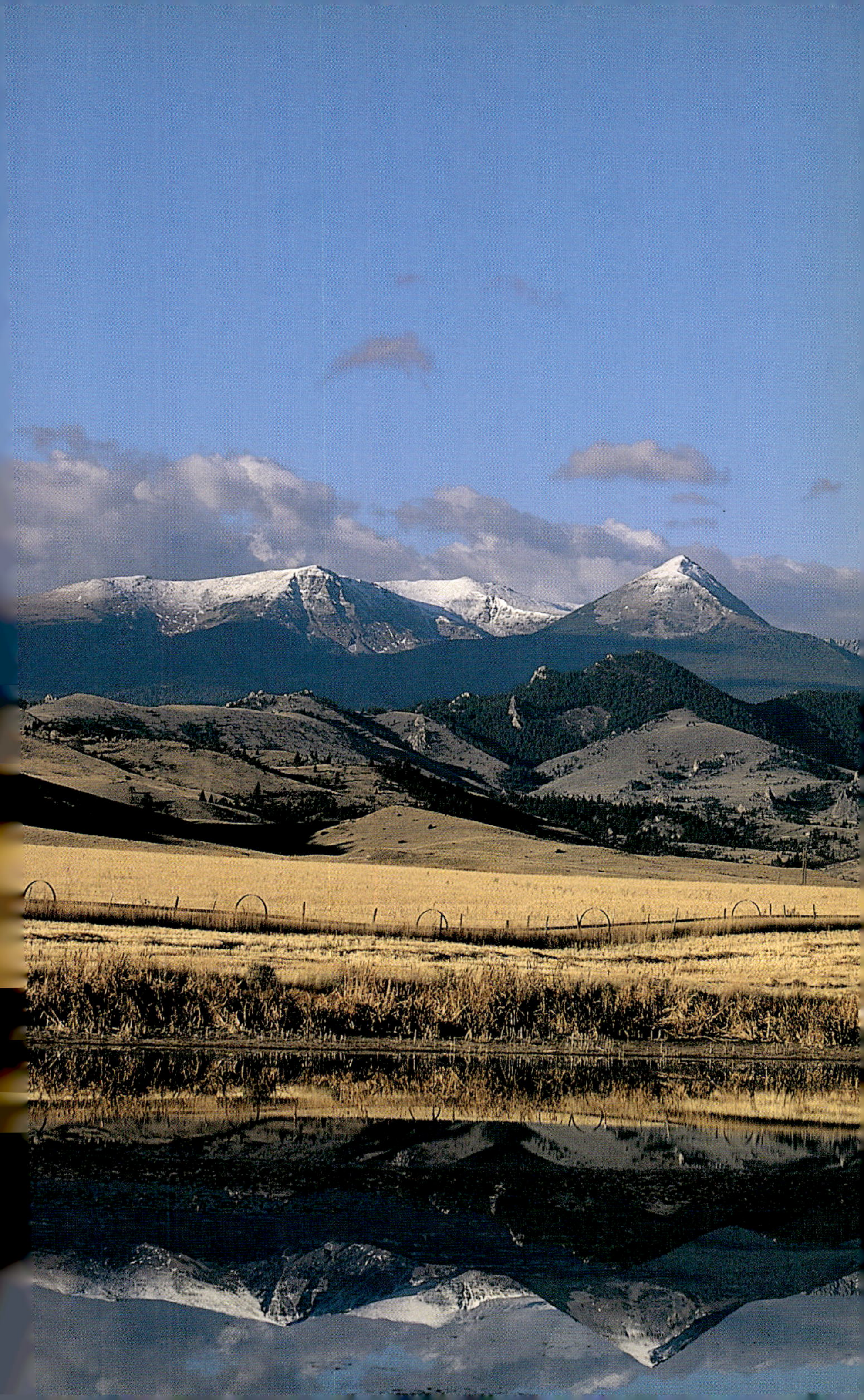

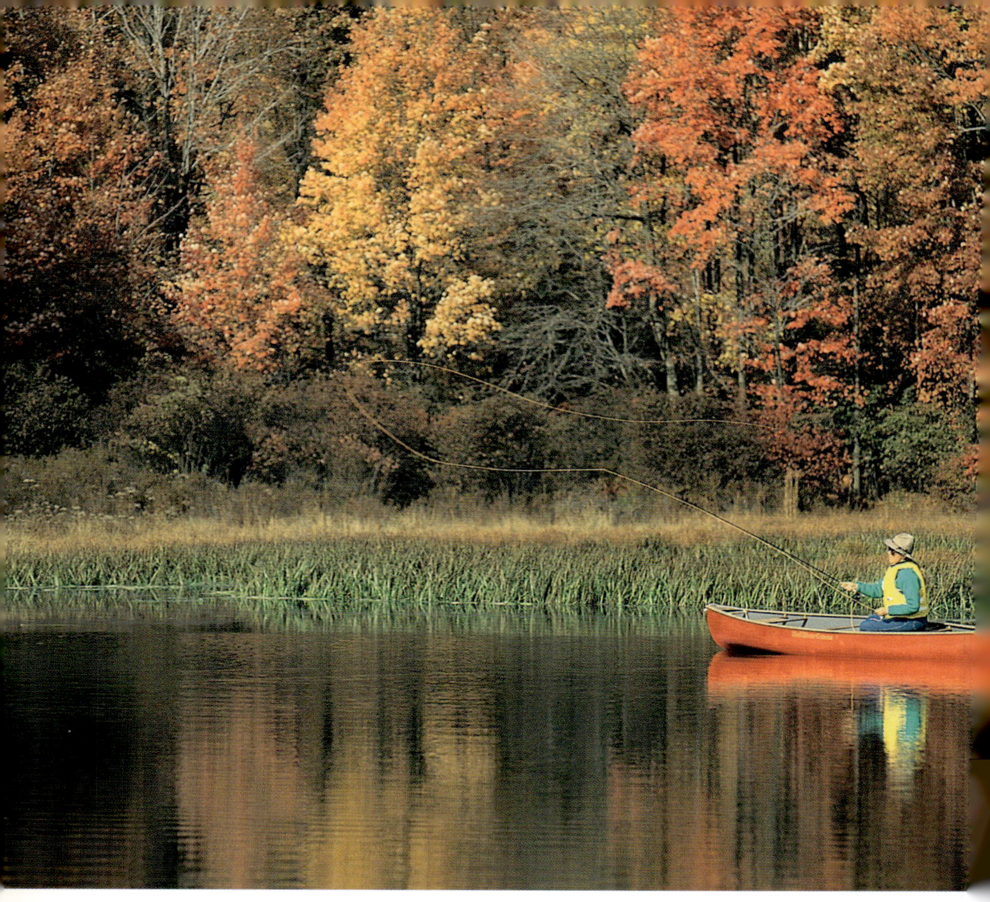

leave the viewer thinking that the earth is slipping to the left or right. Watch for things that distract, like tree limbs that stick out of a person's head or an unwanted light pole that somehow just showed up in a photograph even though you were sure it wasn't there when you snapped the picture. Decide just how much of the sky and foreground you want to include as you compose the image. On gray days try to eliminate as much drab sky as possible and fill the frame instead with the foreground.

We can't emphasize how important it is to change your angle. It's important to move around as you compose an image. Try taking a wide-angle lens and get low. Try lying down on the ground or climbing up a bank and shooting down for a different viewpoint. Your choice of a lens can have a dramatic effect on an image. Wide-angle lenses will get your creative juices flowing. One of our favorite wide angles is a 17mm to 35mm, which gives us great depth of field. A longer telephoto 80mm to 200mm can compress mountains and bring focal points closer to

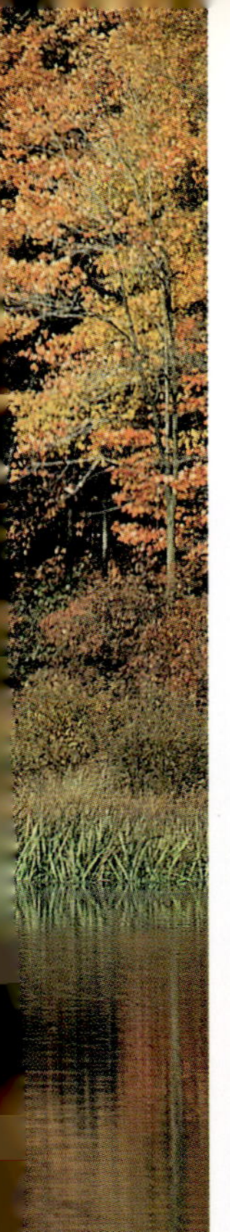

Left: *A well-composed image with a combination of good light and fall colors.*

Below: *A wide-angle lens can give you that creative edge, as it does here in South Africa.*

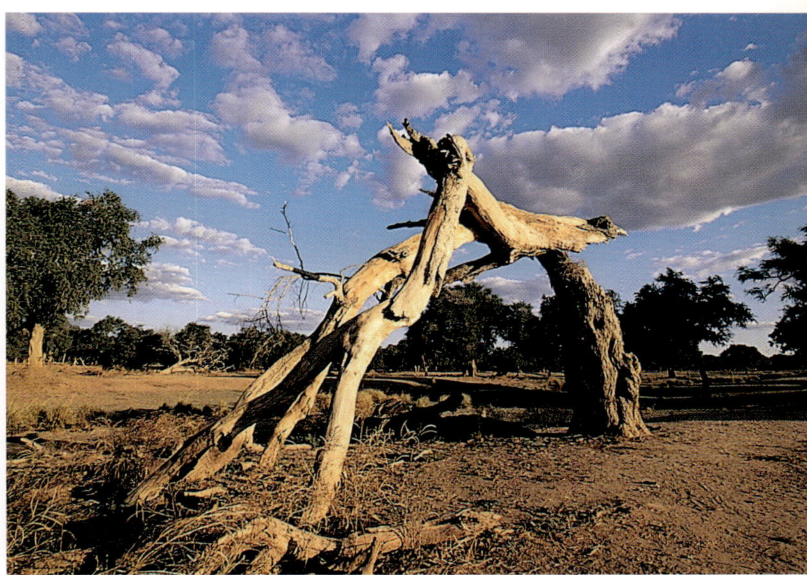

hand. Experiment with different focal lengths, previewing the image and making a final check before you snap the shutter.

Shoot more than one frame. Make this a habit. Never take just one picture of a subject. If you take only one shot and think that you've got it, you're probably going to be disappointed when your images come back from the lab. Things happen. If you don't bracket your exposures, you may have an image that is under- or overexposed. The subject may have moved, people blink, things go wrong. Shoot up the film, bracket if you have the option, and move around. Put the odds in your favor, and you'll be glad in the end that you did.

Your images should have a center of interest and tell a story. They should be strong, bold, and show a sense of depth. There are no set-in-cement rules when it comes to composition. Beauty is in the eye of the beholder, and if you're happy with the image and the way it's composed, then you're the winner.

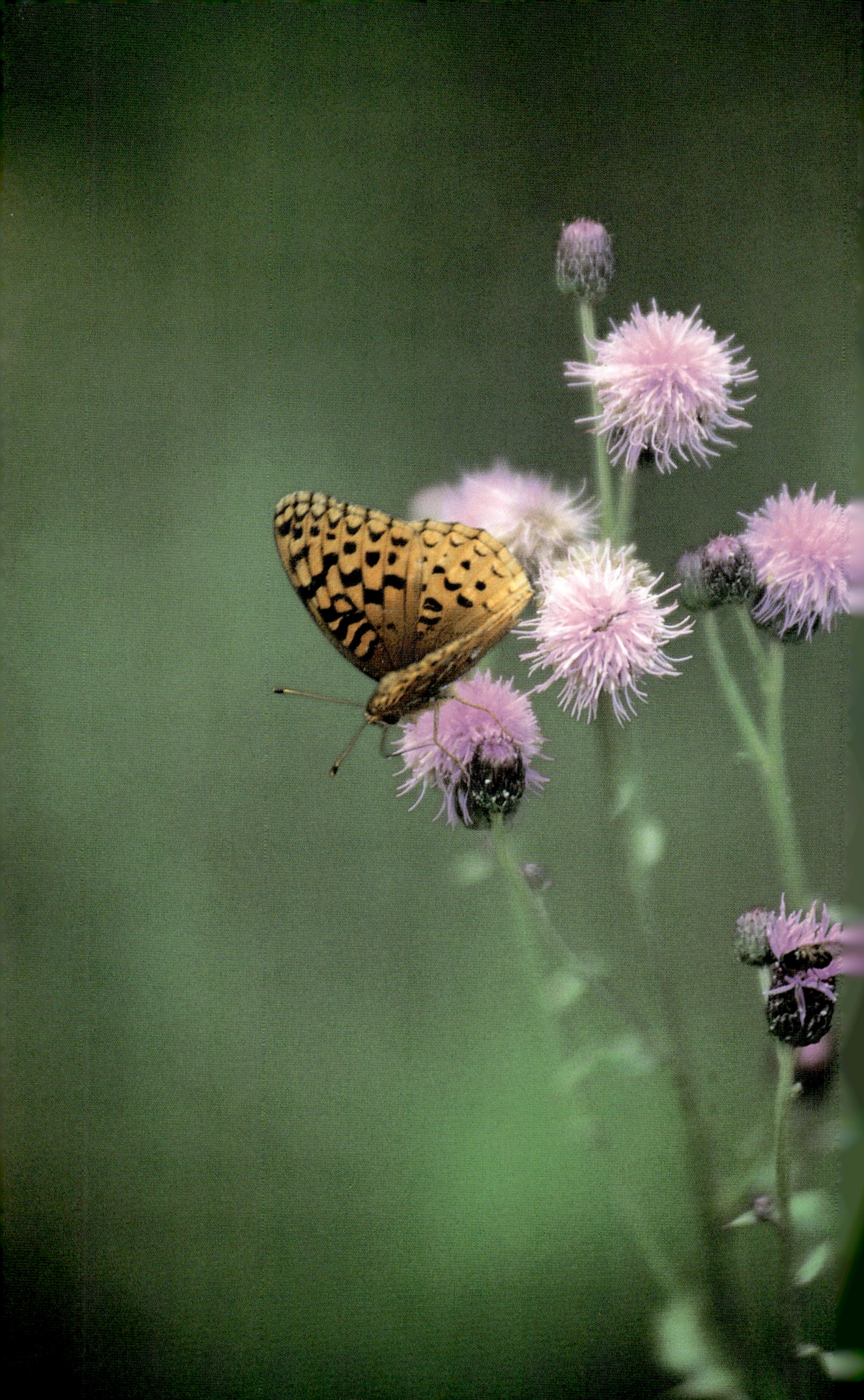

< CHAPTER 4 >

Flash

Your Portable Light Source

Your flash accessory unit is exactly that—a portable light source that can often turn an average outdoor image into a good one. In the past, a lot of photographers refrained from using flash in their outdoor photography because they felt that using one gave the images a flat and unnatural look. With many of the older manual flash units, the photographer had to determine sync speeds and guide numbers, and as a result, there was a lot of guessing. After much experimenting, you could eventually figure out what worked. Then technology gave us TTL, or through the lens, flash metering found on most cameras today.

TTL is a dramatic improvement over the old ways and has taken outdoor flash photography to new levels. TTL balances flash output with the ambient light to give better and more natural-looking exposures even when you are using a filter. A flash in outdoor photography can soften hard shadows, freeze motion, and make you a better photographer. Today's flash units are so smart that they can compensate and solve backlighting problems and ensure that bright or dark

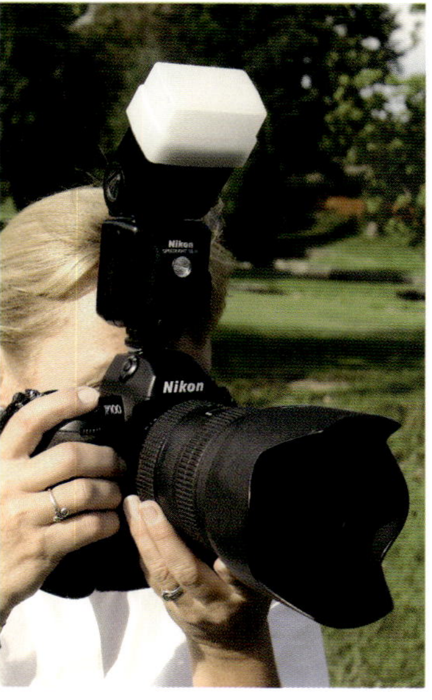

Today's flash units can solve many lighting challenges.

Left: *Cathy captured this moment when the butterfly added another dimension to the wildflower shot.*

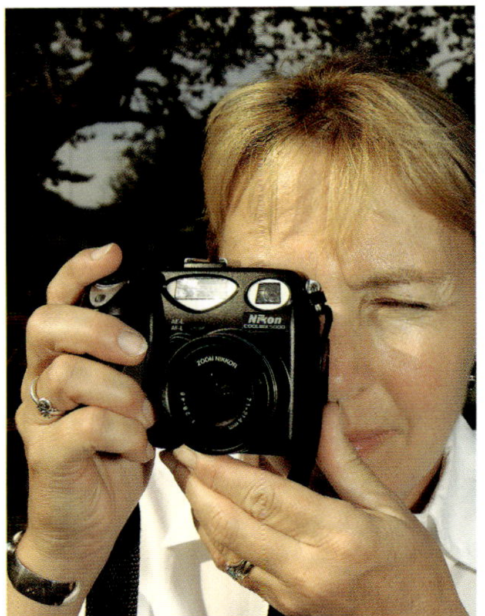

Most modern point-and-shoot cameras have a built-in flash.

foreground subjects are not over- or underexposed. Most modern point-and-shoot cameras, as well as a few SLRs, have a built-in flash, which is OK in tight situations (ten feet or less) where a lot of extra light is not necessary. But if you need to reach out and flood a larger area with light, you'll want to consider an external and more powerful speed light.

Right: *Adding flash can freeze motion caused by a breeze.*

Far right: *Flash freezes the motion of these flowers.*

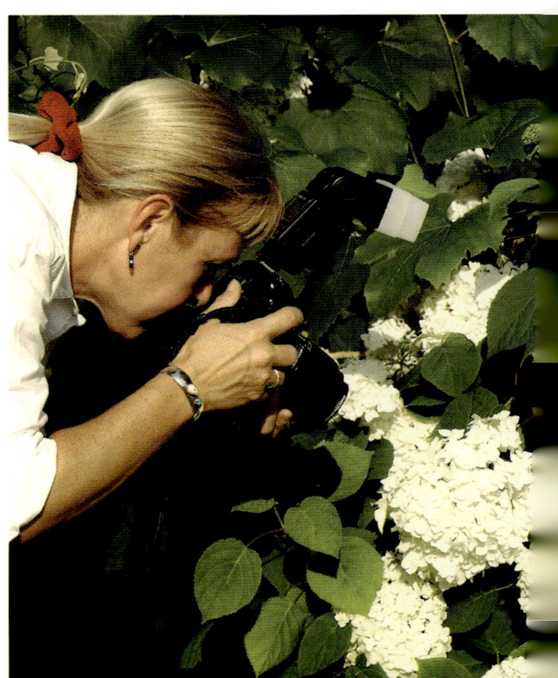

There are times, too, when you want to get close to the subject. Perhaps you are using a macro lens and the built-in flash would throw the light out above the flower or insect, completely missing it. An external flash fitted with the accessory cable can be held at any angle to light the subject or to throw or bounce light onto the subject. To use an external speed light, your camera body needs to have a hot shoe or flash accessory shoe to which you can attach the speed light or cable.

We often rely on our flash to freeze motion for us. For instance, if we are working with wildflowers or closeups of insects on a windy day, it's almost impossible to capture a sharp image because the subject is moving. A short burst of flash will freeze the subject. Most speed lights

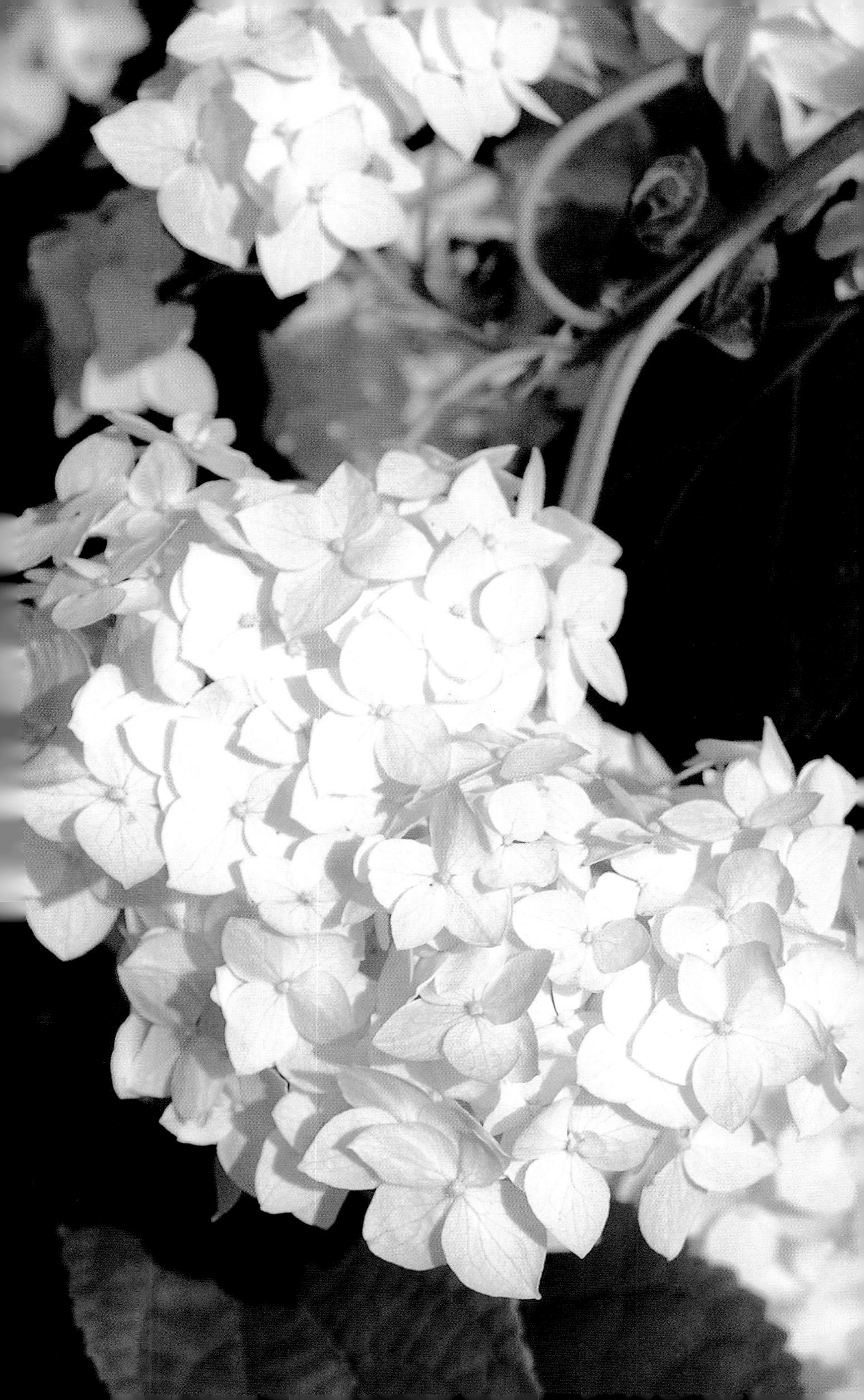

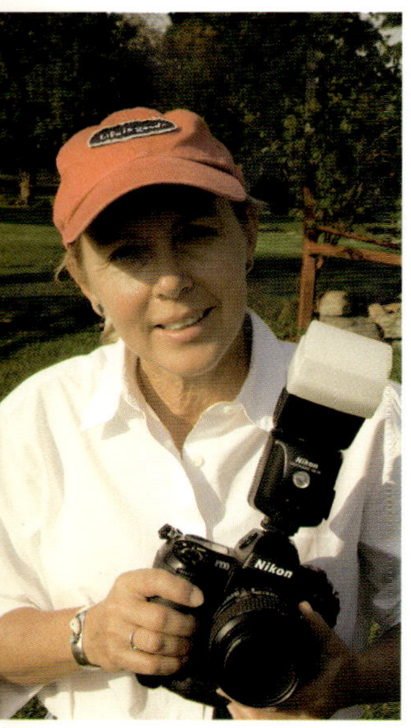

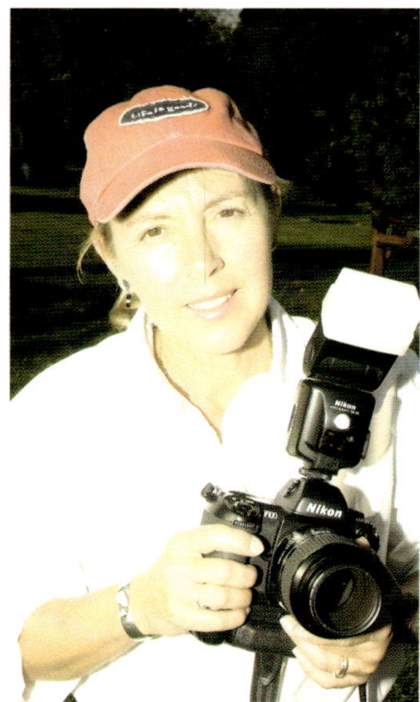

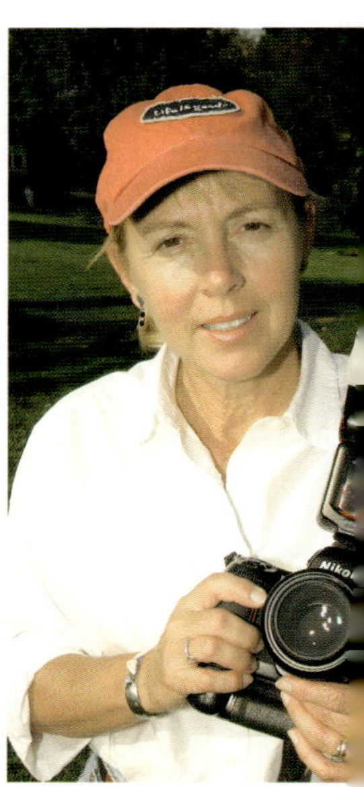

In the photo on the left, with no fill flash, there is a dark shadow from the hat brim, but the center photo has too much fill flash. The photo on the right has the correct amount of fill flash.

offer a flash exposure compensation control, which allows you to increase or decrease the amount of flash output. How much or how little flash is needed will depend on the situation. You may want to bracket your flash and keep notes on your exposures. By referring to your notes later, you'll learn what settings work best in which situations. When using the bracketing option, you'll use up the battery supply in a hurry, so remember to carry extra batteries.

We regularly rely on fill flash to soften dark shadows such as those created by a hat brim, and through experience and note keeping, we know that a minus 1.7 on our speed light will usually give us a natural-looking portrait. When we are working with a wide-angle lens but working close to our subject (five feet or less) and using flash, we rely on a diffuser to spread out and soften the flash. Our Nikon speed light has a built-in diffuser that can be dropped down in front of the flash head. You'll find a variety of diffusers for different camera models at good photo shops. The diffuser spreads out the light to create a more even effect.

If you're using a larger and more powerful speed light as an external light source, it helps to get the flash off the camera. You can use a flash bracket and a dedicated extension cable that will help you reduce red-eye problems as well as spread out the flash burst for a more natural and detailed image. The flash bracket also provides support and helps you stabilize your camera for sharper pictures.

Red eye is a common flash-related problem that most of us have had to deal with at one time or another. It's the result of the light from the flash reflecting off the interior surface of the subject's eyes. It happens in animal shots as well as those featuring people. Most modern point-and-shoot cameras now offer a red-eye reduction or preflash that fires a short burst of light before the main flash fires. With a preflash, the pupils contract before the photo is taken, thus minimizing the red-eye effect.

A good speed light is worth its weight in gold, but like all pieces of modern camera equipment, it has a technical side that you need to become familiar with. Read your owner's manual carefully, and become comfortable with both the camera and the flash. Once you're comfortable using this piece of equipment, you'll see significant improvement in your photos.

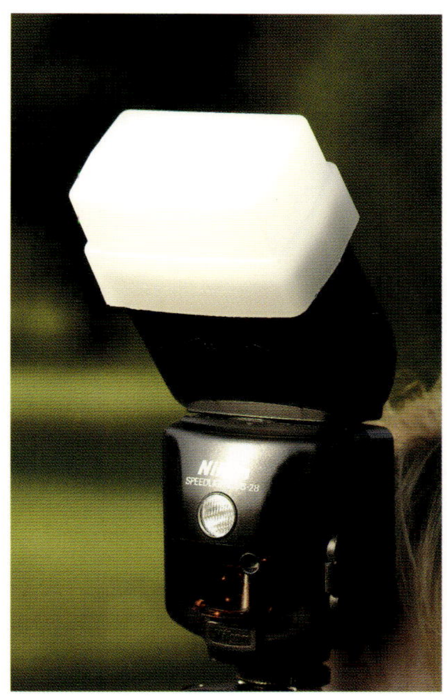

A diffuser will help spread out the light when working with a wide-angle lens.

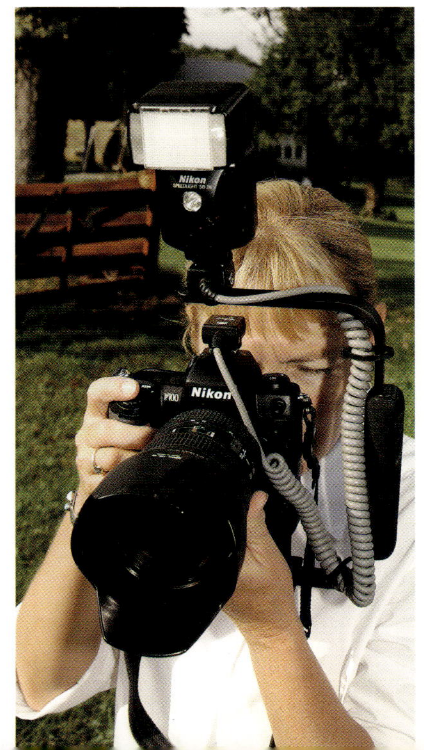

Using a flash bracket and a dedicated extension cable will help you reduce red-eye problems.

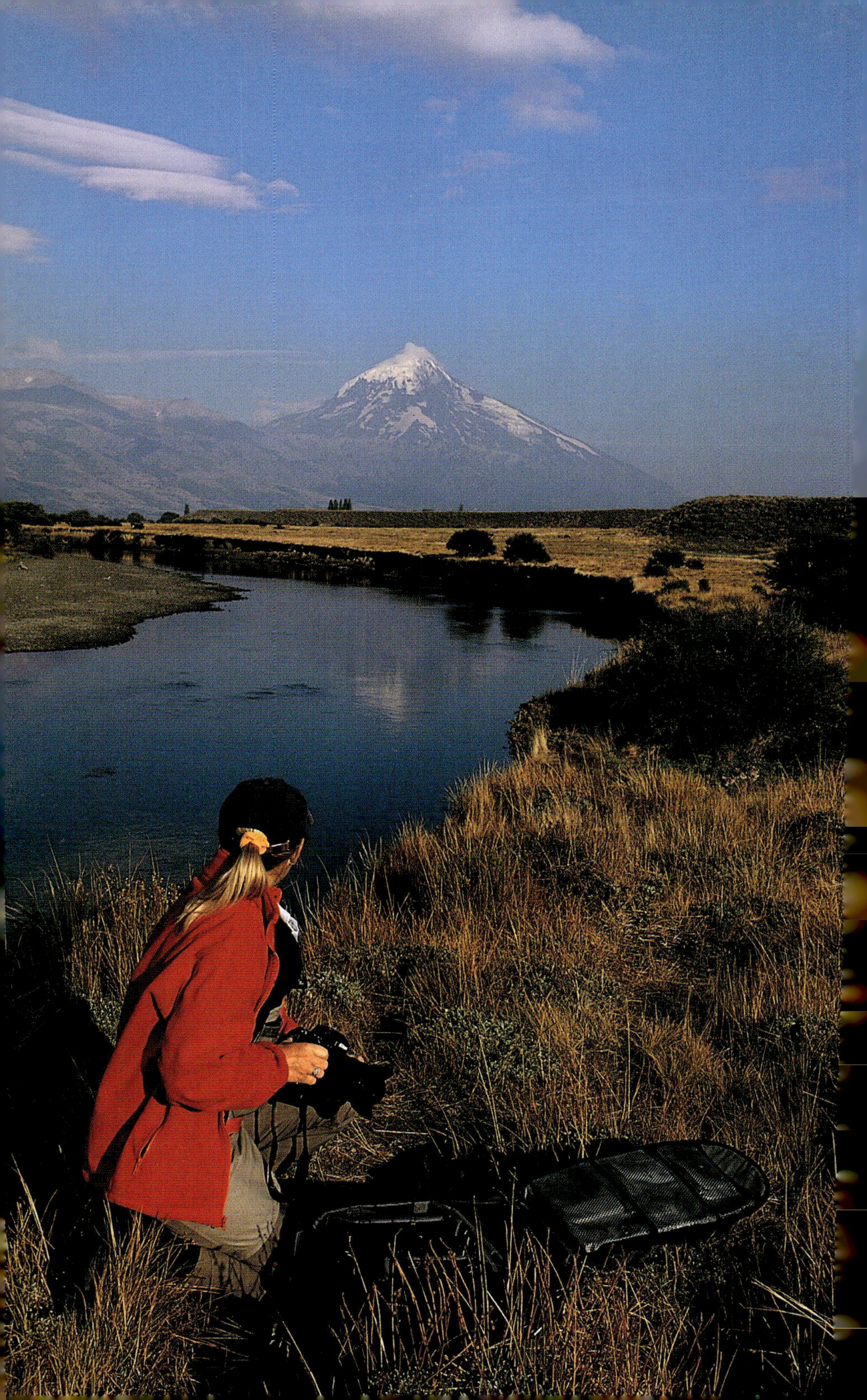

< C H A P T E R 5 >

Your Camera Bag

There are a lot of choices when it comes to camera bags, fanny packs, and backpacks designed to keep your camera and gear handy and safe. The size of your camera bag depends on your camera system and the amount of gear that you intend to carry. The design should be user friendly—you should be able to access your gear quickly, and the bag should keep it all organized. If a photo opportunity comes up and your camera is in the bag, you don't want to be fumbling around with difficult zippers or buckles wasting time and missing a good shot.

There is no one perfect bag because, as photographers, our needs vary. We've tried a couple of guaranteed waterproof bags that haven't worked. They were either not waterproof or so waterproof that we couldn't easily get into them. The hard-sided Pelican cases are just perfect for protecting equipment, but they are hard to get in and out of quickly. Because they are made of high-impact material, they don't give when you're trying to squeeze them into a small space (under the seat or in the overhead bin of small planes), and they are difficult to hike or walk

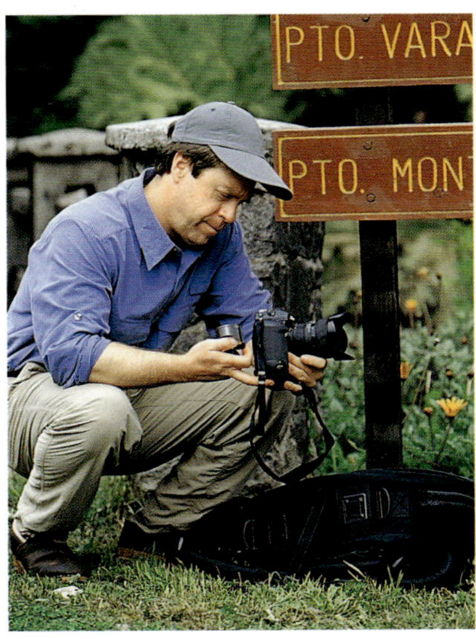

Traveling with your camera requires careful planning.

Left: *This was a rare opportunity with perfect light to photograph the Rio Malleo River and the Lanin Volcano in Argentina.*

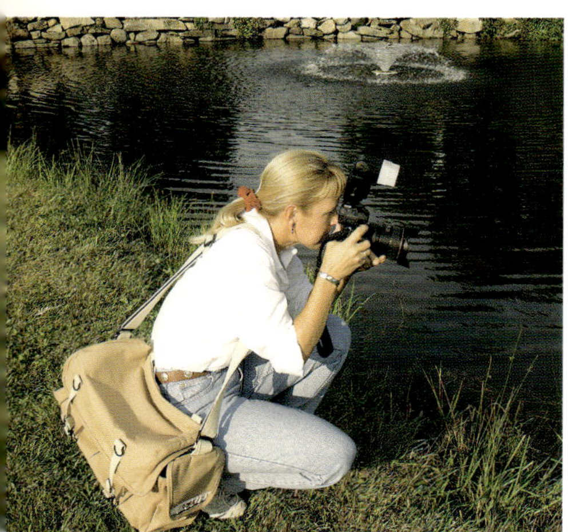

Shoulder bags are popular with a lot of outdoor photographers.

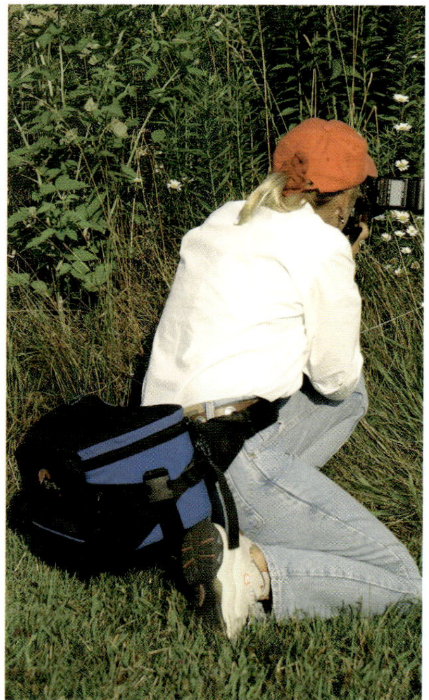

This Lowepro fanny pack is a convenient and mobile pack.

with for any distance. And because they are so well padded, it's hard to fit in any extras. But they do a great job of protecting the equipment.

We carry a small Nikon Coolpix 5000 digital camera in a thin neoprene case that easily fits into a carry-on bag. It goes just about everywhere we go. We load our Coolpix with a one gig card that will hold a lot of images. It has an onboard flash, a short zoom lens, and it does the job when we are restricted or unable to carry more equipment. When we're traveling on assignments and carrying more camera gear, we rely on either a Lowepro fanny pack or a Tamrac Extreme backpack. Both accommodate our larger SLRs and are easy to get into quickly. The Extreme backpack has a weatherproof cover which has been a lifesaver in wet weather.

Since we have found no perfect bag or pack, we end up compromising. We love our photo backpacks when we're hiking and moving around a lot. But they are not as waterproof as we often need them to be. So when we find ourselves working out of a flats skiff or flat-bottomed boat, we put the camera bag on a boat cushion to keep it up off the bottom and to help cushion a rough boat ride. If there is rain or splash from the waves or wind, we'll pull out the always-handy garbage bag and put the pack inside. The photo fanny pack is perfect for walking in the water for any great distance when we want to "go light" with perhaps one camera body, a lens and flash, and half a dozen rolls of film. On the other hand, if we're set up in a blind photographing waterfowl, the shoulder bag or hard-sided case is our choice. In the end, you'll probably end up with more than one system to handle different situations.

Whatever style you decide on, look for a bag with a lot of foam padding to protect and absorb shock and dividers that can be arranged to suit your needs. The better bags are made of tough nylon with heavy-duty zippers and snaps and well-padded, nonslip straps. Make sure the stress points are reinforced and there are enough external pockets to accommodate your needs.

WHAT'S IN THE BAG

Inside our bags we carry the usual SLR bodies and our favorite assortment of lenses. Along with these are filters, a lens-cleaning cloth, an antistatic brush, enough spare batteries to cover the trip (our Nikon film cameras use lithium AAs), two power packs, and a charger for our D1X digital camera. We leave some of these things in the room during the day. We always carry two heavy-duty

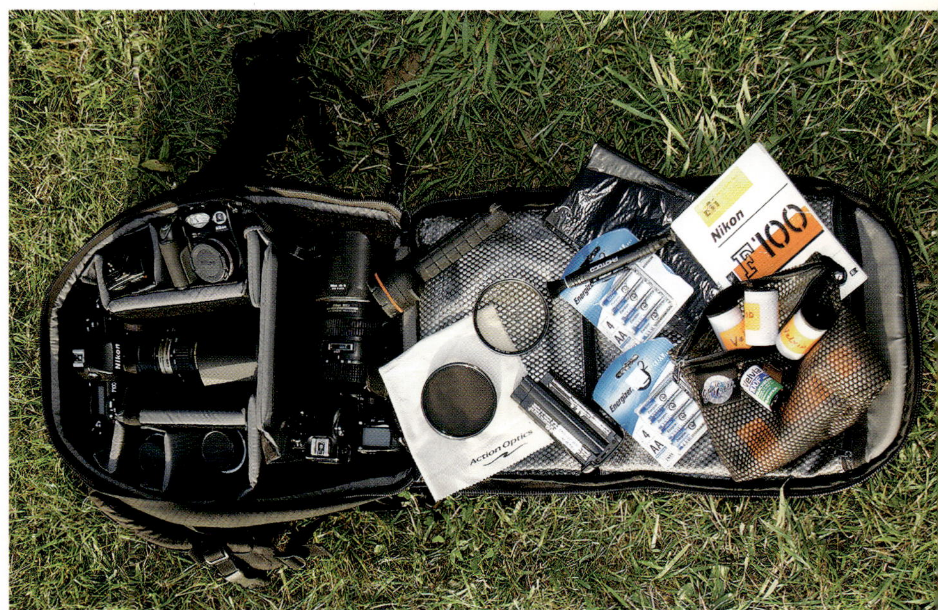

Our camera backpack loaded with gear.

garbage bags and a few (gallon size) Ziploc bags folded and placed in an outside pocket of the camera bag. In the outside back pocket of the pack is a space blanket. It serves many purposes. We have used it as a temporary tarp to shield us from rain or snow when we're changing lenses or film. It's provided us with a temporary blind to shoot from. It always doubles as an emergency blanket. A small Maglite can come in handy, not only for finding things in the dark, but it can serve as a light source as well. If we're going to a tropical environment, we normally carry a supply of moisture-absorbing silica gel to absorb moisture in the pack.

For years we traveled with a Leatherman in our camera bag. It's the perfect all-purpose tool and has gotten us out of a lot of tight spots, but with the new restrictions at airports we can no longer carry it on board. Now we pack it in our checked luggage and put it in our camera bag after we leave the airport. We carry a small roll of duct tape and our camera manual. We hide a small amount of cash in an inside pocket and a photocopy of our passports and our home information, address, phone, and email. If the passport is stolen, the photocopy will help get us back home. If the pack is lost or stolen, the identifying information might help get it returned to us.

TRAVELING WITH YOUR CAMERA

If you plan to travel in third-world countries with your camera gear, dress conservatively. We wear casual unassuming clothes, and our camera bags look well used. Leave the expensive or new clothes at home, or pack them. The less you stand out, the safer you are. Make sure your wallet, tickets, and passports are in inside pockets that can be secured with a zipper or button closure. A photo vest is a convenient item to have and we use them occasionally, but you might not want to suggest that you're a photographer or a journalist.

We encourage you to always carry the camera bag yourself. Porters, friends, taxi drivers will try to help, and most of the time all goes well. But there are going to be times when it doesn't. No one is going to be as careful as you, and accidents will happen. If the camera bag falls off a cart or if you pick it up upside down when you forgot to close it or it slides off the truck tailgate, you've got no one to blame but yourself.

Keep in mind any drastic change in temperature going from inside your room to outside. Often, especially in tropical humid locations, all of our lenses will fog up from being inside an air conditioned room all night. We've found that if we put our camera bags inside a closet or bathroom and close the door, they won't get as cold as they do when sitting in the air conditioned bedroom or living room. By keeping them warm they don't fog up when we take them out in the morning.

TRAVELING WITH FILM

We mentioned in chapter 2 that traveling through airport security is a breeze with a digital memory card since the X-ray screening will not affect the card. Faster film, ISO 800 and higher, on the other hand, can be affected or fogged by a X-ray scan. Fortunately most of us never use film in this range. In our experience, ISO 50 to 400 film has never been affected by scanning. Even after a month in Argentina, traveling by air from one end of the country to the other with our film going through more than twenty scans, it showed no evidence of the scans affecting the film. The consideration between film and digital for us is not so much the ease of passing through the screening process, but the extra weight, bulk, and space required for the film. Although the screening process is quite harmless, it is important to remember not to put any film in the checked luggage. The higher intensity CT scans that your luggage is subjected to will fog all film regardless of speed.

We carry our film in clear 5 x 9 x 2-inch Rubbermaid containers that we buy at the grocery store. We take the film from the original round plastic canister and wrap each one with an extra-small rubber band to hold the exposed leader in place. We then put thirty-five rolls of film in each container. When we get to the airport security, we send the boxes through, and if the TSA agents have any questions they can simply remove the lid and examine the contents. Don't be like a friend who once tried to take forty rolls of film still in the cardboard boxes. The agents had him open each roll for inspection. He protested and ended up spending even more time in security as they then decided to check each and every item in his camera backpack. We remember to put ten empty film canisters in our checked luggage. When we arrive at our destination we fill the empty canisters with film to use through the day.

When your pack or camera bag is sitting out in the bright sunlight for any amount of time, the contents will heat up. If you have a light rain jacket or nylon shell or a towel, lay it over the camera bag. The sunlight will now reflect off the light color and the contents will stay a little cooler. It's important to keep professional film cool, and taking along only enough film for the day and covering the bag when in bright sunlight will make a difference.

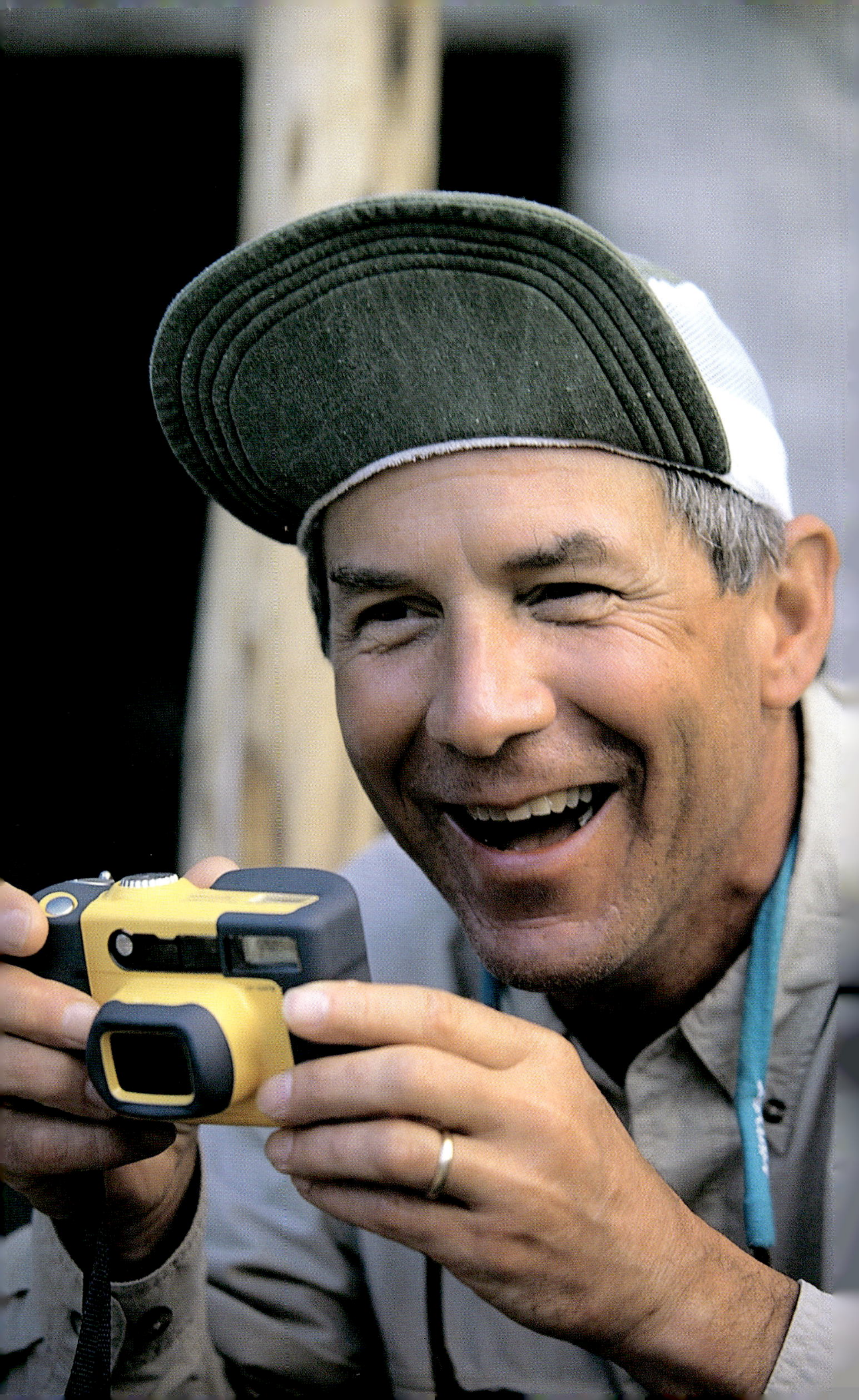

< CHAPTER 6 >

Having Fun with Your Camera

PEOPLE

You would think that people would be easy to photograph. After all, we've all had lots of practice looking at the camera and smiling when someone says "cheese." Unfortunately, it's seldom this easy, and actually wild animals are often easier subjects. For some reason we get self-conscious and uncomfortable in front of a camera. We move around and change expressions and fret about how we look. We stiffen up, smiles start to look forced and unnatural, and the photograph ends up looking staged and cold.

Good images of people don't often happen by accident. A spontaneous photo opportunity is a rarity, but a great photograph happens just often enough to keep us aiming for it. There are some things you can do to help your chances. If you're sure your subject won't mind your shooting, try to catch the subject off guard,

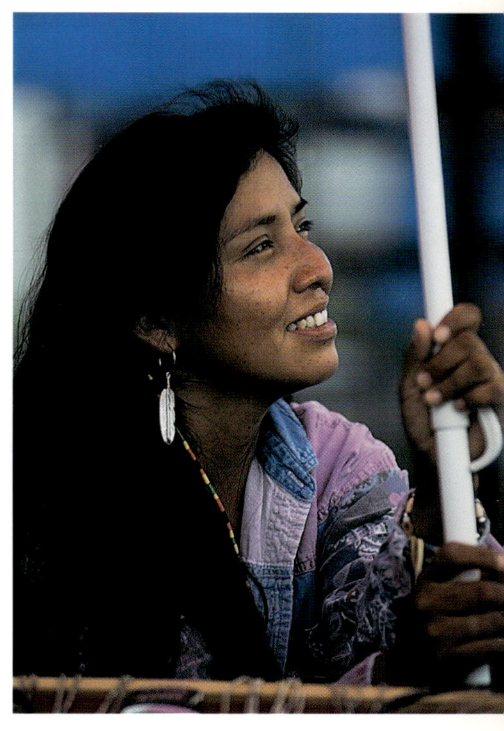

A spontaneous smile helps make this image on the Crow Indian Reservation in Montana.

Left: *This is what photography is all about—Parker Sterner shows his enthusiam for taking pictures.*

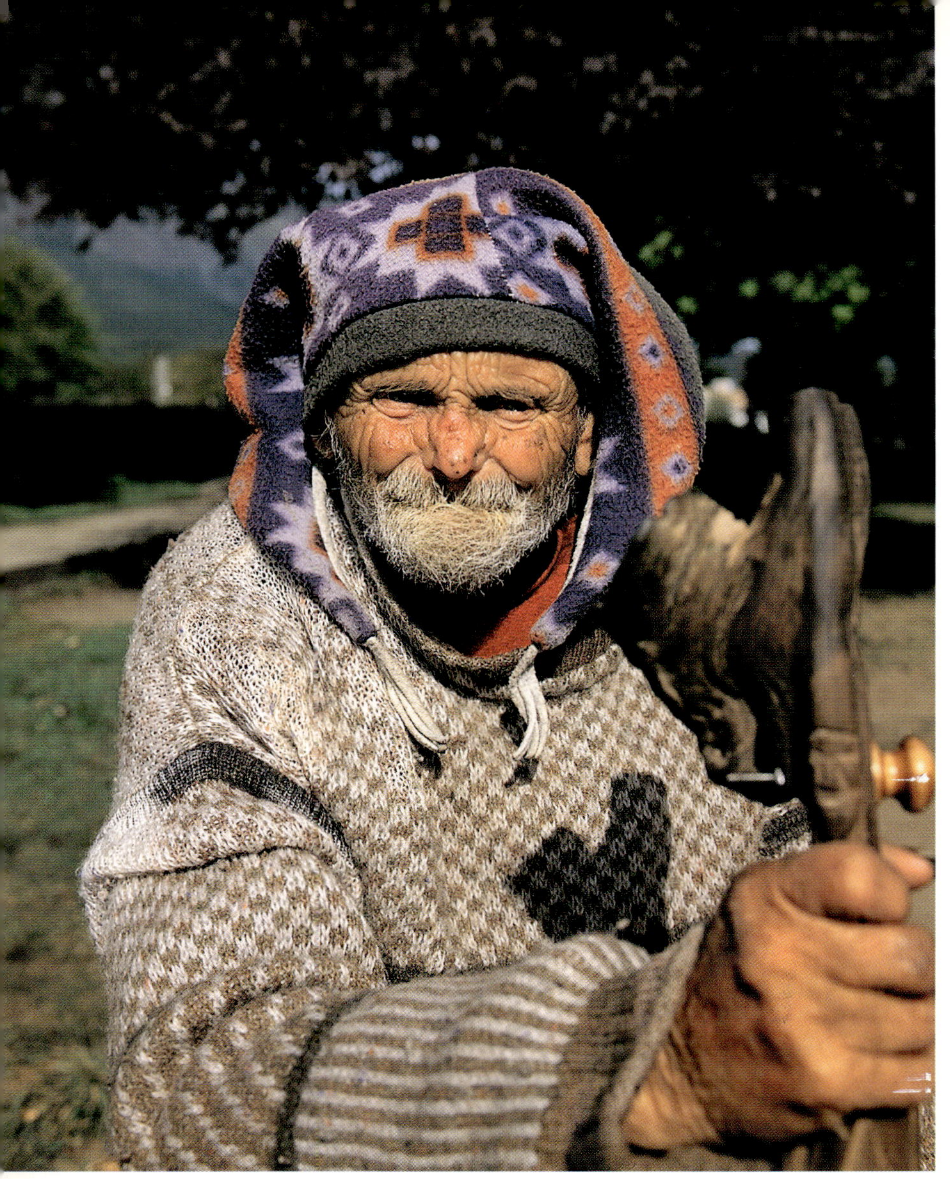

An interesting face, good light, and a fifteen-cent ice cream cone work for us in Argentina.

preoccupied in laughter or engaged in an activity, and unaware of the camera. Whenever you're planning to photograph a stranger or are just not sure, ask permission. A quick way to get into trouble is to stick your camera in the face of someone who

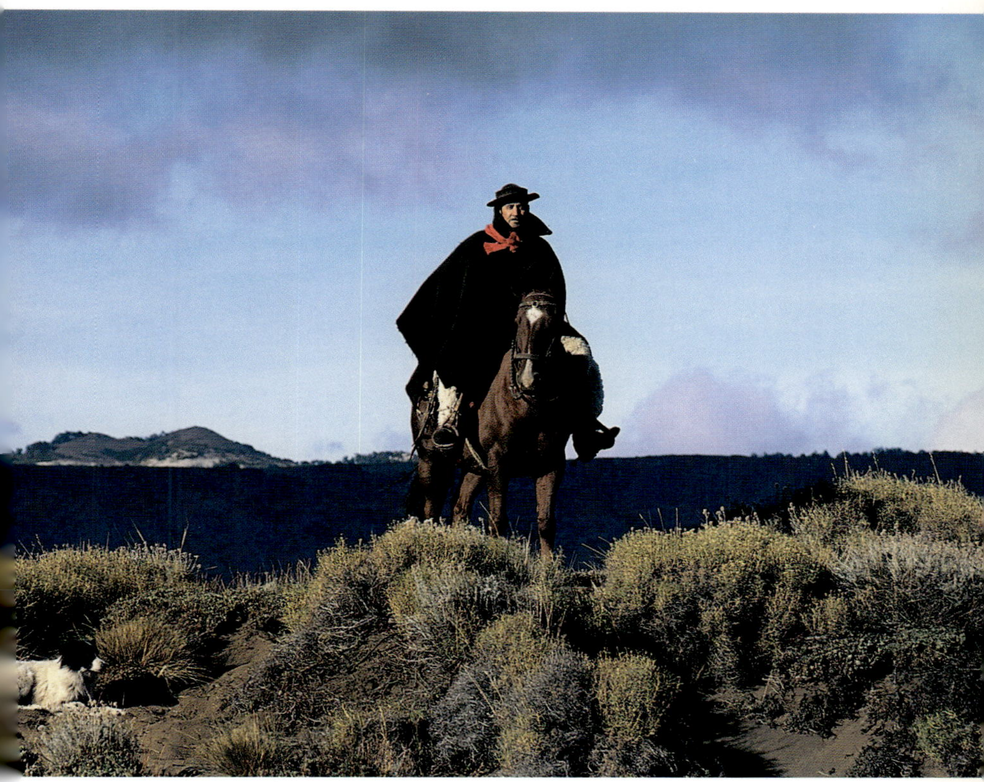

Morning light, a gaucho, his horse, and dog make for a great composition.

doesn't want it there! Most good photographs are the result of some planning: choosing the location, knowing the subject or subjects, and letting everyone know the plan. A good photographer will know what to do to make the subject feel relaxed and will know how to joke in order to create a relaxed atmosphere. A good photographer knows what it takes to get the shot.

When shooting portraits, pay attention and focus on the eyes. They must be tack sharp for a good image. Try posing your subject at a 45-degree angle, slightly turning the body, instead of having the person face straight on. Pay close attention to the background and make sure nothing distracts from the subject. Apply the rule of thirds, and try to keep your subject's head in the upper third of the picture.

A few years ago we were traveling through the small village of El Bolson, Argentina, when we spotted a small, distinctively dressed older man sitting on a bench. He had a most

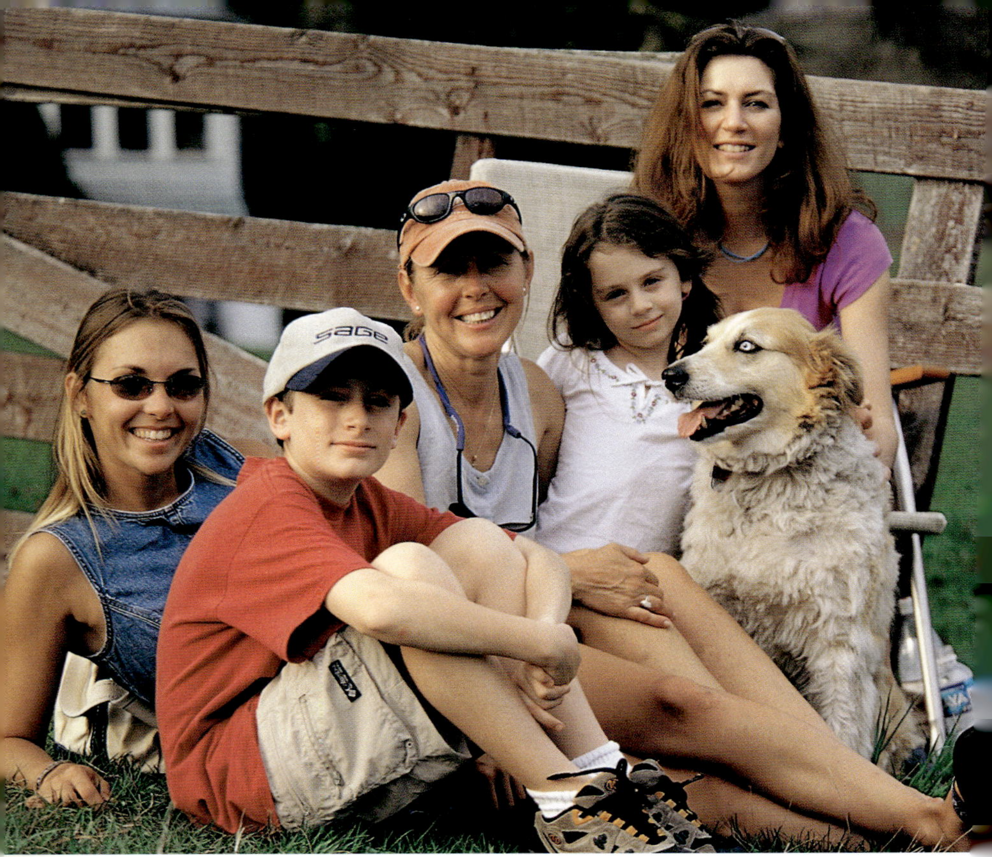

Family shots are fun and easy to do. But keep it light and make sure everyone is looking at the camera.

interesting face, and we knew we wanted his picture. It took thirty minutes—we speaking English and he Spanish—a lot of sign language, and a fifteen-cent ice cream cone before he graciously posed for us. Another day we came upon a gaucho sitting on a horse on a ridge above the Rio Malleo. His dog sat close by. With the mountains behind them, it made a great image. We stopped our car, introduced ourselves, and told him we'd be honored if he would permit us to take his photograph (again in our modest Spanish). He agreed, and we got what has become one of our favorite images from rural Argentina. A year later we returned to the same area and delivered a print to our new gaucho friend, who was very pleased to have a photograph of himself with his horse and dog.

CHILDREN

Kids make great subjects, and having a photographic record of our children growing up in the outdoors is priceless. But kids are people too, and just like adults, they present challenges. The best pictures of kids are almost always taken when they're at their best. It's just impossible to make a tired or unhappy kid look happy. They're too honest and don't know how, nor want, to hide their emotions. So, for instance, if you're hiking with young children, try to get as many images as possible at the beginning of the hike. At picnics, field trips, and amusement parks, take photos early when everyone is fresh, excited, and happy. And, as long as the kids are happy, continue shooting. When they get bored, tired, and hungry, put the camera away. Nobody wants a picture of himself looking out-of-sorts, including the kids. Nor do we want photographs reminding us of the part of the trip when we were grumpy. If you show only the happy times, that will eventually be what everyone remembers about the trip, and the kids will be more agreeable to posing again in the future.

Tight shots of smiling faces are always favorites, but when there's a background in the photo, remember to keep it clean and simple. A background that's too busy distracts from the image. And remember that a little color can improve a photograph. So, if there's a way to get a red hat, an orange parka, or colorful flowers in the photo, do it.

If you want a group shot of you and your group at the campground or at the trailhead and there are other people around, don't hesitate to ask someone you don't know to take the picture. Most people are happy to help out. Or, use a tripod. We have a photographer friend who always tells people their second lens should be a tripod. A tripod will prevent any movement of the camera that could result in blurry photographs. We've found that a monopod is lighter and much easier to use and still does a great job of holding the camera still. If you have to ask someone else to take the photo, be considerate and get the group together and compose the shot before asking. This way you can make sure everyone is in the frame and in focus with the right settings. If there is no one around to ask

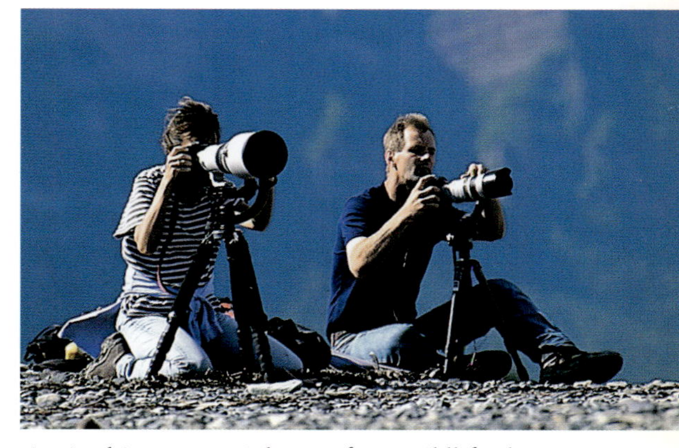

A tripod is an essential part of any wildlife photographer's gear.

and no tripod, experiment with setting the self-timer on your camera and placing it on a fence post or picnic table. Now you can get in the picture yourself before the shutter is released.

When you're taking informal photos and not portraits, photograph the kids playing together, looking at each other instead of at the camera. These shots are more natural, less staged, and livelier. Don't hesitate to try different angles; experiment and let your creativity flow.

Taking pictures of your kids is a great way to introduce them to photography as well. Encourage them to look through the camera and take pictures themselves if they show any interest. Kids love digital cameras because they can instantly see the results on the monitor. And, if they don't get the shot or aren't happy with it, they can erase it and try again. You can help them make their own albums, greeting cards, and CDs with the images they've created.

ANIMALS

Both wild and domestic animals are fun to photograph. Like people, they have personalities, and it's exciting to try to capture their individuality in photographs. Working with animals takes a certain degree of sensitivity, a lot of patience, and at times some caution as well. We quickly learn to expect the unexpected when it comes to photographing animals. Composing an image with people can be as easy as asking them to turn this way or that way, but with animals you are often at the mercy of the moment at hand. Being ready for that moment and responding to it make the difference between a good photo and a great one.

Pets

Pets are the most dependable because they're familiar with us, we can get close, and we know their routines and habits and can have some hope of capturing them at their best. Our dogs and cats can act as dignified as it gets and then turn right around and be the silliest things we ever saw. Photographing their different habits, moods, and personalities is both challenging and rewarding.

For some great shots, try getting down to their level. Lie on the grass and have someone tease your cat with a piece of yarn or a string. A cat reacting and stalking the yarn makes a great subject to photograph at their eye level. Photograph your dog rolling over or doing tricks. Maybe you can find him asleep on the forbidden couch. If you have both a dog

Cats are always fun to photograph. From kittens to adults, they give us wonderful opportunities to have fun with our cameras.

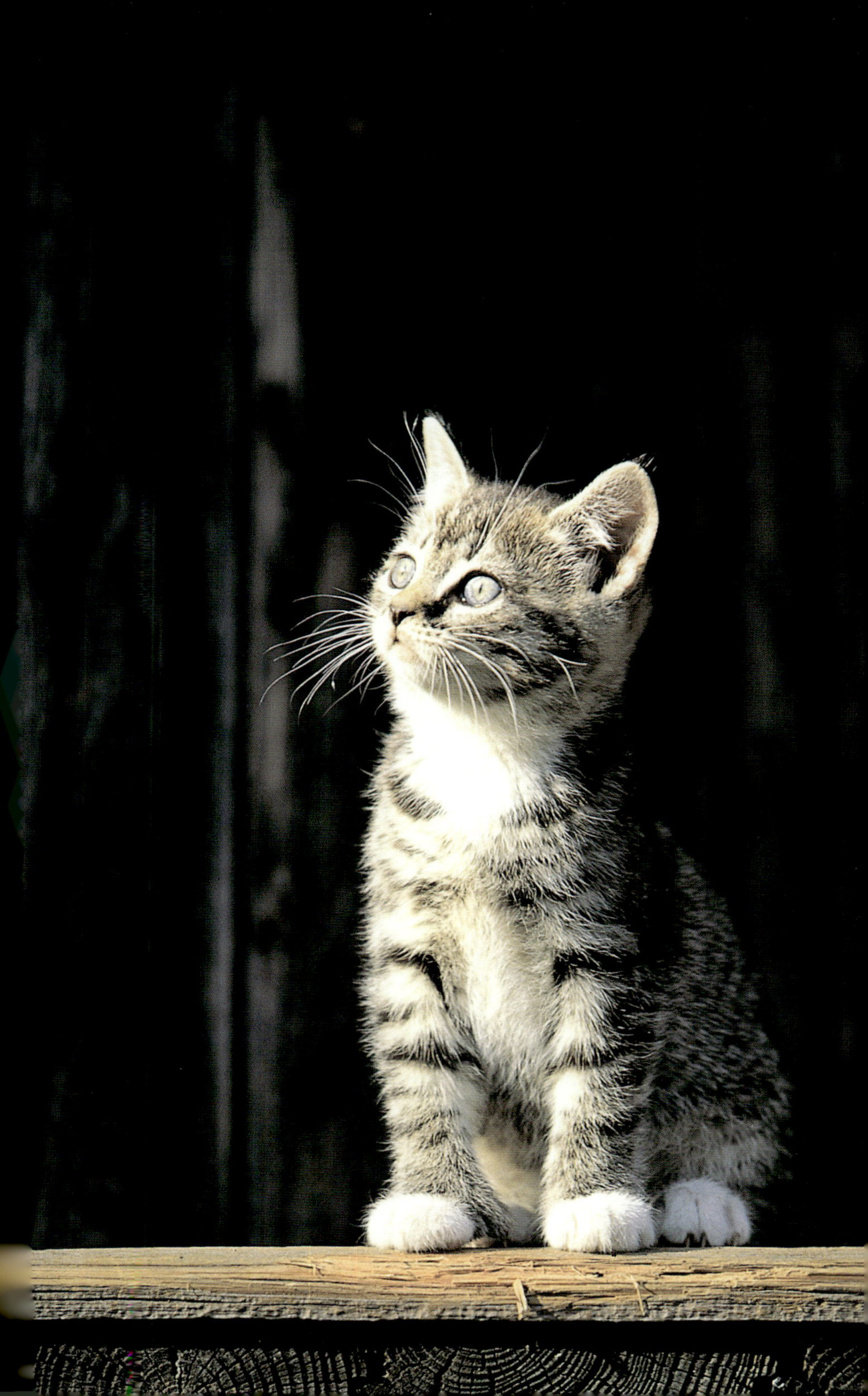

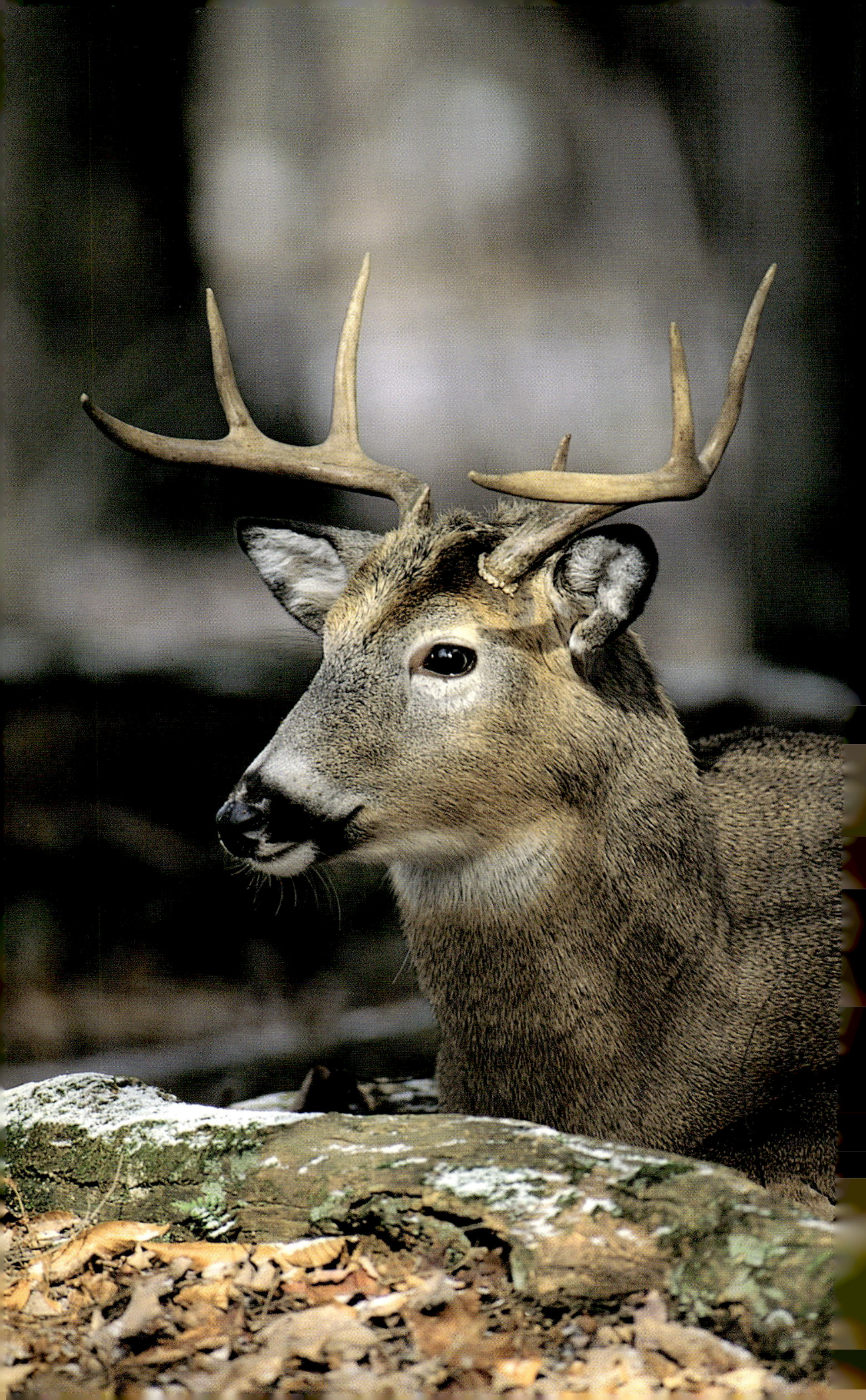

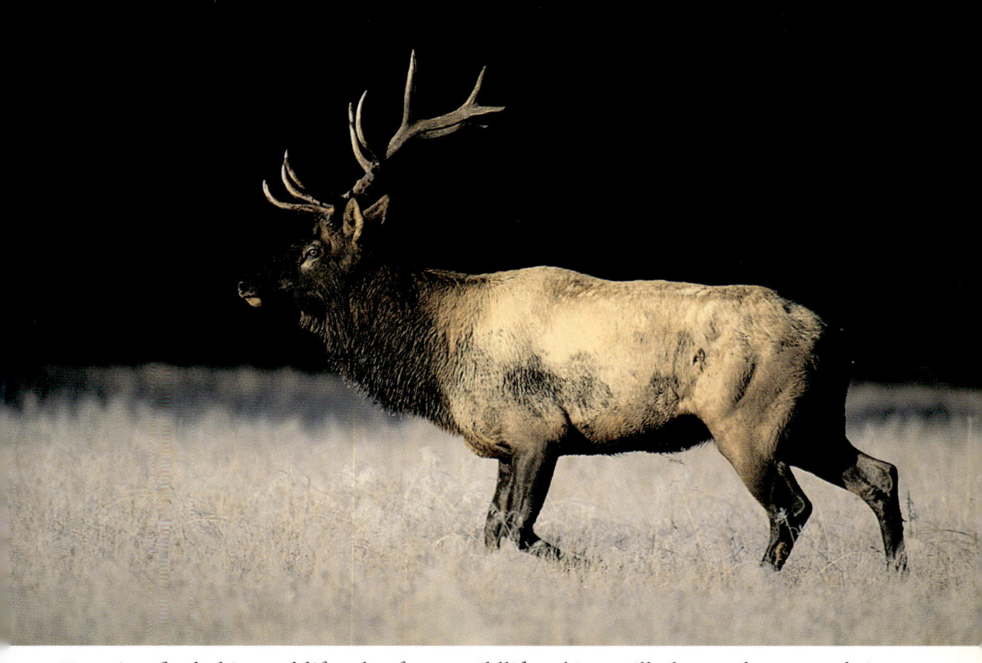

Knowing the habits and lifestyle of your wildlife subject will almost always result in better photo opportunities. This bull elk in Yellowstone regularly made his appearance in this meadow.

and cat, photograph them together. Kids and pets together are always favorites. The key is to be ready, keep a camera handy, and take advantage of the moment.

Wildlife

Wild animals deserve our respect, admiration, and our caution. Wild is the key word, and we photographers should never forget it. It's easy to be cautious as we look through our view-finder at an African lion lying in the grass of the Serengeti plains. He's big and we know he's dangerous, so we make sure we're careful. But a raccoon or squirrel we might take for granted. If we are careless and get too close, we could get a serious bite. Be especially careful around mother animals, both wild and domestic. They will be very defensive and protective of their young.

The best wildlife photographers spend a lot of time researching their subjects. Learning all you can about habits and habitats of wild creatures will almost always result in better photos. If you know that the elk of Yellowstone Park are in rut in the fall

This whitetail buck was an easy subject in Ricketts Glen State Park, where hunting is not allowed.

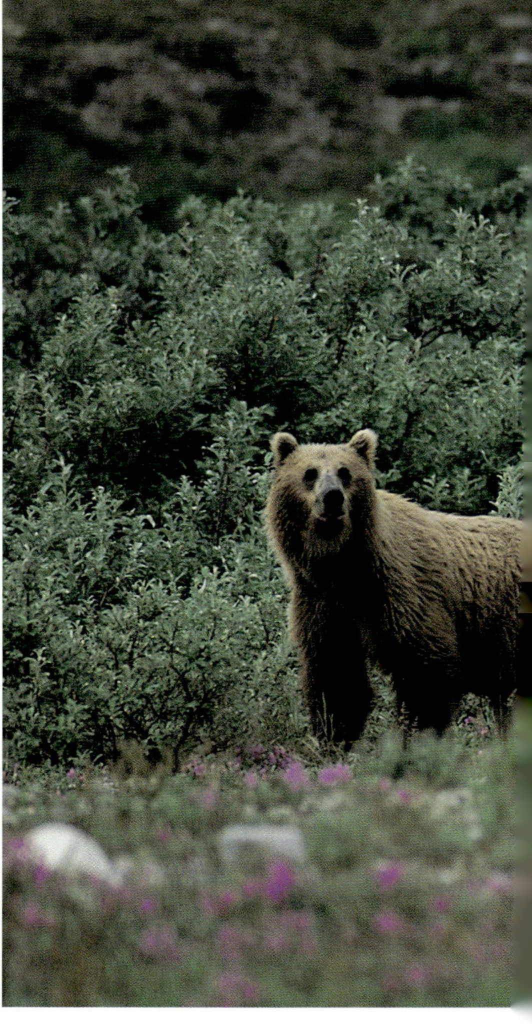

This group of grizzlies gave us a great photo opportunity.

of the year and if you visit the area around Mammoth Hot Springs, you can count on getting some great photo opportunities of bull elk bugling in the meadows in the early-morning light. Sometimes, if we're lucky, there'll be a light dusting of snow on the ground and animals. The elk are in this area every fall, and from past seasons we have learned when to be there and where we should be. We know how close we can safely and legally be to the animals, and we know the routine of the elk, the other photographers, and the Park Service personnel. So it's comfortable for us, and we know we'll get something we can use.

We found ourselves in a similar situation nearer to home, photographing whitetail deer in Pennsylvania's Ricketts Glen State Park. For two weeks straight, we watched a whitetail buck chasing a small herd of doe. We would get up in the darkness of the early October mornings and make the twenty-minute drive to the area of the park where the buck was working. There is no hunting allowed here and the buck was used to seeing hikers and campers. Consequently he paid little attention to the two photographers who would follow along. We would stay until the light was too bright and then call it quits. The result: We learned a lot about how the buck interacted with his harem, and we got great photos.

In Alaska when the salmon run the rivers every summer, along come

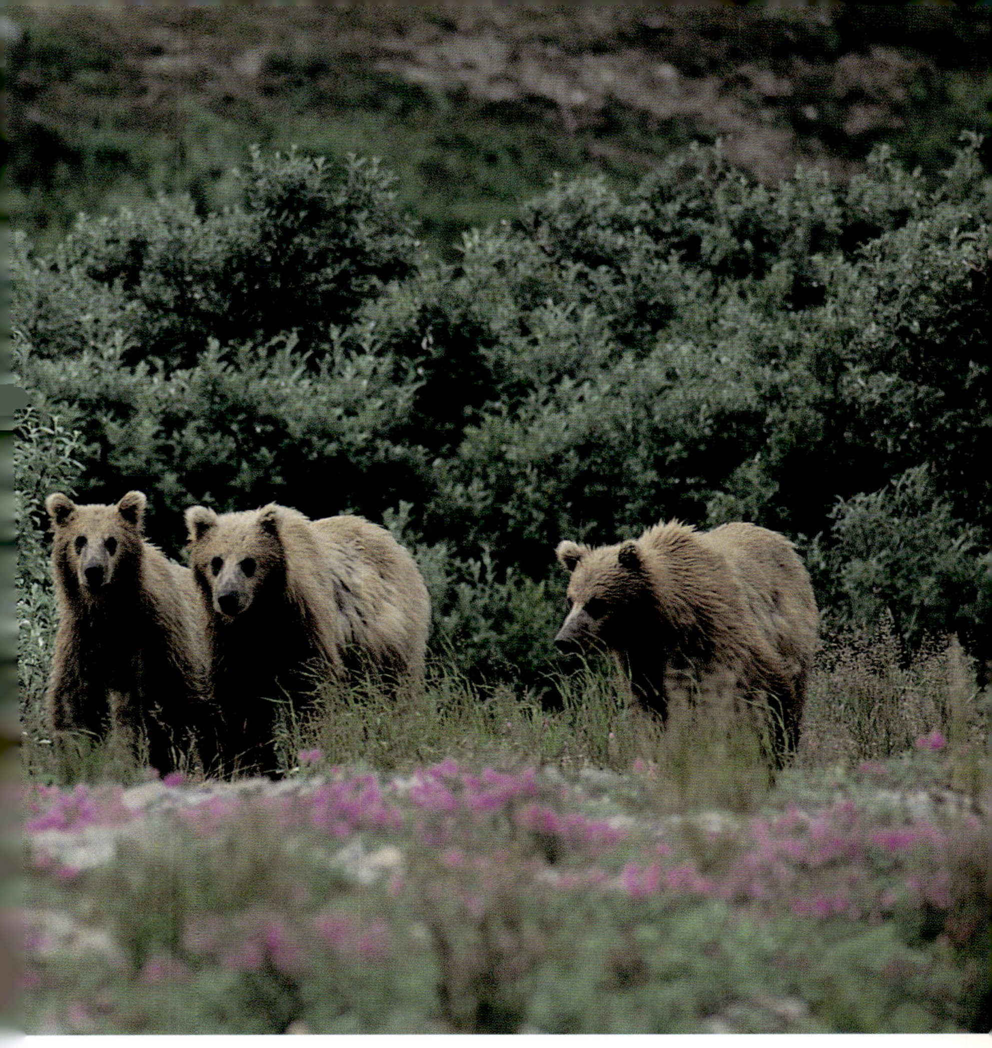

the coastal grizzly bears intent on feeding on the salmon. One morning as we were getting ready to fish, a group of four bears walked through a bed of profusely pink fireweed on their way down to the water. We and a few other fishermen watched as the bears split up and started chasing salmon. It was quite a sight. The next morning we gambled on a repeat performance and were back in the same spot ready with our cameras and tripods when the bears showed up. The light was getting good, and we spent the next hour with them shooting some of our best bear stuff.

If you get serious about photographing wildlife, especially the larger species, you will need a longer lens. It takes a lens in the range of

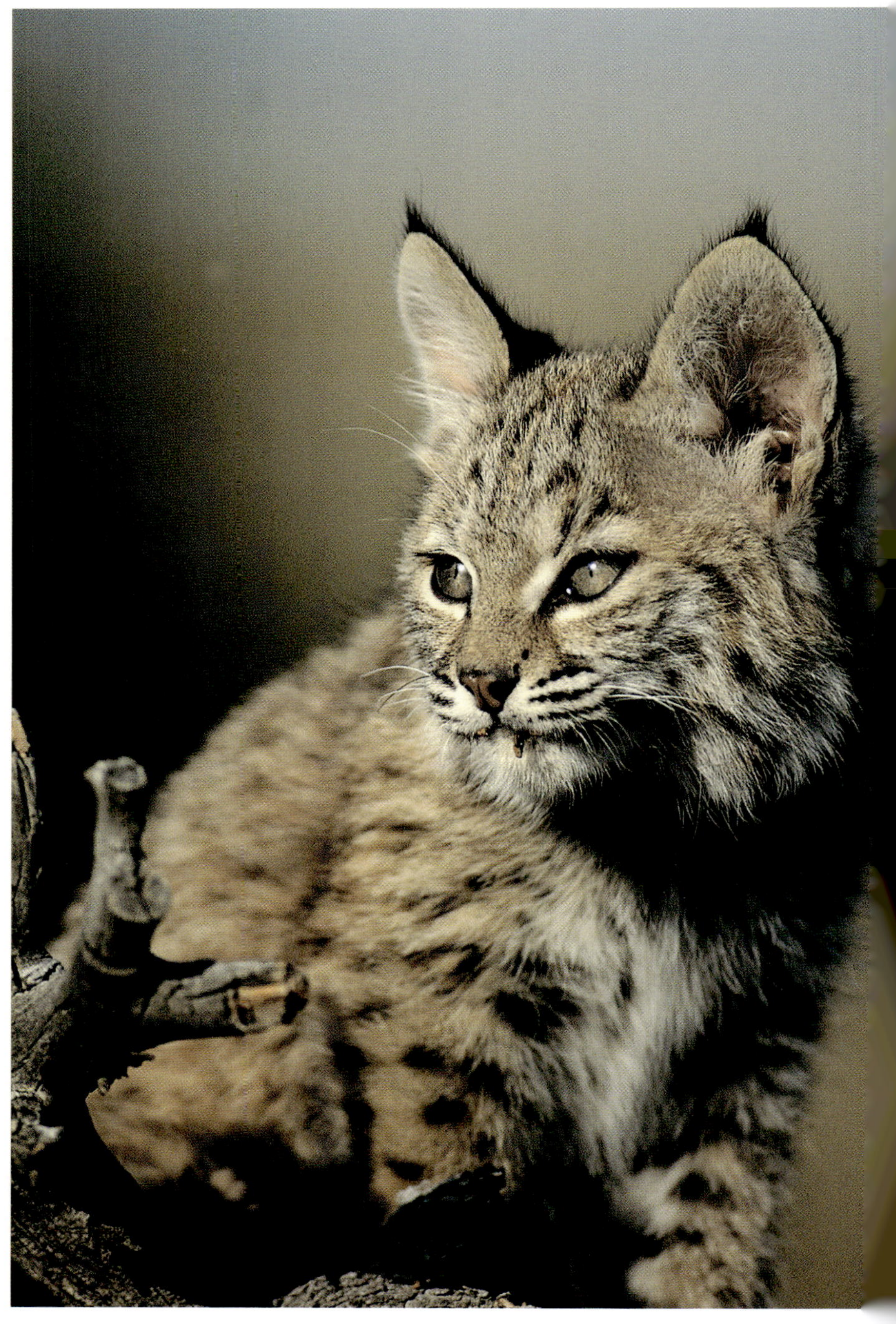

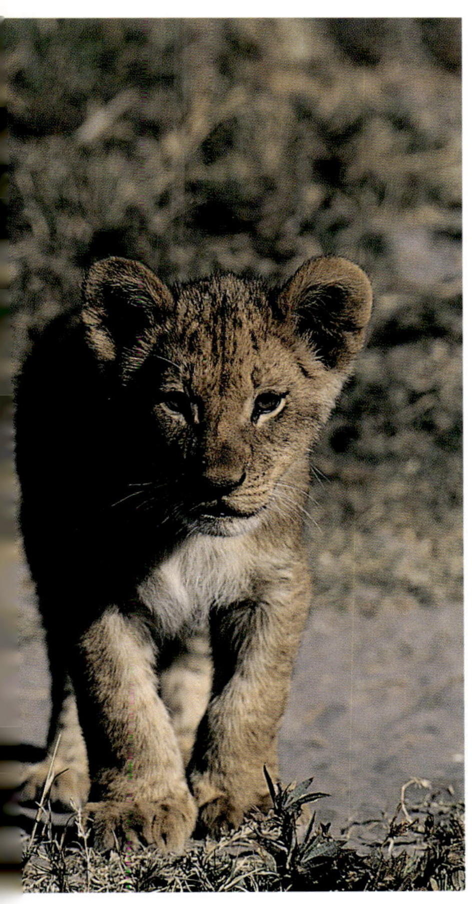

A young lion cub in South Africa.

300mm to 500mm to get close enough for tight shots. This lens should be fast, f/2.8 to f/4, for low light situations. Lenses in this range can be pricey, especially the newer auto focus models, but if you hope to get tack-sharp images, they're worth every penny. A tripod or monopod is as important as the lens. If you're going to set up and be in one place, a tripod is an absolute must. But if you're moving and following the animal, a monopod will be lighter and easier to quickly shoot from. It's important not to make the animal nervous. Wear clothing that blends in with the environment. Most animals have a great sense of smell, so leave the aftershave and perfume at home. Move slowly and quietly, being careful not to disturb or startle them. If they are truly wild and not used to having people around, once they notice us, they take off.

A good zoo can present us with unique photo opportunities. Many exotic animals that we find in zoos we shall never see in the wild. In some zoos the animals are restricted to small quarters with not much natural environment for an interesting backdrop. But there are zoos and safari parks that offer wide open spaces and natural-looking habitat. These are your best bet for photographing animals in natural-looking settings.

Game farms and rehabilitation facilities can also be good locations for wildlife photography. If you're stuck dealing with close or unattractive quarters, use a longer lens and

This young bobcat was photographed with a 300mm lens in early-morning light.

shoot tight. Head shots of animals will often look more natural if we blur out the background by using a shallow depth of field. Use a tripod or monopod to steady your camera for sharper images.

Birds are very popular with most outdoor photographers and can be found almost anywhere from the backyard to the wildest places, but photographic success usually calls for research and patience.

Working with shy species, a blind is a real asset in getting close. If you study the migration of waterfowl you can plan to be in the right place at the right time. Many nature preserves have waterfowl blinds for visitors to use, but these areas are popular with both photographers and birdwatchers, so reservations may be required at certain times of the year. Learning to use a duck or goose call can improve your results on waterfowl.

If you plan on constructing your own blind, choose your site carefully. You'll want the blind to be on the flyway, as close as possible to the birds, but not so close that you disturb your subjects. Whenever possible, construct the blind using natural materials (wood, leaves, branches, and burlap) and leave it on the site for the birds to get accustomed to. When a blind of this type is not possible, we often work from natural blinds, a brush pile or the cover provided by the edge of a corn field. Get there early, before the birds arrive, wear camou-

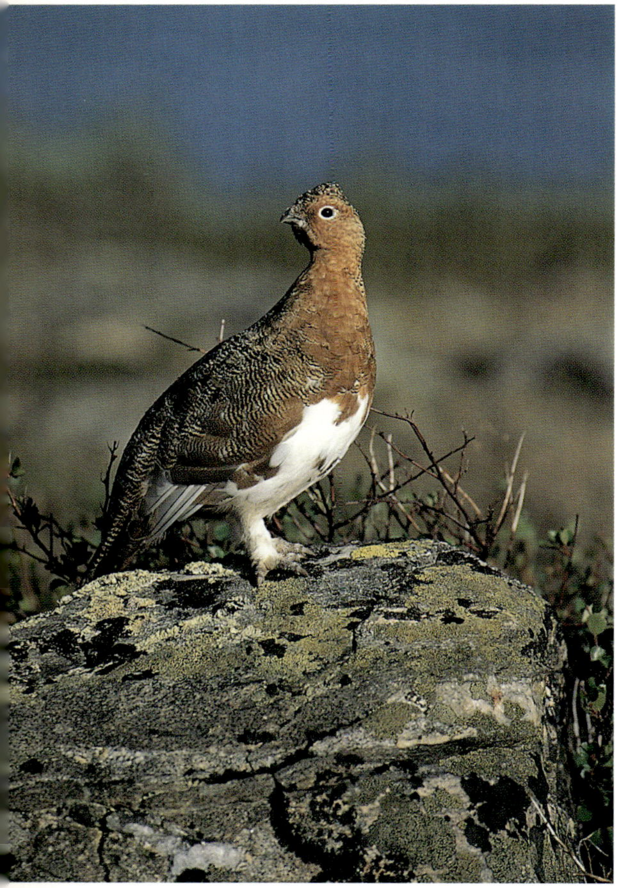

An arctic ptarmigan is unafraid and willing to have its picture taken.

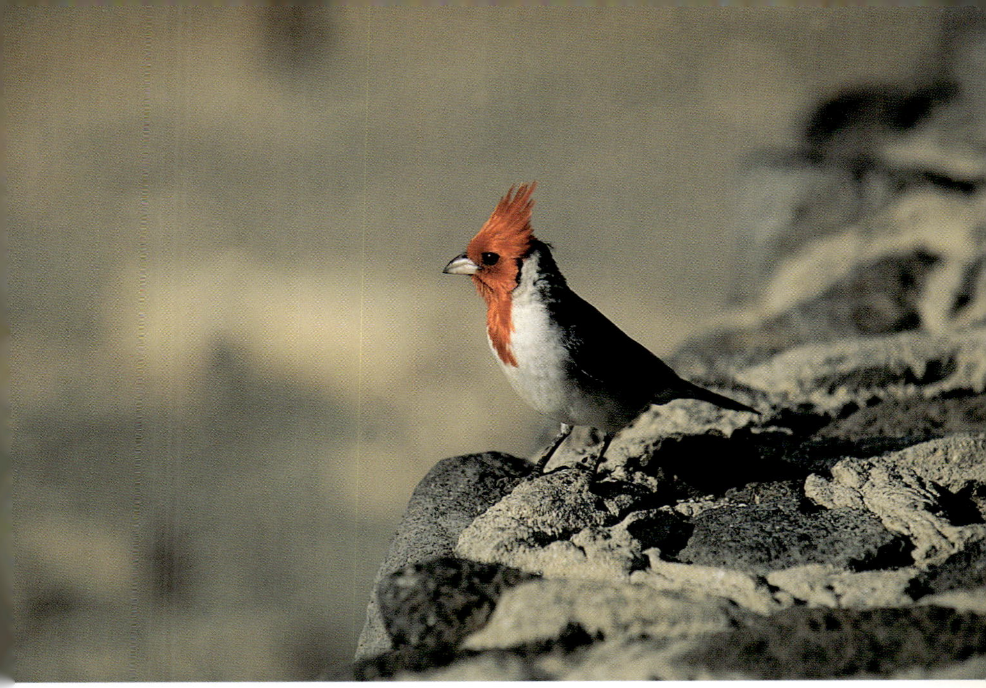

Colorful birds make great subjects for your camera.

flage clothing, and be very quiet when you are in the blind.

Bird feeders attract many species and are good spots for photo shoots during the winter feeding season. Often the birds will grow accustomed to us and will become less shy than the truly wild birds that don't frequent feeders. There are lots of possibilities with feeders. If the feeder is away from the house, you may be able to use your car as a blind, which will provide some protection from the weather as well. If the feeder is close to a window, you may want to shoot from inside. Just before a winter storm, birds will become very active at the feeders. Several times during the winter at our house we'll see a redtail hawk sitting in a nearby tree waiting for a smaller bird to make a mistake. There are pileated woodpeckers in the woods nearby, and we're pestered with squirrels in the feeders too, but they can be funny and photogenic at times. We've even had wild turkeys eating on our picnic table. You may be surprised at who's coming for dinner!

Insects are amazing and interesting and present us with photographic challenges. A macro lens (60mm or 105mm) is a good choice for close-up work, but a less expensive alternative is the screw-in close-up lens, which fits like a filter, threading and screwing onto the front of a normal lens. You'll need a steady tripod, a flash, and a shutter-release cable. Because you're shooting at a high degree of magnification, you'll need to make sure the equipment and the insect stay stationary. This is an area that requires the maximum depth of field from our light and film for in-focus images.

So many of the insects we want to photograph simply will not hold still. We've found that if we capture them and store them in a small insect collecting jar, which we put in the freezer or a cooler filled with ice for a few minutes, they become more cooperative. The colder temperatures make them lethargic. After a couple of minutes in the cold, we can position the bugs on a leaf or branch, and they will cooperate for a short time. Once the insects warm up, they become active again and try to escape, so be prepared to recapture them if you don't get the shot the first time.

To capture these sunflowers on an August morning in Montana, both the flowers and the camera neeed to be perfectly still.

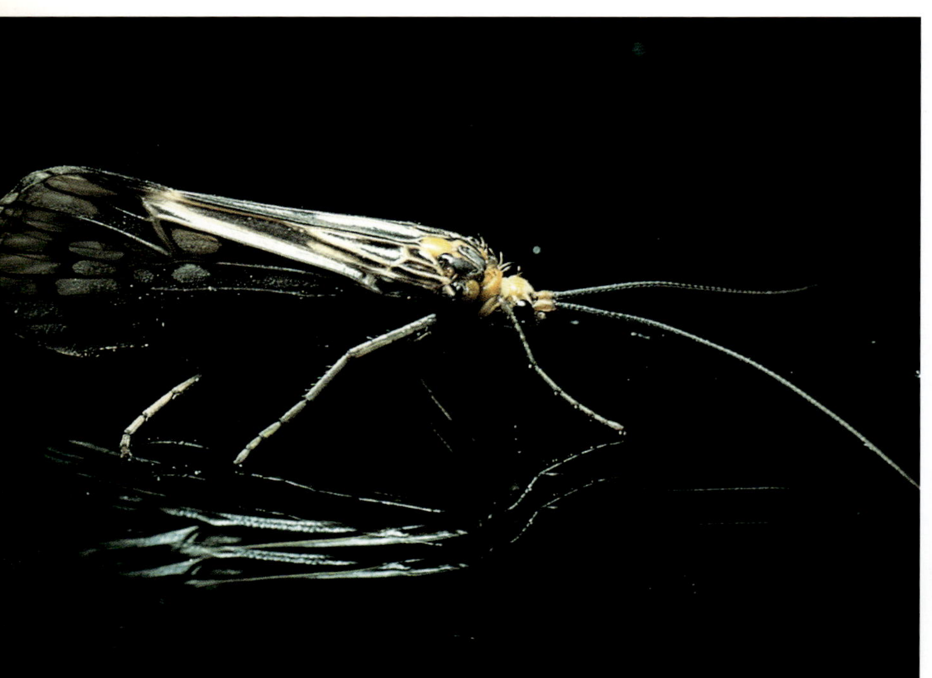

A 105mm macro lens helped capture this adult caddisfly.

A 60mm macro lens and the saturated colors of Fuji Velvia capture a group of yellow salsify flowers in Argentina.

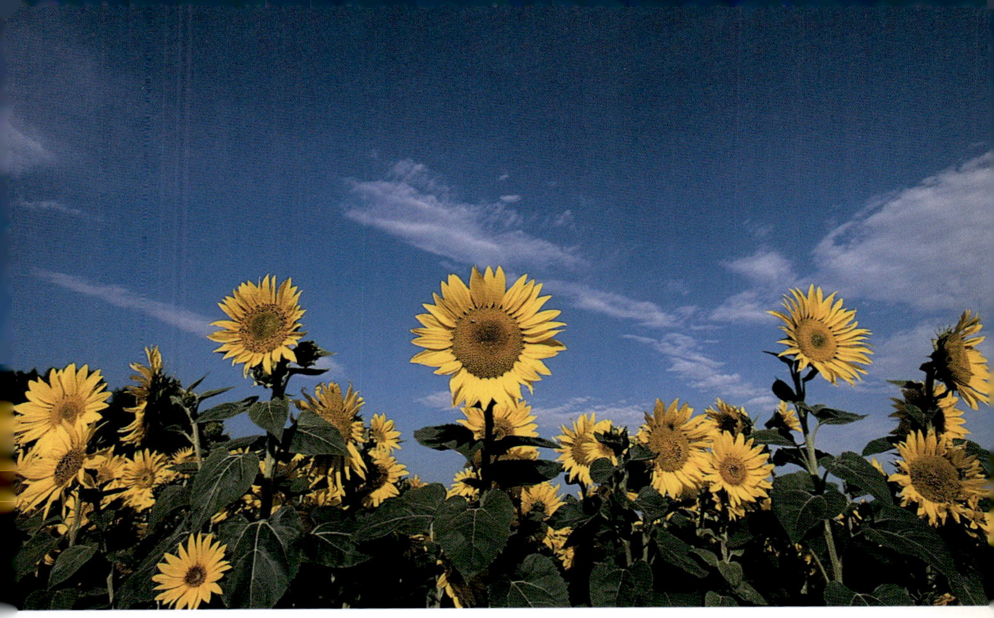

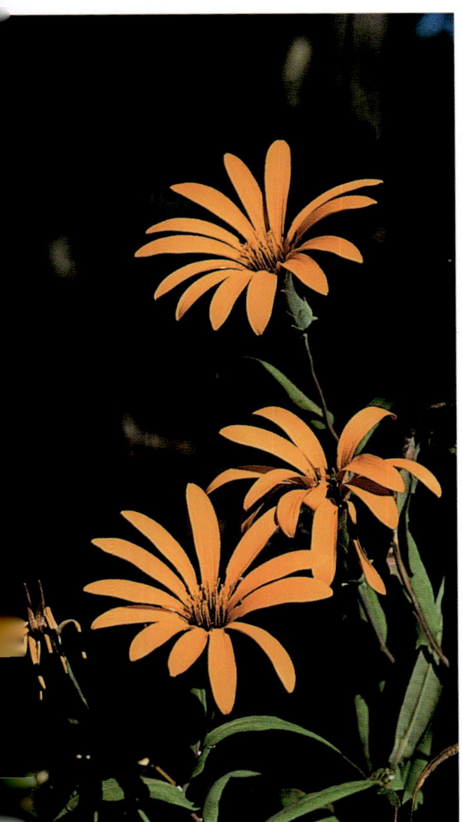

FLOWERS

Flowers in their own way present us with many of the same problems we face in photographing insects. We'll need our macro or close-up lenses as well as our tripod and flash. We can be creative with a wide-angle or fish-eye lens as well. The most important things that we look for in wildflower photography are, once again, light and composition. Just like the insects, if we're using close-up magnification we need both the camera and the flowers to be dead still. The slightest breeze becomes our enemy. Our best work happens on those dead calm mornings when the warm morning light just begins to illuminate the flowers. Another plus is to find the flowers covered with frost or dew. If you're shooting film for your flower photography, try Fuji's Velvia for its highly saturated color.

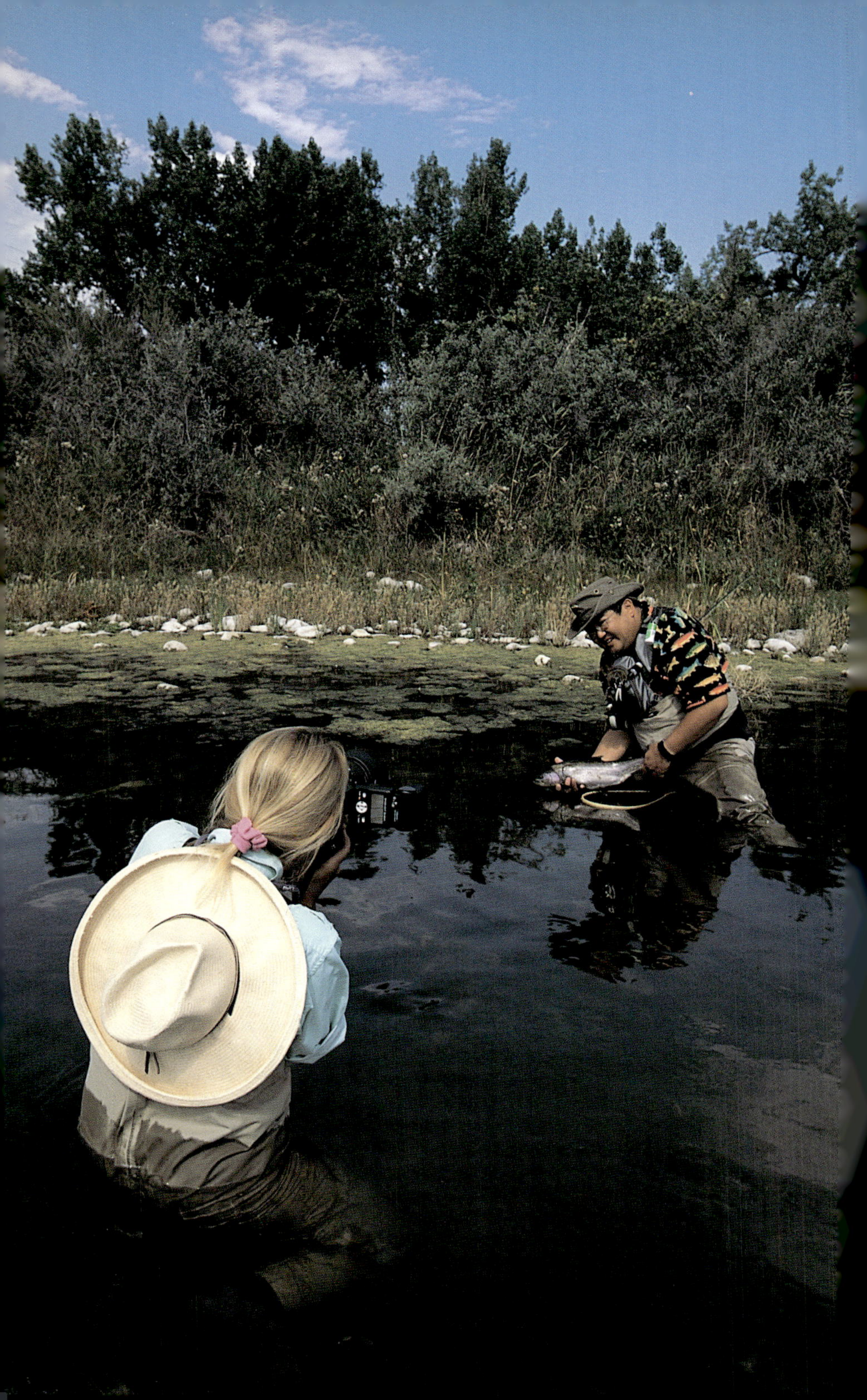

< CHAPTER 7 >

Taking Better Fishing Photos

We promised our fishing friends that if we were to ever write a book on photography, we would include a chapter on taking better fishing photos. This is a subject that is special to us, primarily because most of our commercial work is for the fly-fishing industry. Over the years as we have hosted fly-fishing trips, we have seen a lot of film shot by friends who travel with us. Most of the mistakes we see relate to the basics of photography and are simple and easy to correct. But before we get into the techniques of taking photos of fish, let's take a minute and talk about the fish.

Most anglers enjoy a picture of themselves holding the fish of the day or the fish of a lifetime. Since many anglers choose to release the fish, a photograph is the perfect way to remember it while at the same time allowing it to live and be caught again. How we treat the fish during the photo session is essential to its

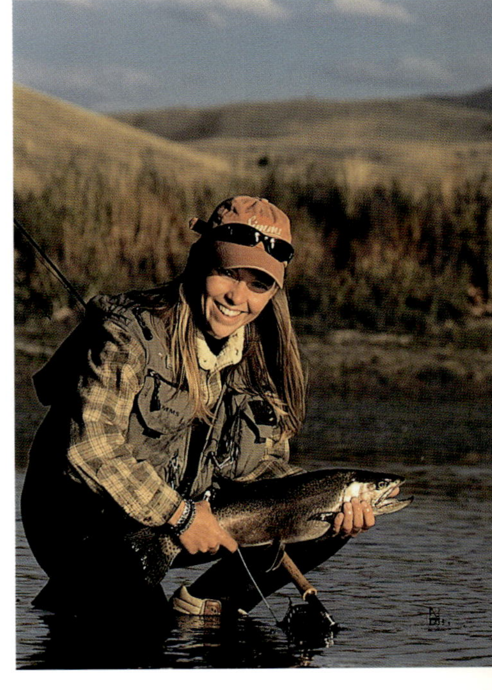

A nice fish, smiling face, and good light give us a well-composed grip-and-grin image.

Left: *Cathy stays low in the water to photograph Ron Taniwaki with a nice Bighorn River trout.*

survival. Keep the amount of time handling the fish to a minimum. Remember that, unlike us, fish breathe under the water not out of it, so keep the fish in the water.

USE A NET

Preparation is the key to both getting a good fish photo and releasing a healthy fish. Whenever possible, use a net, especially for trout. A fish landed in a net is a fish under control. With a net, we can safely keep the fish underwater, allowing it to breathe while we decide how and where to take our picture. We've seen, on more than one occasion, fish flopping around on shoreline rocks or in the bottom of the boat with anglers or guides hurrying to get the camera ready. This has got to be traumatic and injurious to the fish. We remember one time when the angler, after beaching his fish and grabbing his camera, realized that he had forgotten to put in a new roll of film. What he should have done is simply release the fish, but instead the flustered angler fumbled in his pockets to find the new roll of film, then removed the exposed film and loaded the new as the fish lay on the bank. When the photo was finally taken, the frustrated angler released the fish, which slowly floated downstream belly-up. Had the fish been resting in a net in the water, it would have survived, even though the angler should have had the camera loaded with fresh film and ready to go.

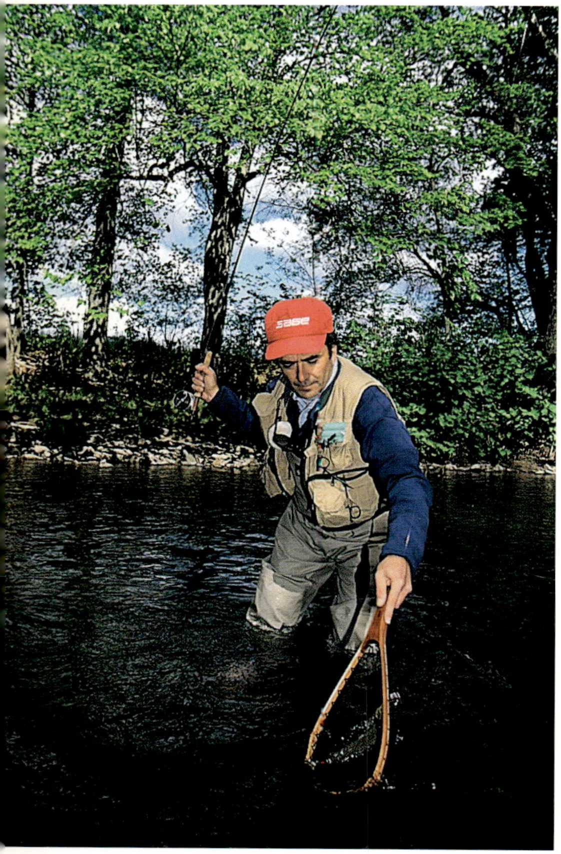

Whenever possible, use a net, especially for trout, to keep the fish under control.

COMPOSE YOUR IMAGE

Important to both taking care of the fish and getting the best photograph is being ready. If

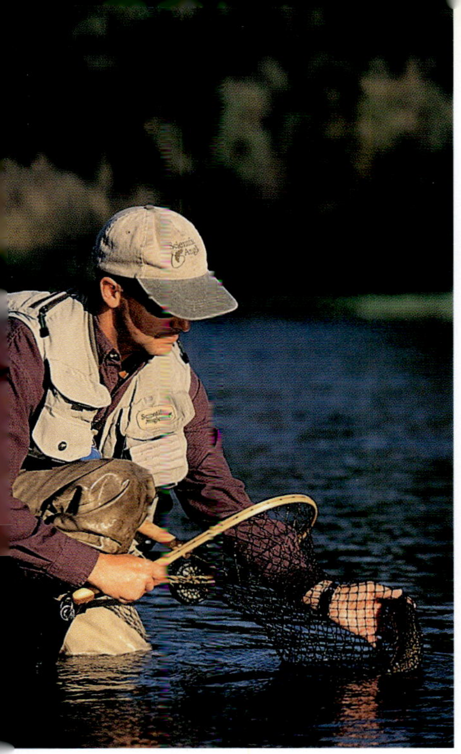

Compose your image before you lift the fish out of the net.

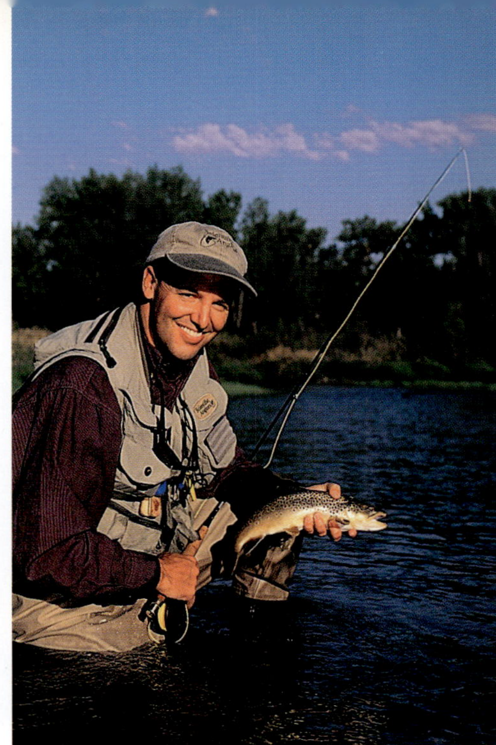

Make sure you have a happy-looking face before you click the shutter.

you're going to take a picture of a friend holding a fish, compose the picture before your friend lifts the fish out of the water. Start off by checking the light source, where the light is coming from and where it is falling on the subject. Use the rule of thirds—place the angler at the left or right side of the composition and not directly in the center of the image. As you look through your viewfinder, check to make sure that the horizon is straight and that there is nothing distracting—like tree limbs or fly rods sticking out from behind the angler's body or head. Blue skies make a great backdrop. Gray skies render a washed-out looking image. If you're working with gray skies and the situation permits, have the angler kneel and hold the fish while you stand shooting slightly downward at the angler and fish. The water will then become the backdrop and will give you a better-looking picture.

GET CLOSE

Being too far away from the subject when you snap the shutter is an easy mistake to make. You'll end up not being able to identify either the angler or the fish. The next time, you may decide to fix the problem of being too far away by having the

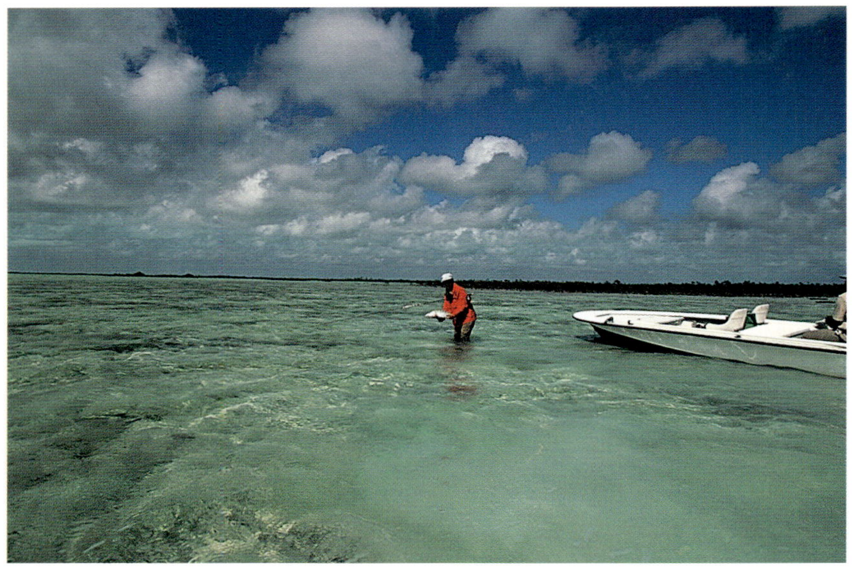

A common mistake that many photographers make is to stand too far away—the angler and fish are not identifiable.

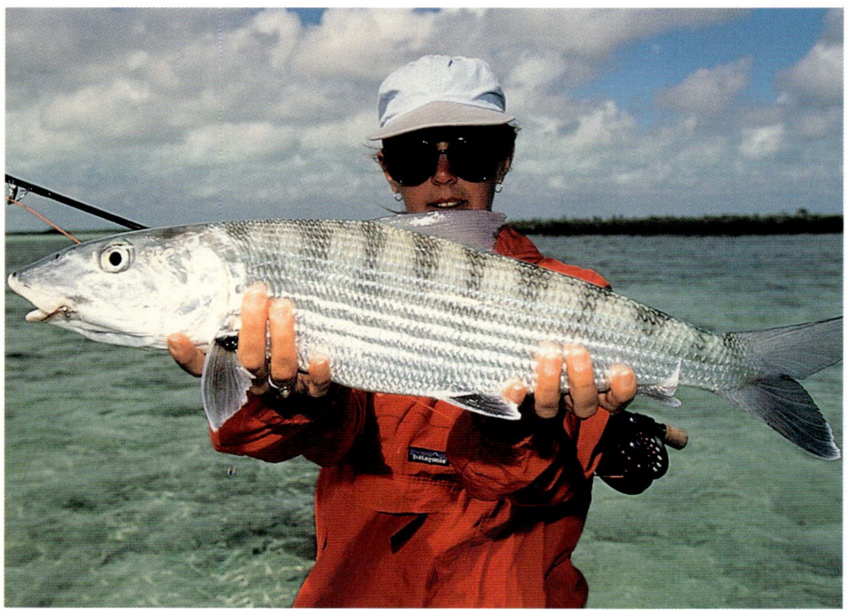

Another common mistake is to get too close. In this example, the angler is holding the fish way out in front, which can distort the hands and the fish.

This is a much more pleasing image, where the angler and fish are in a more proper position.

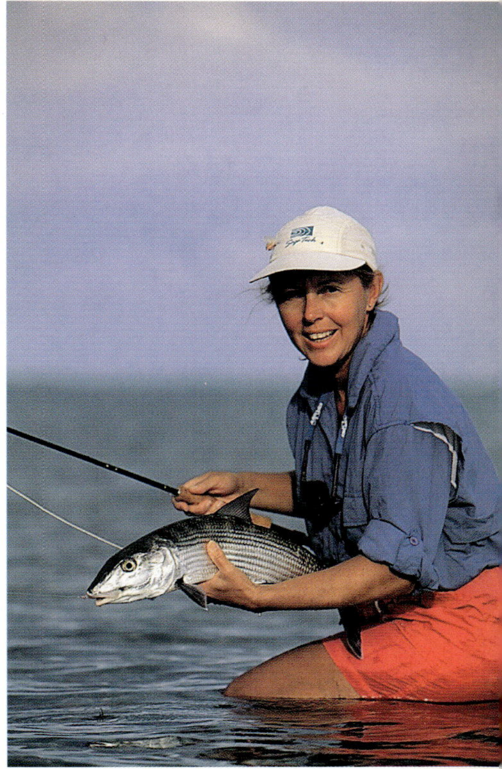

angler hold the fish way out in front of him. Now you get a *really* big fish being held by a *really* little guy. So how do you get the right perspective? Make the adjustment from your side of the camera. Get closer. If you're after a shot of the angler and the fish, fill up most of the frame with them. While you're composing all this, the angler can be kneeling and holding the net so the fish is upright and under the water. When you're ready, have the angler take the fish out of the net and, at the count of three, lift the fish for the photo. If the angler holds the fish fairly close to his body and out in front, you'll get the shot. For something different, try having the angler give you a side profile of himself or try tilting the head of the fish slightly down toward the water. These different angles often result in pleasing photographs.

TURN ON THE FLASH

If the angler is wearing a hat with a brim, you may get unwanted shadows on the subject's face on sunny days, especially between the daylight hours of 10 A.M. and 2 P.M. These shadows can be dark enough to make the angler in the photo hard to recognize. What happens is you, the photographer, can see under the brim, but the camera, because it's reading metered light, does not. Try having the angler remove the hat, or better yet, turn on your fill flash to remove the shadows.

If your camera has the option, try bracketing the flash. By trial and error, we've found that a minus 1.7 setting on our flash gives us just enough fill flash to properly light the angler's face under a hat. While having a flash built into the camera is certainly simple and easy to use, a flash unit that can be removed from the camera body and held at differ-

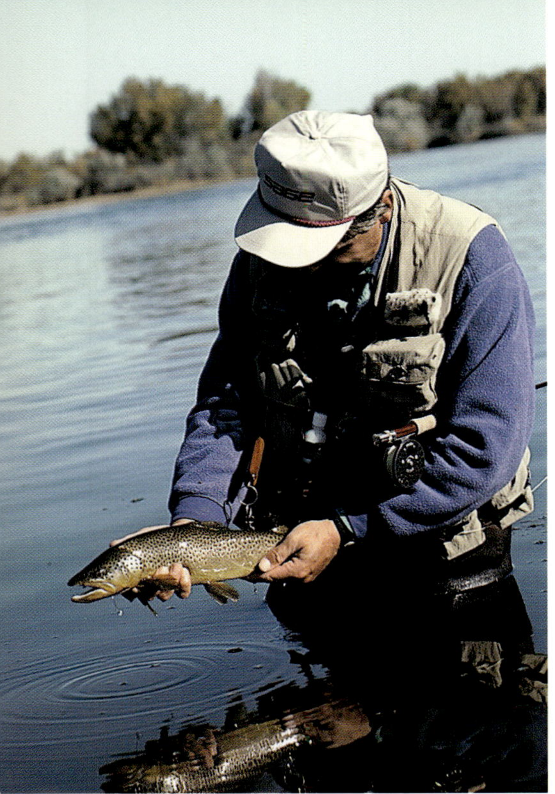

This is an example of a poor grip-and-grin photo: You cannot see the angler's face, and the horizon is angled.

ent angles and levels will provide a better directed burst of light on the subject, resulting in better shape and detail. Direct flash (with a built-in) can be too harsh.

The settings needed for your flash will depend on the flash unit and the speed of the film. You will want to experiment with your flash until you find the right combination for a well-exposed image. Remember, too, if the angler is wearing sunglasses, ask him to remove them before you click the shutter. The flash may bounce off the glasses, and being able to see his eyes will make a more pleasing picture. Use and get to know your flash and you'll be pleased to see the difference it makes in your photographs—inside and outside.

HOLDING THE FISH

Fish are slippery. This slippery coating, which helps protect the fish from infection, makes them hard to hold. Keep your hands and net wet, and that will help keep the protective coating from being rubbed off the fish. Turning the fish upside down for a moment underwater will temporarily disorient it and will often make it easier to hold. A calm fish will be more cooperative when lifted out of the water a few seconds to be photographed. Be ready. Check to be sure that you are photographing the broadside of the fish and not the white belly or back of the fish. The photographer has some creative license here, and by experimenting you'll find a position for the fish that appeals to you.

Once the photograph is taken, you'll want to get the fish ready to release. If the fish has been resting in the net, it may be revived and ready to go. Hold it quietly in the water

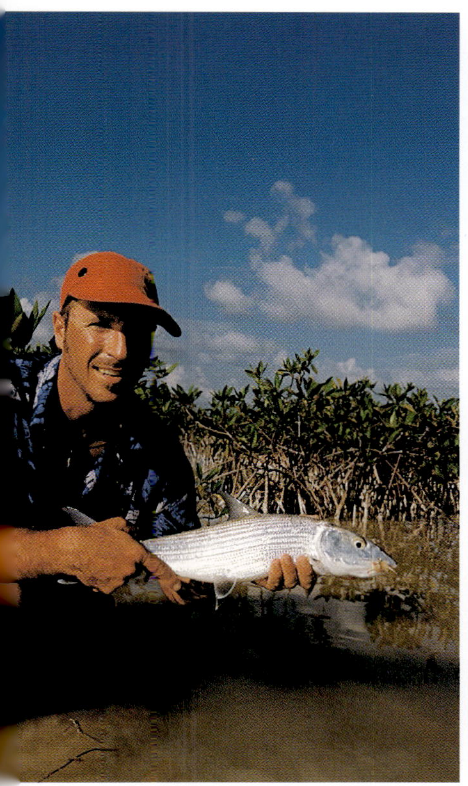

A saltwater image without fill flash.

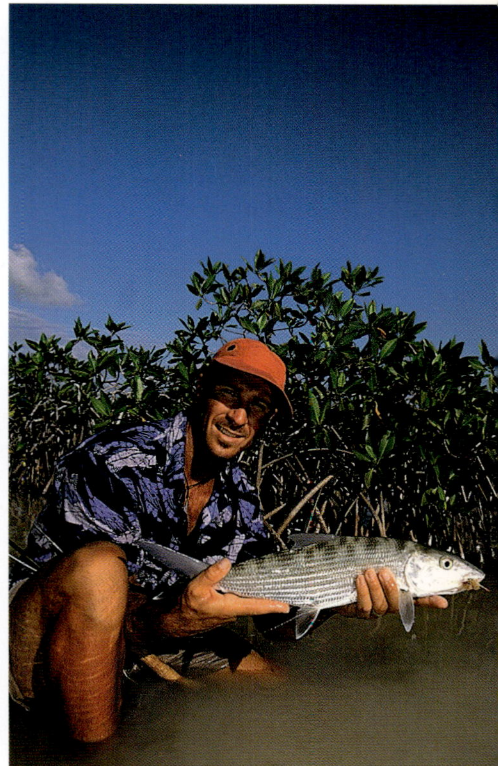

A saltwater image with fill flash. Saltwater fish can be highly reflective, and too much flash can blow out the highlights of the fish. You may need to experiment until you find the right amount of flash output for the proper exposure.

until it starts to fin, and once you see it's moving strongly, let it slip gently through your fingers.

A COUNT OF THREE

When we look through our viewfinder and are satisfied with the composition, we use a count system that works well for us. For instance, Cathy is holding the fish underwater as I compose the picture. When I'm happy with the composition (I've mentally checked to make sure her hat is back and light is on her face, or I've set the fill flash, her sunglasses are down, and her position is good), I'll say something like, "OK, 1 . . . 2 . . . 3 . . . ," and on three she lifts the fish out of the net to a position we've predetermined, smiles, and I

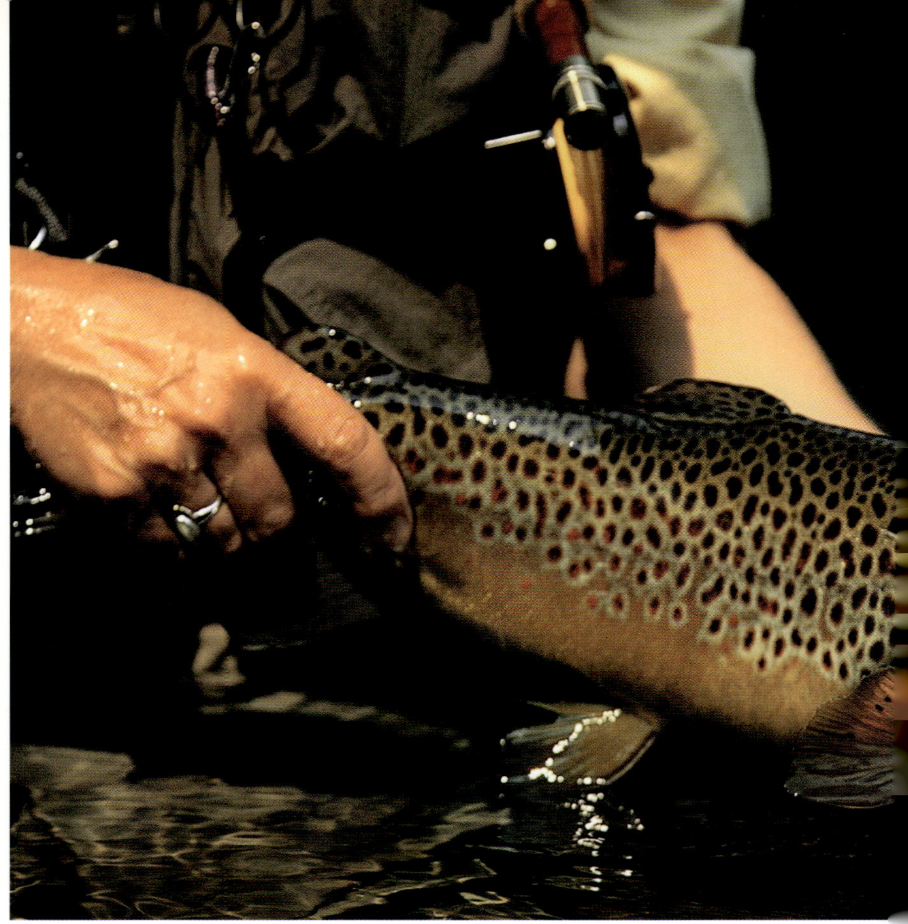

Make sure you have a firm grip ahead of the tail, and do not remove the fly until you are sure you have the photograph. That way, if the fish gets loose, you can retrieve it.

quickly fire off three or four frames. Then she places the fish back in the net to rest underwater. We may go through this routine two or three times, often bracketing our exposures or checking our monitor if we're shooting digital to make sure that we have the image. With each set, we may switch lenses or adjust the angle of the angler, the fish, or the rod, repositioning all components so we get the best light and composition.

WATCH FOR GLARE

Take note of any light that may be reflecting off the scales of the fish. This may happen with bright saltwater fish like bonefish and tarpon. Try having the angler turn the fish slightly one way or another to find the best angle to eliminate the unwanted glare. Be careful with your flash, because it, too, can bounce off those shiny scales and overexpose the image.

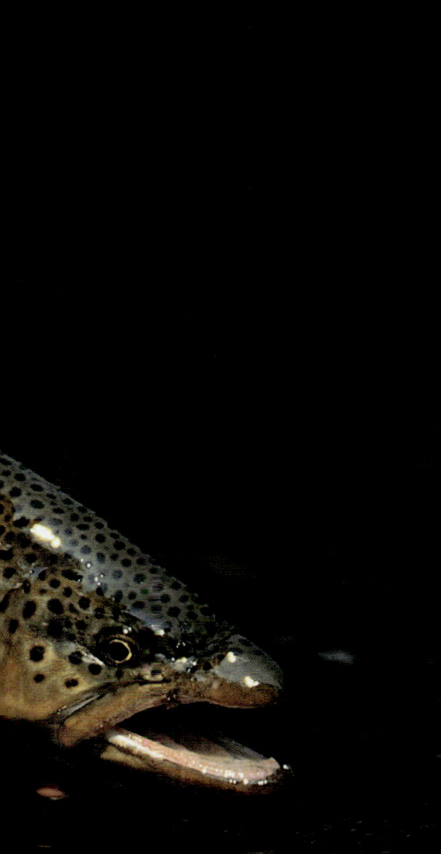

EXPERIMENT WITH CLOSE HEAD SHOTS

We all enjoy seeing a photo of a proud angler, smiling and holding a big fish. But it's fun to focus all your attention on the fish as well. Try moving in close and shooting just the fish. You can experiment with different angles and lenses. Be creative. Maybe you have a macro lens or a

Below: *Even with good light you have to be careful of reflections off a fish's scales. Try moving the fish to different angles or use your polarizing filter to eliminate the glare.*

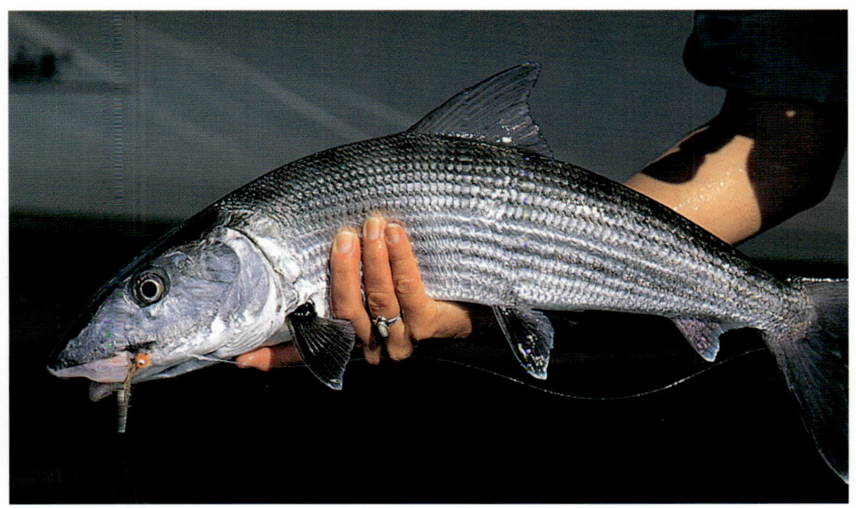

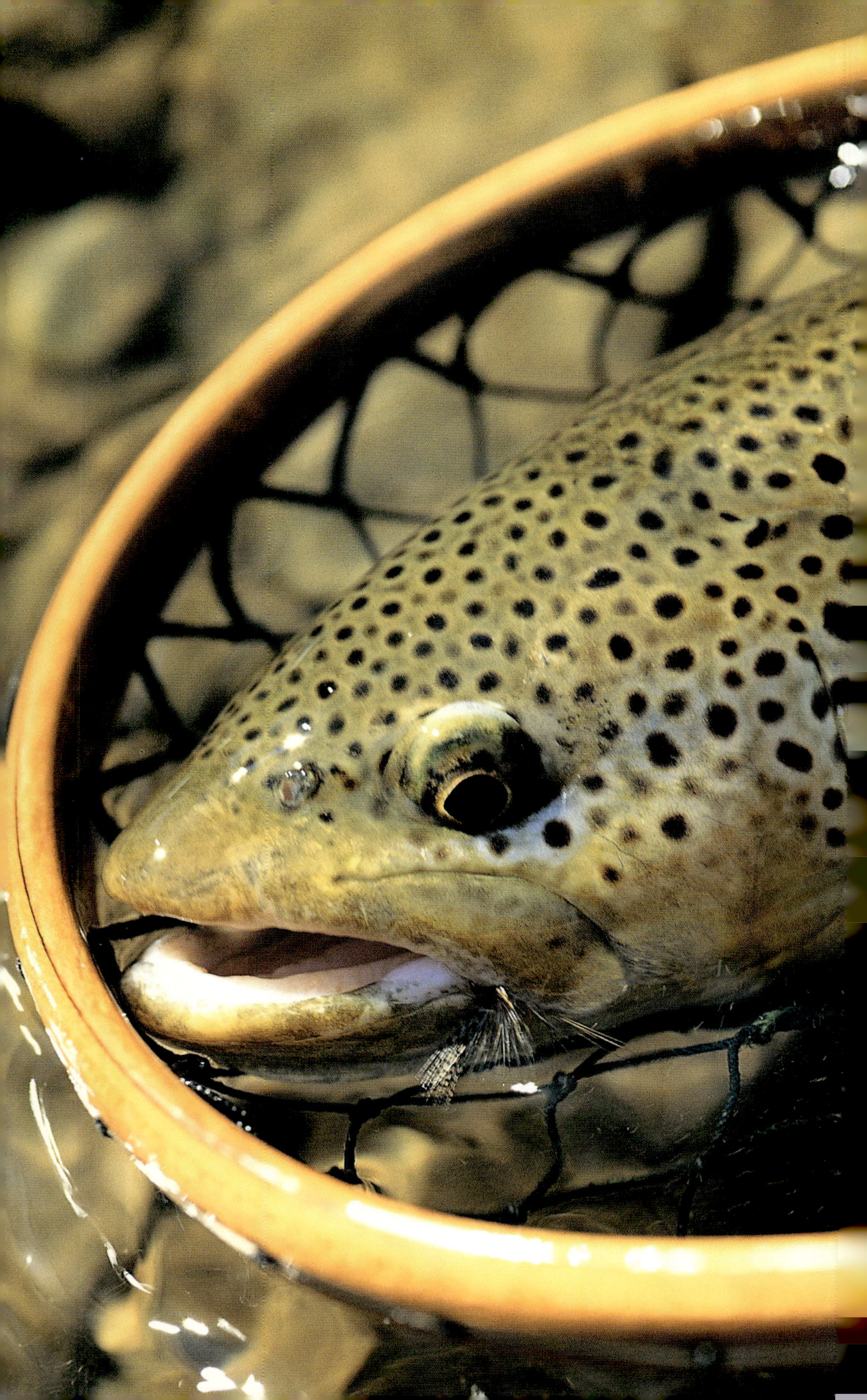

macro setting on your digital camera. If so, try getting very close and shooting just the head of the fish. As you move in, though, be careful that your shadow does not interfere with the photograph. If you have a fisheye or super-wide lens, you can have a lot of fun shooting close shots of fish. A word of warning though—it's easy to distort the subject with a super-wide-angle lens. Experiment. With a little practice you can create some stunning, eye-catching fish images. Brian O'Keefe, a well-known fly-fishing photographer, is a master of close-up, wide-angle fish shots. There is no mistaking an O'Keefe shot when you see one.

WATCH FOR REFLECTIONS

Tight shots and reflections of fish are fun to shoot and make interesting images. It's important to remember that in the best images, the water is still and the fish are close to the water. Check out backwater and areas that are protected from the wind. The water here will be still and reflections will be good. Experiment with getting down low to the water and using different angles, choosing the ones that look best to you. Try including both the fish and the net for a different aspect. Take advantage of any color—a bright shirt sleeve or some streamside wildflowers can add interest to your composition.

ACTION SHOTS

Action shots often happen on the spur of the moment, but there are ways to be prepared. We remember a saltwater trip to Boca Paila, on Mexico's Yucatan coastline. It's one of our favorite saltwater destinations because of the variety of fish species and the beautiful environment of the Yucatan. Our friend, Barry Serviente, was along, and we were hoping to do some snook fishing, which we knew from prior trips could be pretty exciting. Snook like to frequent mangrove shorelines, lying in wait under the cover of the mangroves to ambush unwary bait fish that swim by.

Most snook will jump when hooked and we were hoping for some jump shots. Our guide was poling along a shoreline that had produced some good snook before, so going on a hunch, we got out of the boat and waded along behind, hoping that Barry would have a hook-up. It didn't take long before he hooked a fish and, as we had hoped, it jumped three times. We were ready and the camera was focused, the light was right, and we got a great jump shot. It doesn't always go that way,

A 105mm macro lens gives a tight head shot.

but with a little patience and perseverance, it sooner or later pays off. It takes a fast shutter speed of 1/250 to 1/500 to freeze motion, so using a faster film of ISO 200 to 400, you can get the image you want.

Getting action shots can often mean anticipating the action. If you're in a boat with an angler fishing for tarpon, knowing that this fish loves to jump and dance across the water will help you be ready with the camera. There's one second when the fish jumps when he's at the top of the jump just before starting back down. That's the second you want to be clicking the shutter. When he's coming straight up and falling straight back he'll be harder to keep tack sharp. But for that brief moment when he hesitates, if you're ready, composed, and focused, you can get a great jumping fish shot. And make sure you've got plenty of shots left on the roll of film. It's so frustrating to be in the right place at the right time, the action starts, and you realize too late that there's only two or three frames left on the roll of film.

KEEP YOUR CAMERA DRY

We're often asked how we keep our cameras dry when fishing. If you want to keep it simple, there are a lot of waterproof point-and-shoot cameras that are small enough to fit in a pocket of your fishing vest. They take great pictures both in and out of the water, so getting them wet is not a concern. If the camera you want to carry is small but not waterproof, you can seal it in a freezer-weight Ziploc bag and put it in a wader pocket. We have a small Nikon Coolpix digital that we've carried around the world this way. Most of us have fallen in

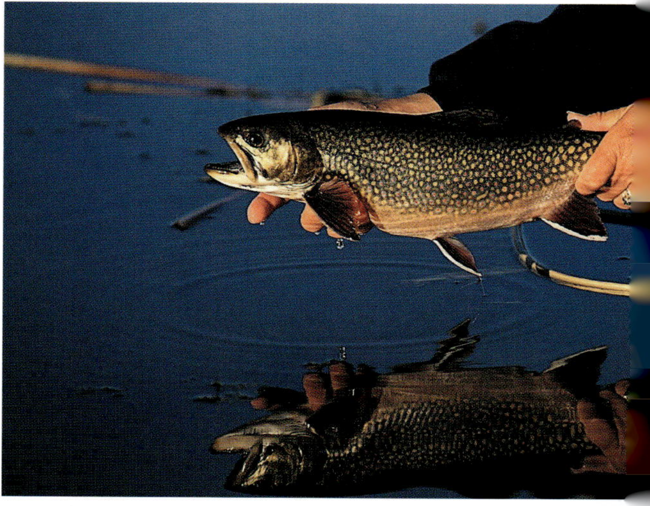

If you hold the fish low to the water and use a low camera angle, you can get some interesting reflections.

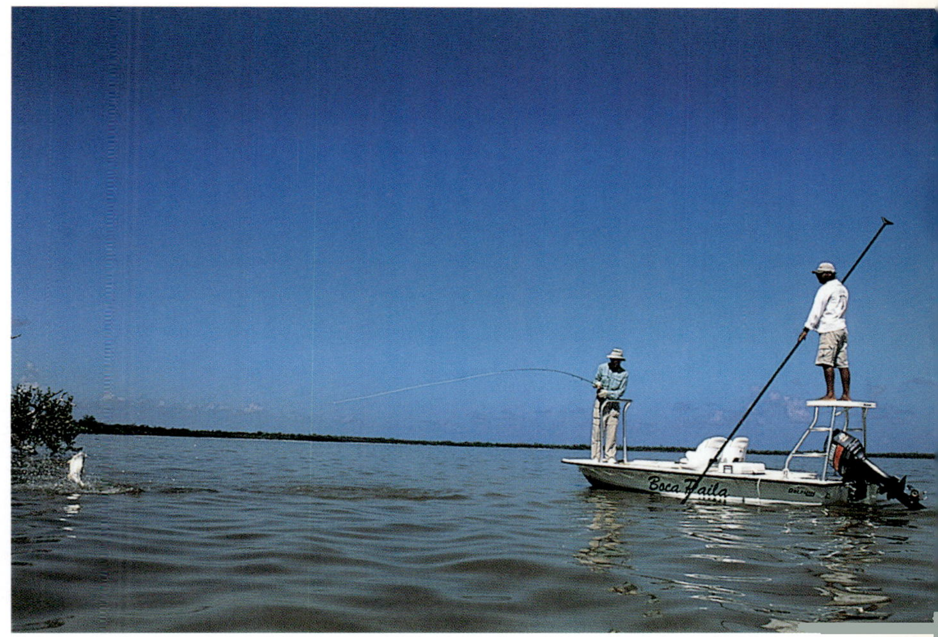

Patience pays off with this jumping snook in Mexico.

while wading, but we won't have a problem with the heavy-duty Ziploc bags. The plastic canisters that film comes in are waterproof, but we still put our film and extra batteries in the Ziploc bags to be on the safe side.

If we are working with our larger 35mm system that includes extra lenses, filters, and flashes, all of which are not waterproof, we use a backpack designed for photographers. It is not waterproof, so we're very careful when wading. We've got a nylon shell that fits over it when we're walking with it in the rain, and we always keep a large garbage bag inside that we can slide the pack into during heavy rain. A fanny pack is a great way to carry camera gear if you're wading on a saltwater flat, but it's easy to forget and wade in too deep or, without thinking, kneel down in the water. Ziploc bags inside the fanny pack may save the day.

Great fish images, like all good images, are the result of light and composition and the time to take them. Take your camera along when you fish, and try to take some time away from the fishing to use it.

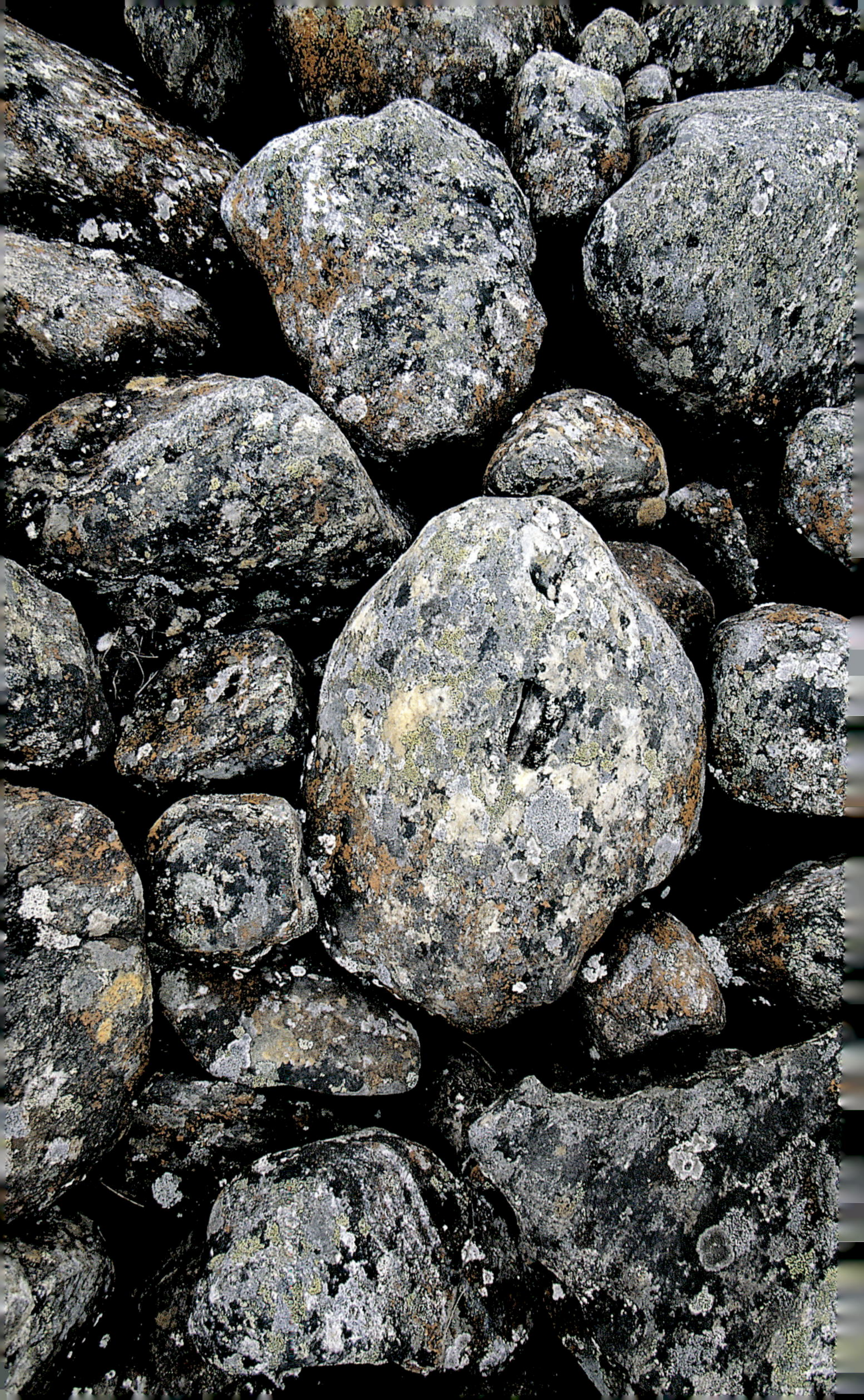

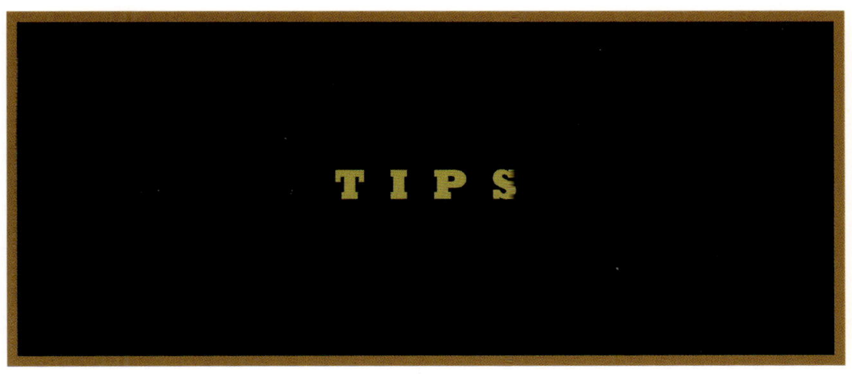

TIPS

Pack your camera, take it with you, and use it.

Keep your film in a cool place—film exposed to heat may lose its color accuracy.

Carry as much film as you may need—you may not be able to buy it once you get to your destination.

Use a tripod or monopod for sharper images.

Always look for the best light available.

Do not shoot directly into a hot sun.

Move around and try different angles for more creative compositions.

Use your flash outdoors for removing unwanted shadows.

Turn your flash off if it's snowing—the light will bounce off the snow and will not illuminate your subject.

Use a UV filter to protect your lens.

Use a circular polarizing filter to eliminate glare on reflective surfaces.

Use a lens cloth and keep your lens clean—dirt that shows up on

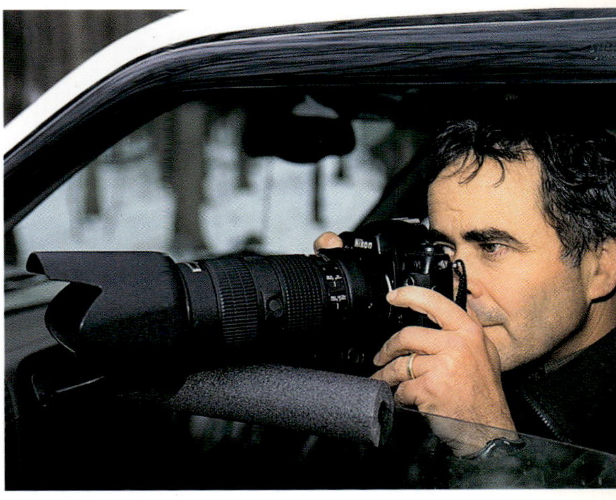

A piece of foam on a car window will help steady your camera.

Left: *Mother Nature paints and the photographer seizes the moment to create a pleasing image.*

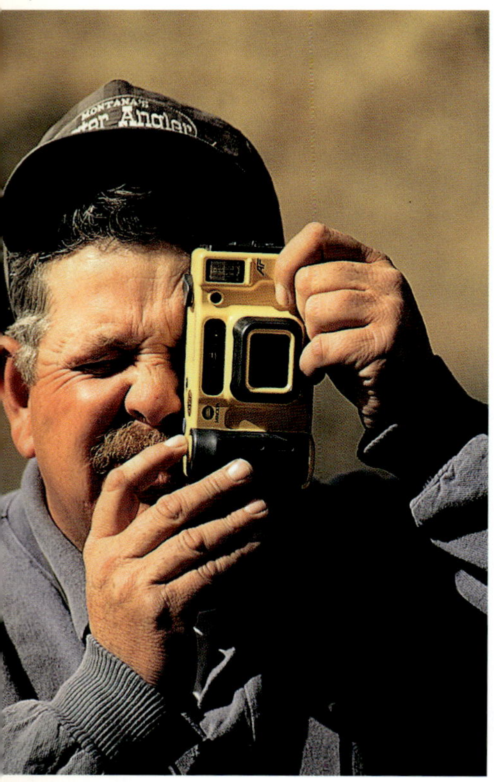

Shoot both vertical and horizontal images to add a different look to the same shot.

your filter may show up on your images.

Keep your camera dry—moisture and electronics don't mix.

Carry extra batteries for your flash and your camera, and make sure they are fresh.

Bracket your exposures if you can.

Make sure your horizons are straight as you compose your image.

Watch for anything in your viewfinder that may distract from your image.

Choose a subject to photograph that you are comfortable with, and learn all that you can about it. Shoot as much of it as you can.

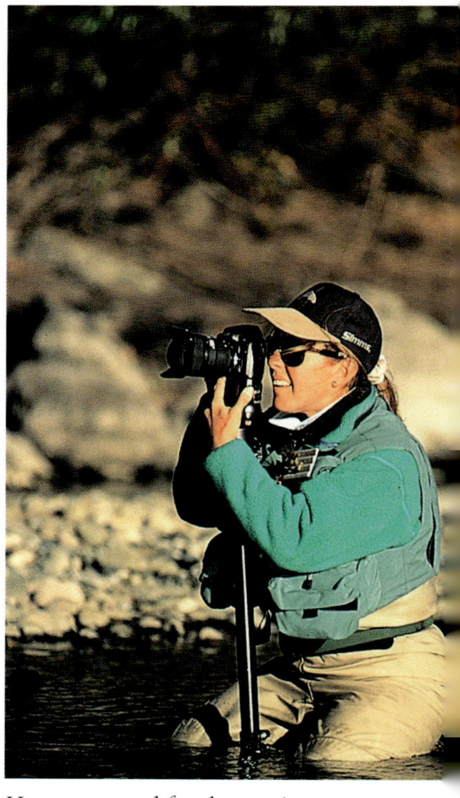

Use a monopod for sharper images.

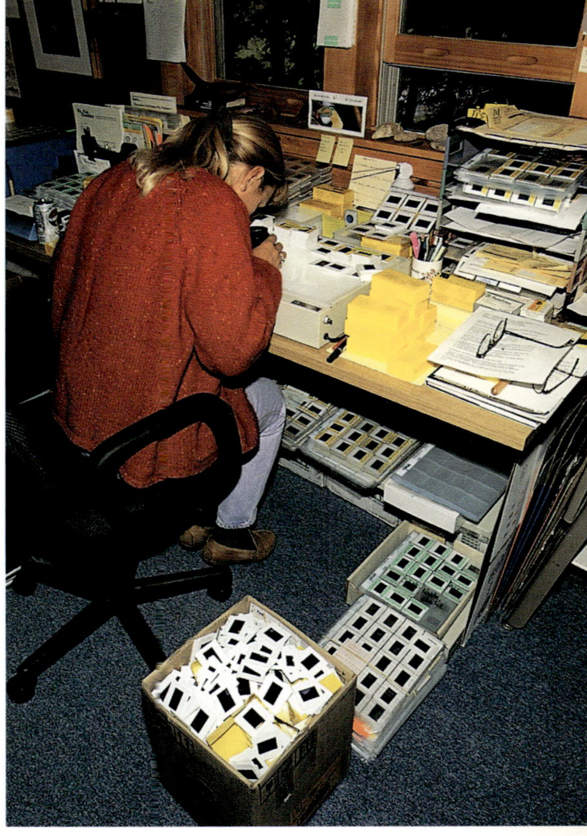

Throw your bad images away and keep the good ones.

Keep a notebook with exposure and light information for future reference. You can learn a lot from your mistakes.

You can also learn from others. The *National Geographic* photographers may be the best in the world. Check out their work.

Make a checklist of your photographic equipment before you travel and use it as you pack—don't forget the film.

Never open your camera back until you have rewound the exposed film.

If you see the shot, take it—you may lose the light in the next few seconds.

Learn to be patient with light, your subject, and yourself.

Put together a slide show for your friends and family. It's better entertainment than TV.

If you want to publish your images, start with regional magazines. Don't be put off by rejection. Beauty is in the eye of the beholder, and what one editor thinks is just OK another may find is exactly what he has been looking for.

If you're shooting digital, learn to use photo-editing software. You now have your own darkroom.

Sacred Roots Spiritual Classics

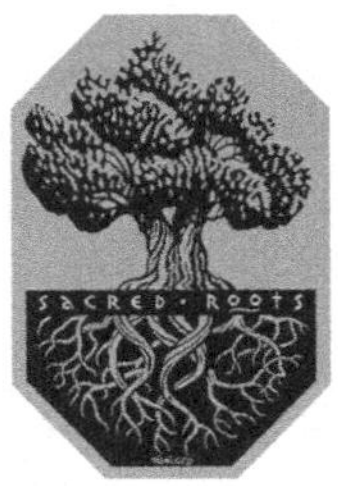

"Toward Ten Thousand Tozers"

Becoming a Community of Disciples:
Guidelines from Abbot Benedict and Bishop Basil

Sacred Roots Spiritual Classics 2

Greg Peters

What "They" Say . . . What Will You Say?

"Today, when societies are frayed or unraveling, it is hard to imagine people living in close proximity, working and praying together. That is what Christian monks have been doing since the early days of Christianity. By trial and error, with the Gospel for their guide, they gained wisdom that is handed on in the Rules of Basil and Benedict. Greg Peters has distilled their teaching in a very helpful way. Now to live it—together."

~ Fr. Hugh Feiss, OSB,
Monastery of the Ascension (Jerome, Idaho)

"Greg Peters, along with his old friends Basil and Benedict, have provided us with a worthy guide to becoming followers of Christ. In this book we learn to live together in a peaceable order. We learn to lead kindly and to follow faithfully. We learn to work, to welcome, and to worship. If we would not only read these Rules, but experiment with them as we rub shoulders with one another, we might just become a force for Christ as powerful today as Basil and Benedict were long ago."

~ Evan B. Howard, PhD,
Director of Spirituality Shoppe:
A Center for the Study of Christian Spirituality,
author of *A Guide to Christian Spiritual Formation:*
How Scripture, Spirit, Community, and Mission Shape Our Souls

"For thousands of years the Rules of Sts. Basil and Benedict have guided monks and nuns in following Christ and building community. In *Becoming a Community of Disciples* Greg Peters makes this tried and true wisdom available to Christians in all walks of life. Here readers will find actual texts from both Rules which relate to leadership, community, hospitality, virtue, prayer, and discipline, followed by discussion questions which will enable them to apply this wisdom to present life challenges."

~ Sr. Colleen Maura McGrane, OSB,
Editor, *The American Benedictine Review*

Becoming a Community of Disciples: Guidelines from Abbot Benedict and Bishop Basil

ISBN: 978-1-955424-03-5

Published jointly in 2021 by TUMI Press and Samuel Morris Publications

TUMI Press is a division of World Impact, Inc.

TUMI Press
The Urban Ministry Institute
3701 E. 13th Street, Suite 100
Wichita, KS 67208

Equipping Leaders. Empowering Movements.

Samuel Morris Publications:

Samuel Morris Publications
Sacred Roots Project at Taylor University
236 W. Reade Avenue
Upland, IN 46989

Samuel Morris Publications publishes texts in service to the evangelical church's life together and its ongoing pursuit of a deeper conformity to Jesus Christ (Galatians 4:19).

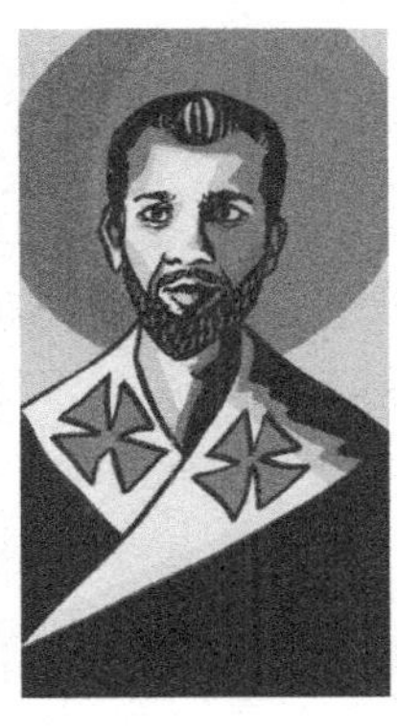

Table of Contents

Acknowledgments ix

Introduction 1

Chapter 1
Legislative Teachings – Organization of the Monastery . 13

Chapter 2
Legislative Teachings – The Role of the Abbot . . . 27

Chapter 3
Legislative Teachings – Other Monastic Offices . . . 39

Chapter 4
Spiritual Teachings – The Tools of Good Works . . . 47

Chapter 5
Spiritual Teachings – Personal Behavior 55

Chapter 6
Spiritual Teachings – Virtues and Discipline 65

Chapter 7
Spiritual Teachings – Prayer 99

Chapter 8
Spiritual Teachings – Hospitality 107

Afterword 113

Resources for Application 119

Soul Work and Soul Care:
Learning to Be Intentional about Our "Rule of Life" . 121

Continuing the Conversation 142

Map of Important Places:
Benedict of Nursia and Basil the Great. 144

A Letter to God's Friends and Fellow Warriors
On Why We Read the Sacred Roots
Spiritual Classics Together. 145

The Nicene Creed with Scriptural Support 161

From Before to Beyond Time:
The Plan of God and Human History 165

About the Sacred Roots Project 168

Scripture Index 173

For my former and current students in the Torrey Honors College of Biola University, who have modeled how to read spiritual classics well and put them into practice in their lives

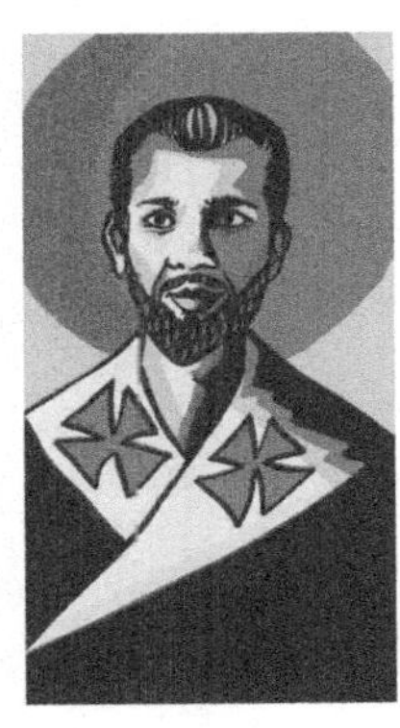

Acknowledgments

I would like to thank for Fr. Luke Dysinger, OSB, of St. Andrew's Abbey, Valyermo, California, for permission to use his translation of the Rule of Benedict, originally published by Source Books. I would also like to thank my wife Christina for assistance in developing the discussion questions and to my son Nathanael for transcribing the selections from the Rule of Basil.

Theology & Ethics

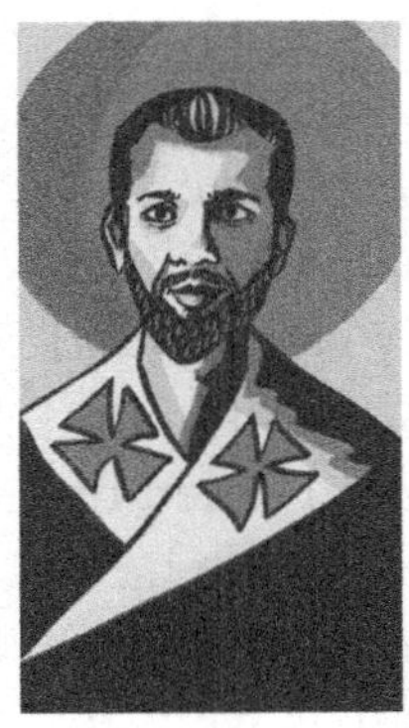

Introduction

Meet My Mentors—Dad, Basil, and Benedict

I was raised by hardworking parents. In fact, my father is one of the hardest working people I know. Now approaching his mid-80s he has certainly slowed down, but during my childhood and teenage years he worked long hours. More or less, my dad only worked a few jobs in his entire life. As I recall he worked a short while for a car dealership, getting recently-arrived new vehicles ready for the sales lot; he spent nearly four years in the United States Navy as a radar man on a destroyer, trying to tell the difference between whales and Russian submarines; and then he mostly worked at the local paper mill, first owned by Mead and then by Rock-Tenn. The paper mill in Lynchburg, Virginia, where he worked making paper from recycled magazines and newspapers, not wood. In its heyday the mill had two paper machines and a large number of finishing machines. The paper machines took the cocktail of water and pulp and efficiently made huge rolls of brown paper. These were big rolls of paper, perhaps only three or four could fit on a semi-trailer. The finishing machines took these big rolls of paper and made other paper products. Not things like ruled notebook paper or envelopes, but thick paper stock products used in the backs of mirrors, in car doors and in hardback books, for example. Those rolls of paper were glued together by a machine called the laminator until they were the right thickness for whatever use they were bound and then cut to size by machines with ominous-sounding names, like "the slitter." Though my dad worked different jobs at the plant over the decades, for most of my life he was a "pallet maker." Though he no longer actually made the wooden pallets, he made sure the right pallets were at the right machines at the right times so that the finished products could be shipped to their final destination.

So what made my dad a hard worker in this environment? Well, throughout most of my childhood and teenage years the plant was wildly successful, so much so that my dad worked seven days a week most weeks of the year. He would take a week or two of vacation in the summer, perhaps a week in the spring to do some spring cleaning around the house but otherwise my dad was at work. One week he worked the daylight shift (7 a.m. to 3 p.m.) and the next week he worked the evening shift (3 p.m. to 11 p.m.). Pallet makers did not have the miserable 11 p.m. to 7 a.m. shift but sometimes my dad would have to work late anyway. The paper and finishing machines ran 24/7 so he could not leave until everything was in order for those middle-of-the-night projects. In spite of all this, I do not recall my dad ever complaining. I am sure he did complain at times but I just do not remember it. Rather, my dad dutifully went to work, day in and day out, doing his job and when he did come home, he took care of his family and his home. He also did those tasks without much complaint!

Turns out my father's lifestyle was somewhat monastic. That is, like monks and nuns who live in a monastery, he had a fairly predictable routine and followed that routine with due diligence. As well, as an employee at a large company he learned obedience to his superiors and as part of a team he learned to get along well with others. If my dad failed to do his job it affected others and vice versa. But my dad's experience is not particularly unique. Many people around the globe work jobs where they must work hard and where they must work well with others. Unless someone is self-employed or is the person in charge, then all employees must learn how to be obedient workers and failure to do your job well often results in termination. In these ways, and in other ways too, most of us do a lot of things that monks and nuns do.

But perhaps even more than this, all of us rub shoulders every day with other people—including family, friends, co-workers and even complete strangers. In other words, it is fairly impossible to navigate our daily lives without interacting with others. Now, I must confess, that I am not a big people person. That is, I rather enjoy being alone or, at best, with just my immediate family. I can often do without large crowds and I find most small talk uncomfortable so I tend not to be overly chatty with complete strangers or people that I hardly know. But my vocation as a professor and pastor means that I must interact with people every day, so I have had to learn how to be in relationship with others. And is this not true for all of us? No matter our personal opinions when it comes to how we relate to others, all of us have to live our lives, to some extent, connected with others. And I would say that this is even truer for Christian believers than it is for others.

The Bible assumes that Christians will be united to one another. The earliest Christians modeled it for us when "They devoted themselves to the apostles' teaching and to fellowship, to the breaking of bread and to prayer . . . All the believers were together and had everything in common. They sold property and possessions to give to anyone who had need" (Acts 2:42, 44–45; NIV). And when the Apostle Paul wrote to the believers in Corinth he said "I appeal to you, brothers and sisters, in the name of our Lord Jesus Christ, that all of you agree with one another in what you say and that there be no divisions among you, but that you be perfectly united in mind and thought" (1 Cor 1:10; NIV). So, as Christians, we take these passages seriously and we try to be in good relationship with our brothers and sisters in the Lord. We live in community with one another in the power of the Holy Spirit who unites us to one another in love (Eph 4:1–7). We are quick to forgive when we sin against one another (Eph 4:32). In short, we strive to live together as a family, having been brought into this family through our adoption as sons and daughters of God (Gal 4:4–7). But like any family, there will be seasons when we do not get along well with others in the family. To do things well and to honor God best we need to be taught how to be in good relationship with one another, both our sisters and brothers in Christ and those with whom we interact each and every day. We need to become disciples together.

There are different ways that we can choose to learn things. For example, you have a minor repair issue on a car and you are convinced you can fix it yourself. In the past you may have just gone for it. Just dive in and see what you could figure out using your own "know-how" and experience. Or you could have bought or borrowed a printed car repair manual that was unique to your vehicle. With the Internet you can probably look up that manual or even one on the car manufacturer's website. Now, though, with websites like YouTube we can watch a video that some nice person posted, walking us step by step through the necessary repair. Something similar is true when we think about how to learn to be Christian disciples together. We can jump right in and figure things out as we go. Or we can turn to the Scriptures, which have so much to teach us about being a disciple of Jesus Christ. And we can also read other books that have taken the teachings of the Scriptures and used them as their foundation to describe how we are to be Christian disciples. This book is an example of the last way. That is, I will use the writings of Basil of Caesarea (d. 379) and Benedict of Nursia (d. 547) to illustrate how we can become better disciples of Jesus with one another. Let me be completely clear: I do not think these authors are saying something better than what we can learn from the Bible, but I do think that they take what is in the Bible and make it practical for those of us who are in relationship with others and who are called to be faithful followers of God.

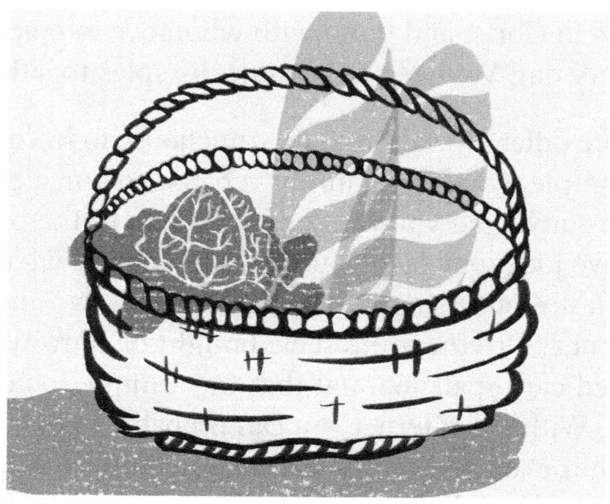

Benedict lived in a cave for three years; his food was lowered to him in a basket.

Basil, born in a town called Caesarea, is one of the most significant and important early Christian authors. Along with his brother Gregory of Nyssa (d. 395) and friend Gregory of Nazianzus (d. 389), Basil helped to firmly establish Christianity and Christian monasticism throughout Asia Minor (modern Turkey) by way of his writings. Basil's spiritual writings evolved in three stages. The Morals were written when Basil lived as a solitary monk across a river from his sister Macrina. The work is a collection of quotations from the New Testament that seem to speak about monastic practices and is divided into eighty topics. The *Asceticon* has two versions: the *Small Asceticon*, composed of 203 questions; and the *Great Asceticon* that includes 55 "Long Rules" and 313 "Short Rules." There is quite a bit of overlap between the "Long Rules" of the *Great Asceticon* and the *Small Asceticon*, and many of the "Short Rules" are also in the *Small Asceticon*. The "Long Rules" are Basil's most complete statement about monasticism, allowing us to understand Basil's full vision for the monastic life, but the so-called "Rule" of Basil (which is primarily the *Small Asceticon*) is the one that was translated into Latin and had the greater impact on the Christian Church in the west, of which we are a part.

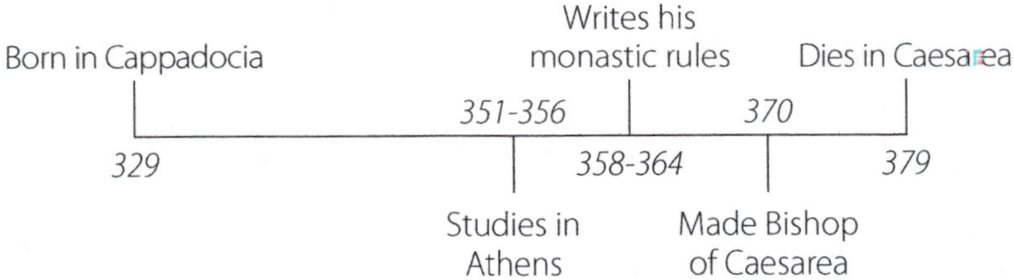

Benedict was born in Nursia, which is in central Italy. According to Gregory the Great (d. 604), who wrote his life, Benedict was sent to school in Rome but after seeing the sinfulness of his classmates he quit his studies, left his family home, gave up his inheritance and sought to please God alone. He chose to become a monk so that he could lead a holy life. This led him to live in a cave at Subiaco, about forty miles east of Rome. Gregory tells us that on the way to Subiaco, Benedict met a monk named Romanus who gave Benedict a monastic habit; that is, the long dark gown worn by monks. Over the next three years Romanus brought Benedict food, lowering it to him in a basket. In time Benedict's holiness became well-known by the other Christians living in the area, leading them to copy his way of life. A local monastery asked Benedict to become their leader. He agreed to be their Abbot, but in time "the monks under his rule grew furious . . . It was hard for them to have to change their attitudes."[1] After the monks tried to poison Benedict (!) he left the monastery and returned to his cave. Soon Benedict founded other monasteries near his cave. Yet, due to ongoing difficulties, Benedict placed all the monasteries he built under the leadership of other monks and moved south to start a new monastery. This monastery is called Monte Cassino and is his most famous monastery. It caused him to write his *Rule*.

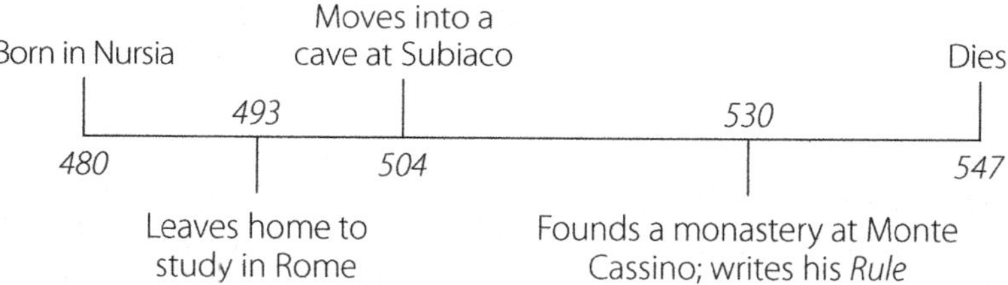

So, the goal of this book is to introduce you to some of what is in the Rule of Benedict and the "Rule" of Basil. I will do this by including texts grouped under eight different headings, which in turn are grouped under two higher level headings:

Administrative Teachings

Organization of the Monastery
The Role of the Abbot
Other Monastic Offices

---

1 Terrence G. Kardong, *The Life of St. Benedict by Gregory the Great: Translation and Commentary* (Collegeville: Liturgical Press, 2009), 21.

Spiritual Teachings

The Tools of Good Works
Personal Behavior
Virtues and Discipline
Prayer
Hospitality

Like the Bible, both rules are broken down into chapters and verses. In this way, you can always choose to read only a part of a chapter, picking up at the next verse when you return to the text. Texts from Christian monastic history almost always contain unfamiliar words. These words are unknown to us because we are not monks or nuns and because these rules were written about 1500–1700 years ago. When a word is used that is particularly unfamiliar, I will put its meaning in a footnote. Further, to ease discussion of the texts and to make this volume more user-friendly, I have consecutively numbered all the chapters of the selections.

My hope is that these texts will change your life like they have changed mine. I was introduced to Christian monasticism in my last semester of college and I have not gotten over it yet. That was twenty-six years ago! I love the Bible, of course, and I love all kinds of books, but the rules of Benedict and Basil have been extremely helpful in teaching me how to live well with others and how to be a better Christian.

I try to read a little bit of these rules every day. Why? Because I have seen how they help me love my neighbors better, love my friends and family better, love my fellow Christians better and, most importantly, love God better. As I mentioned above, I am not very good at meeting people naturally and being in a relationship with them. But I have learned so much from Benedict and Basil that I want to share it with you. Though you might not understand everything they are saying at first (I surely did not!) the more you read them the easier it becomes to see what they are saying. Basil and Benedict can teach us so much about living well as a human being in this big community called "the world" (and our own, smaller communities) that we must read what they have to say to us. Just like my dad, we are all kind of monks and nuns anyway, so why not read these helpful monastic rules.

The Text

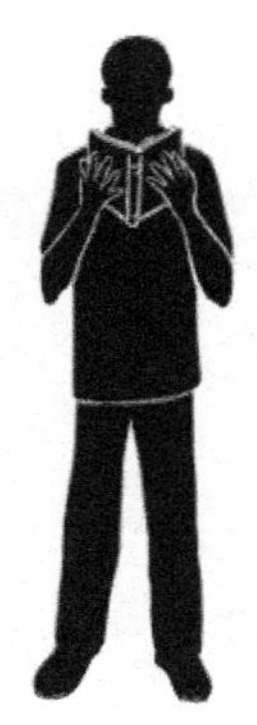

THEOLOGY & ETHICS

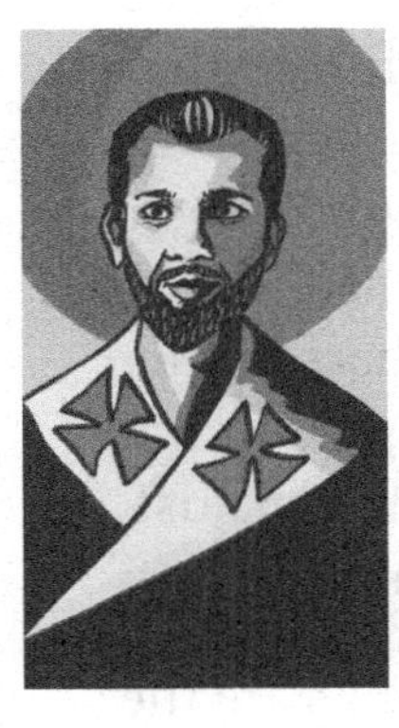

Chapter 1

Legislative Teachings – Organization of the Monastery

Every monastery is an organization and all organizations need rules in order to run smoothly. Monastic legislative texts are these rules and they are intended to guide the community in its corporate life together. In a world where everyone wants to do what is right in his own eyes (see Judges 17:6), legislative texts ensure that everyone's experience is, more or less, the same. They do not take away one's individuality but create space for individuals to flourish in community together. Congregational leaders today would do well to institute legislative procedures for their communities so that there is a shared ethos among all members. This will likely help to keep at bay the marginalization of particular populations within the community for it creates a more level "playing field," if you will.

The Various Kinds of Monks (RBen §1)

1 It is clear that there are four kinds of monks.[1] 2 First are the "*cenobites*": that is, those who live in monasteries and serve under a rule[2] and an Abbot.[3]

3 The second kind are the "*anchorites*," that is hermits: no longer in the first fervor of their way of life, they have undergone long testing in the monastery; 4 they have been trained to fight against the devil through the help and training of many others. 5 And well-armed, they go forth from the battle line held by their brothers to the solitary combat of the desert; now able to fight safely without the support of another, single-handed against the vices of flesh and thoughts with God's help.

6 The third and most detestable kind of monks are the "*Sarabaites*," who have neither been tried by a Rule nor taught by experience *like gold in the furnace* (Prov 27:21); instead they are as soft as lead, 7 faithful servants of the world in their works, obviously lying to God by their tonsure. 8 Living in twos or threes, or even singly without a shepherd, they enclose themselves not in the Lord's sheepfolds but in their own. Their law consists in their own willful desires: 9 whatever they think fit or

---

1 Monk – one called to a unique expression of Christian living consisting of prayer, study, and work, often in community with other monks in a monastery (see further Greg Peters, *The Monkhood of All Believers: The Monastic Foundation of Christian Spirituality* [Grand Rapids, MI: Baker Academic, 2018], 1).

2 Rule – the written rule of life which organizes the community, describes each person's role, and establishes codes of conduct within the monastery. See resource section for further information.

3 Abbot – the leader of the monastery. "Abbot" comes from the Greek word abba that means "father."

choose to do, that they call holy; and what they dislike, that they regard as unlawful.

Four Kinds of Monks	
Cenobites	*Live in monasteries; serve under a Rule and an Abbot.*
Anchorites	*Formerly lived in monasteries; now live in isolation.*
Sarabaites	*Never lived in monasteries; never served under a Rule nor an Abbot; call holy whatever is right in their own eyes.*
Gyrovagues	*Wanderers without a fixed monastery, Rule or Abbot.*

10 The fourth kind are the monks called "*gyrovagues*," whose whole lives are spent in province after province, spending three or four days in monastery after monastery as guests: 11 always wandering and never stable; slaves of self-will and the attractions of gluttony[4]; in all things they are worse than the Sarabaites.

12 Concerning all of these and their most miserable way of life it is better to remain silent than to speak. 13 Leaving them then, let us proceed with God's help to make provision for the cenobites—the strong kind of monks.

Whether All Should Receive Necessary Things Equally (RBen §34)

1 As it is written: *Distribution was made to each one according to his need* (Acts 4:35). 2 We do not mean by this that there should be personal favoritism (may it never happen!) but rather that infirmities should be taken into consideration: 3 thus one who requires less should give thanks to God and

4 Gluttony – the sin of eating too much.

be not saddened; 4 and one who requires more should be humbled because of his infirmity—not exalted by the mercy shown him, 5 and in this way all the members may be at peace. 6 Above all, the evil of murmuring must not appear for any reason, through any word or sign whatever: 7 if someone is found guilty of this he is to be subjected to very severe discipline.

The Sick Brothers (RBen §36)

1 Care of the sick must rank before and above everything, so that they may truly be served as Christ Himself, 2 for He said: *I was sick and you visited me* (Matt 25:36) 3 and, *Whatever you did for one of these who are least, you did for me* (Matt 25:40). 4 But the sick are themselves to consider that they are served out of honor for God, and they are not to sadden their brothers who serve them with superfluous demands; 5 Yet they are to be patiently borne with, because from such as these a more abundant reward is acquired. 6 The Abbot shall therefore exercise the greatest care that they not suffer any neglect.

7 These brothers who are sick are to be assigned a separate room and a God-fearing attendant who is also diligent and solicitous.[5] 8 Baths may be offered the sick whenever this is helpful, but those who are healthy, especially the young are to be allowed this less frequently. 9 Additionally, the sick who are very weak may be allowed to eat meat to recover their strength; but when they are better, all are to abstain from meat as usual.[6]

---

5 Solicitous – caring.

6 It was unusual for monks to take frequent baths, and they often did not eat meat.

10 Moreover the Abbot is to maintain the greatest care that that the sick are not neglected by the cellarers[7] or attendants. For he is responsible for whatever is lacking in his disciples.

Daily Manual Labor (RBen §48)

1 Idleness is the enemy of the soul; and therefore the brothers should be occupied at certain times in manual labor, and at certain other hours in sacred reading.

2 We therefore believe that the times for each may be ordered thus: 3 from Easter [i.e., in the spring] to the first of October, on coming out after Prime they are to labor at whatever is necessary from the first until about the fourth hour; 4 from the fourth hour until about the time they say Sext they are to devote themselves to reading; 5 after Sext upon arising from table they are to rest on their beds in complete silence, or if anyone wishes to read to himself he may read, but without disturbing the others; 6 and None is to be performed rather early at the middle of the eighth hour; then they are again to work at whatever needs to be done until Vespers. 7 If, however, local necessity or poverty require that they themselves are occupied with gathering the harvest, they should not be saddened; 8 for they are then truly monks when they live by the labor of their hands, as did our fathers and the apostles. 9 But everything is to be done with proper measure on account of the fainthearted.

7 Cellarer – the monk who watches over the monastery's belongings.

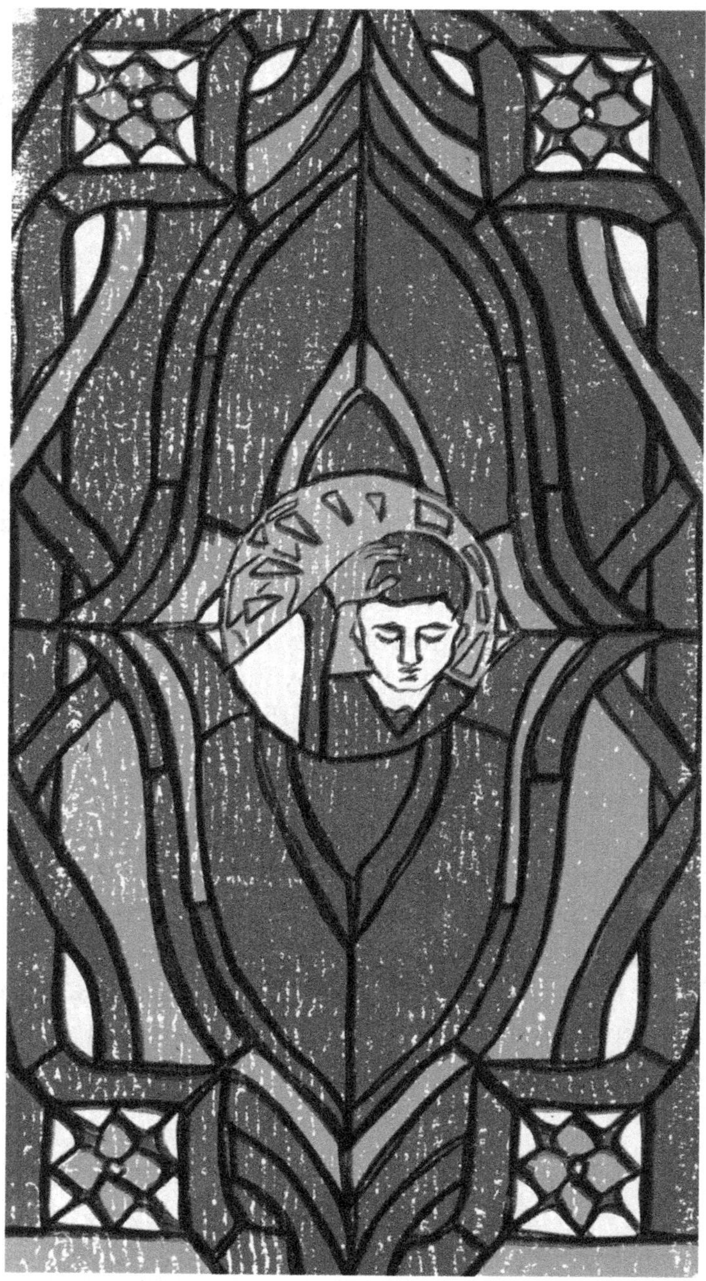

"Care of the sick must rank before and above everything."

10 From the first of October until the beginning of Lent they are to devote themselves to reading until the end of the second hour: **11** at the second hour Terce is to be said, and until None all are to labor at their appointed work. **12** But at the first signal for the hour of None all are to cease from their work, and prepare for the sounding of the second signal. **13** After the meal they are to devote themselves to their reading or to the psalms.

Hours of Prayer		
Name	*Our Time*	*Their Time*
Prime	*6 a.m.*	*First Hour*
Terce	*9 a.m.*	*Third Hour*
Sext	*12 p.m.*	*Sixth Hour*
None	*3 p.m.*	*Ninth Hour*
Vespers	*6 p.m.*	*Twelfth Hour*

14 In the days of Lent, however, from morning until the end of the third hour they should devote themselves to their reading, and afterwards work until the end of the tenth hour at their assigned tasks. **15** In these days of Lent each is to receive a book from the library, to be completely read straight through: **16** these books are to be given out at the beginning of Lent.

The Christian Year			
	Season	*Emphasis*	*Time of Year*
Cycle of Light	*Advent*	*Remembrance of God's Promised Messiah*	*The Four Weeks before Christmas*
	Christmas	*The Birth of Christ and His Revelation to the World*	*December 25 until January 5*
	Epiphany	*The Revelation of Christ's Mission to the World*	*January 6*
Cycle of Life	*Lent*	*Christ's Lowliness and Submission to the Father*	*The Forty Days before Easter, Not Counting Sundays*
	Holy Week	*Christ's Final Week, Crucifixion, and Burial*	*The Week before Easter*
	Easter	*Christ's Victory over Evil, Sin, and the Devil in His Resurrection*	*Easter Sunday*
	Pentecost	*The Descent of the Holy Spirit and the Birth of the Church*	*The Seventh Sunday after Easter*

17 Above all, one or two seniors should be deputed to
make the rounds of monastery at the hours when the
brothers are devoted to reading; **18** and they are to see
that there is not found any brother giving in to *acedia*,[8]
who devotes himself to idleness or idle story-telling, and
does not apply himself to his reading: he is thus not only
useless to himself, but a distraction to others. **19** If one is
found (may it not happen!) he is to be corrected once and
then a second time, **20** and if he does not amend he is to
be subjected to the chastisement of the Rule, in such a
way as to inspire fear in the rest. **21** And no brother may
associate with another brother at inappropriate hours.

8 Acedia – laziness.

22 On Sunday all are to devote themselves to reading except those assigned various duties. 23 But if anyone is so negligent and lazy as to be unwilling or unable to meditate or read, he is to be given work to do so that he is not idle.

24 Brothers who are sick or weak are to be assigned such work or crafts that they will not be idle, and yet will not be oppressed by heavy labor and so driven away. 25 Such infirmities are to be taken into consideration by the Abbot.

Rank in the Community (RBen §63)

1 They are to keep their rank in the monastery which the time of their entry and the merit of their lives determines, or as the Abbot constitutes. 2 For the Abbot is not to disturb the flock committed to him, nor, acting as if his power were unlimited, establish anything unjustly: 3 instead he is always to ponder that for all his judgments and deeds he will have to give an account to God (cf. Luke 16:2). 4 It is therefore, in that order which he has constituted or which the brothers already have in relation to each other that they are to approach for the kiss of peace and Communion, intone[9] psalms, and stand in choir: 5 And in absolutely every place, age is not to decide the order or be prejudicial to it; 6 for Samuel and Daniel were children when they judged the elders (1 Sam 3; Dan 13:44–62). 7 Therefore, with the exception of those whom (as we have said) the Abbot, after taking advice promotes, or demotes for certain reasons; all the rest are to have the order of their entry: 8 thus, for example, one who enters the monastery at the second hour of the day must know that he is junior to one who came at the first hour, whatever his age or dignity.

9 Intone – sing.

9 But children are to be kept under discipline in all matters and by everyone.

10 The juniors, therefore, are to honor their elders, and the elders love the younger. **11** In calling each other by name, no one is to address the other by his simple name; **12** rather, the elders are to call the juniors "brother," and the younger call their elders *nonnus*, which means "reverend father." **13** But the Abbot, since he is believed to represent Christ, is to be called "Lord" and "Abbot"; not for his own sake, but out of honor and love for Christ. **14** Let him ponder this, and behave in such a way as to be worthy of such honor.

15 Wherever the brothers meet one another the junior is to ask a blessing of the elder. **16** And when a superior passes by, the subject is to rise and give him a place to sit; nor should the junior presume to sit unless his senior bids him: **17** let it be as it is written, *outdo one another in showing honor* (Rom 12:10).

18 Small children and adolescents in the oratory or at table are to keep with discipline to their proper ranks. **19** But outside or wherever else they may be, they are to receive care and discipline until they reach the age of reason.

Places of Honor (RBas §10)

Q: When the time requires it, what should we observe concerning *places of seating* and *reclining* (Matt 23:6; cf. Luke 14:7–8)?

R: **1** Since we have a charge from the Lord who directs us to humility in all things, **2** in which he even declares that when we take our seat at a dinner we should seek *the lowest place* and not occupy a higher place (Luke 14:8–10), 3 we ought to realize that when we who have the same purpose and goal all come together, especially if we are giving proof of our humility among the many or the great, it is fitting that each desire to take in advance the lower place, according to the Lord's command.

4 But on the other hand, if the matter comes into contention over this and one tries to displace the other even if from a lower place, it is most unacceptable, 5 for an occasion of turbulence and disquiet arises from this, and if no-one begins to yield to the other, and if they are stirred to fight over it, they will be just like those who fight over the first seats.

6 Wherefore we ought carefully to consider and follow what is fitting for each of us in this matter, and assuredly yield to him who is entrusted with the responsibility of hospitality, 7 and also keep order and comply with him in other matters as well as the order of seating, that the saying may be fulfilled in us, *let all* you do *be done decently and in order* (cf. 1 Cor 14:40).

Serving Sick Brothers (RBas §36)

Q: In what disposition ought we to serve the sick brothers?

R: 1 As offering our service to the Lord himself who said: *When you did it to the least of these my brothers, you did it to me* (Matt 25:40). 2 Yet it helps us to preserve such a disposition in our ministry, if those who receive services from us are such to whom service is deservedly offered. 3 So those who preside ought to take care that they to whom service is done are not such as indulge the flesh and the stomach, 4 but instead are found proven in the love of God and Christ Jesus as those who through their own patience and the merit of their life deserve the services of their brothers, 5 whereby they are a boast for Christ and a reproach to the devil, as was holy Job.

Care for Tools and Utensils (RBas §103)

Q: How must workers care for the tools or utensils they use for work?

R: 1 First they must use them as God's instruments, that is, as consecrated to God. Second, as being unable without them to obtain the benefits of their own devotion and zeal.

Ability to Perform Assigned Duties (RBas §131)

Q: When someone serves in the kitchen on his own day, but works beyond his strength, so that he is hindered and unable to perform his own work for days afterward, should we assign him such an office?

R: 1 We already said above that the one entrusted with the arrangement of tasks and the one who presides ought to note carefully the strength and capacity of each, 2 and, as each is suited, so also assign the task, lest he should hear what is written: *those who frame toil by decree* (Ps. 93:20). 3 The one obeying, however, must not contradict, for the limit of *obedience* to be observed is unto *death* (cf. Phil 2:8).

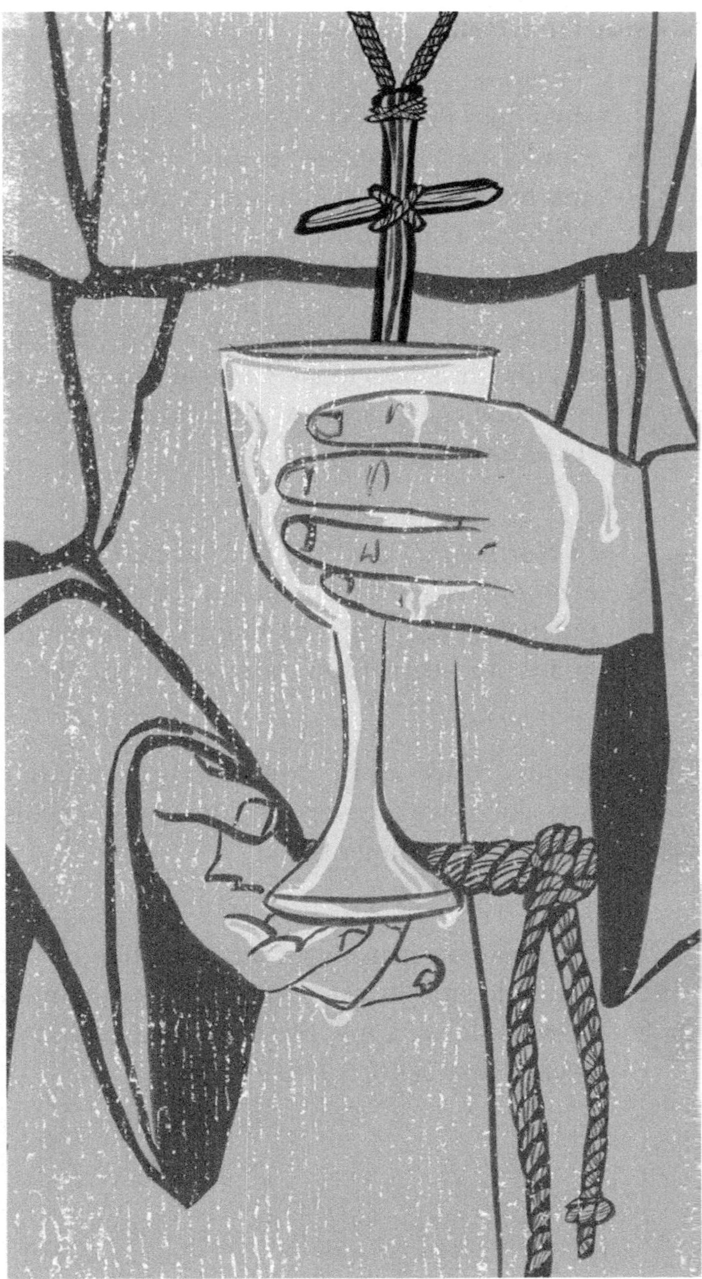

Unhappy monks attempted to poison Benedict's cup.

Discussion Questions

How does Benedict's view that some kinds of monks are "detestable" compare with people and practices today that hinder authentic Christian community?

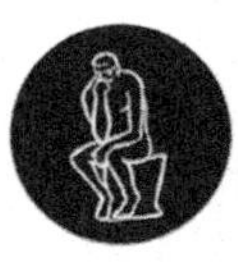

Idleness is a dangerous thing not only for monks but for Christians today. Compare and contrast how monks and present-day Christians guard themselves against this pitfall.

In North America's "me-first" society, can everyone be equal? How does the monastic practice of keeping rank within the monastery guard our hearts from the spirit of our age?

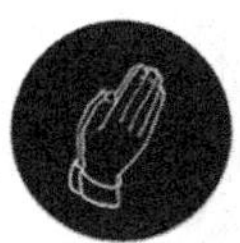

In our "throw-away," consumeristic culture, how could we recover a greater care for tools as "God's instruments"?

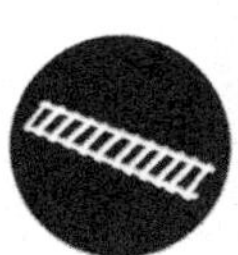

What can we learn from the disciplined schedule and the seasonal rhythms of monks? How could we apply these practices to our twenty-first-century lives?

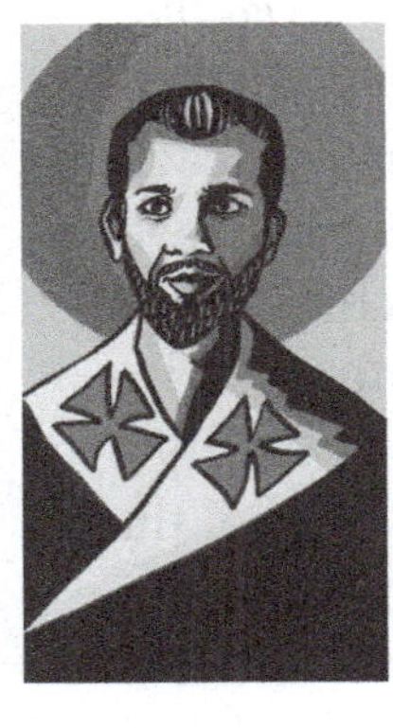

Chapter 2

Legislative Teachings – The Role of the Abbot

Since every monastery has an elected leader (an abbot if it is a men's community or an abbess/prioress if it is a women's community), it is good for the community to have a set of guidelines for this leader. We do not have to look too far today to see that power tends to corrupt leaders. And since all leadership positions come with power, it is possible that all leaders will abuse their power. Guidelines for leaders are meant to limit their exercise of power for the good of everyone, making it possible for the community to thrive holistically. All congregational leaders need to be aware of the ways that they may be tempted to abuse their power and, therefore, should not only be eager for there to be guidelines for leadership but should strive with all their might to follow them well. Experience shows that leaders thrive in the midst of limitations. When there are no limitations, chaos often occurs.

Qualities the Abbot Must Have (RBen §2)

1 An Abbot who is worthy to govern a monastery must always remember what he is called and fulfill the name "superior" in his deeds. 2 For it is Christ's place that he is believed to hold in the monastery, since he is addressed by His title, 3 as the apostle said: *You have received the spirit of adoption of sons by which we cry, "Abba, Father"* (Rom 8:15). 4 Therefore the Abbot should never teach or enact or command anything contrary to the precepts of the Lord; 5 rather his commands and his teaching, like the leaven of divine justice, are to suffuse the minds of his disciples: 6 The Abbot is to remember always that his teaching and the obedience of his disciples—both of these matters—will be examined at the fearful judgment of God. 7 And the Abbot must know that the shepherd will be considered at fault if the father of the household finds that the sheep bring no profit. 8 If, on the other hand, he has exercised all pastoral diligence over a restless and disobedient flock, always striving to heal their unhealthy ways; 9 then their shepherd will be absolved at the judgment of the Lord, and will say to the Lord with the prophet: *I have not hidden your justice in my heart; I have declared your truth and your salvation* (Ps 40:11), *but they condemned and spurned me* (Isa 1:2, Ezek 20:27); 10 and then the sheep disobedient to his care will be punished by overpowering death.

11 Therefore, when anyone receives the name of Abbot he is to govern his disciples by a twofold teaching: 12 namely, all that is good and holy he must show forth more by deeds than by words; declaring to receptive disciples the commandments of the Lord in words, but to the hard-hearted and the simple-minded demonstrating the divine

precepts by the example of his deeds. **13** And all of the things that he teaches his disciples are contrary [to the divine precepts]—his own deeds should indicate that these are not to be done, *lest while preaching to others, he himself be found reprobate* (1 Cor 9:27); **14** and God says to him in his sin: *How can you recite my justice and declare my covenant with your mouth? For you hated discipline and cast my words behind you* (Ps 50:1–17). **15** And also: *How could you see a speck in your brother's eye, and not have noticed the plank in your own?* (Matt 7:3).

16 He is not to distinguish between persons in the monastery. **17** He should not love one more than another unless he finds him better in good deeds or obedience. **18** One born free is not to be put before one who enters religion from slavery, except for some other reasonable cause. **19** Although, according to the dictates of justice, the Abbot may see fit to change anyone's rank. Otherwise let each keep to his proper place, **20** *because whether we are slaves or free, we are all one in Christ* (Gal 3:28, Eph 6:8) and under one Lord serve equally in bearing arms: *for with God there is no partiality among persons* (Rom 2:11). **21** Solely in this are we distinguished before him: if we are found better than others in good works and humility. **22** Therefore, let equal love be shown to all; and there should be imposed upon all, according to their merits, the same discipline.

23 For in his teaching the Abbot should always observe the apostle's norm, where he says: *use argument, exhort, rebuke* (2 Tim 4:2). **24** That is, he must adapt to circumstances, mingling gentleness with sternness, alternating the strictness of a master with the loving affection shown by a father: **25** thus he should sternly argue with the undisciplined and restless; he will exhort the obedient, the mild, and the patient to advance in virtue; and the negligent and arrogant we admonish him to rebuke and correct. **26** He must never disregard the sins of offenders; but as soon as they sprout, cut them out as best he can by the roots, remembering the fate of Eli, the priest of Shiloh (1 Sam 2:11–4:18). **27** Those of honorable and perceptive dispositions may for the first or second time be corrected with words of admonition; **28** but the shameless and hard, the arrogant or disobedient are to be checked by whipping or other corporal punishment at their first offense, knowing that it is written: *The fool is not corrected with words* (Prov 29:19), **29** and again, *Strike your son with a rod and you will free his soul from death* (Prov 23:14).

30 The Abbot must always remember what he is, remember what he is called, and know that from him to whom more is committed, more is required (Luke 12:48). **31** And he must know how difficult and arduous is his received task of ruling souls and serving different temperaments: complimenting some, rebuking others, using persuasion with still others; **32** and according to the unique qualities and intelligence of each he must so conform and adapt himself that not only will the flock committed to him suffer no loss, but he will truly rejoice in the increase of a good flock. **33** Above all he must not, by disregarding or undervaluing the salvation of the souls committed to him, be more solicitous for transitory, earthly, and perishable things; **34** rather let him always ponder that he who has received the ruling of souls must render an account of them (cf. Luke 16:2). **35** And that he may not plead as his excuse a lack of resources, let him remember what is written: *Seek first the Kingdom of God and his justice, and* *all these things will be added unto you* (Matt 6:33), 36 and again: *Nothing is lacking to those who fear him* (Ps 34:9).

37 And he must know that he who has received the ruling of souls, must prepare himself to render an account of them: 38 and whatever the number of brothers under his care, he should know for certain that on the Day of Judgment he must render an account of all these souls to the Lord—and without doubt of his own soul as well. 39 And therefore, always fearful of the future judgment of the shepherd concerning the flock entrusted to him and thus carefully considerate of others, he will also be solicitous[1] of what he must render that is his: 40 and so, in obtaining by his admonitions the amendment of others, he will also amend his own vices.

Summoning the Brothers for Counsel (RBen §3)

1 Whenever anything important has to be done in the monastery, the Abbot is to convoke the whole community, and himself declare the proposed action: 2 and having heard the counsel of the brothers, he is to ponder it over within himself and then do what he judges most appropriate. 3 Now, we have said that all should be called to council because it is often to the younger that the Lord reveals what is best. 4 But the brothers are to give their counsel with all the submissiveness of humility, and not presume insolently to defend their own views: 5 it is, rather, on the Abbot's decision that the matter depends, so that when he has judged what is most beneficial, all may obey. 6 Yet, even as it is natural for disciples to obey their master, so it is appropriate for him to settle everything with foresight and justice.

1 Solicitous – caring.

7 In everything, therefore, all are to follow the Rule as their master: from it no one at all should have the temerity[2] to turn aside. 8 No one in the monastery may follow the will of his own heart, 9 nor may any presume to brashly contend with his Abbot, whether within or outside the monastery. 10 But if he presumes to do so, let him be subjected to the discipline of the Rule. 11 Moreover, the Abbot himself must do everything in the fear of God, observing the Rule, knowing that without any doubt an account of all his judgments must be rendered to that most impartial judge, God.

12 If less important matters are to be done for the good of the monastery, he is to take counsel only with the seniors, 13 as it is written: *Do all things with counsel, and you will not afterwards repent of it* (Sir 32:24).

Those Who, without Permission, Associate with the Excommunicated (RBen §26)

1 If a brother presumes without permission from the Abbot to associate in any way with an excommunicated brother, or to speak with him, or to send him a message, 2 he will incur the same kind of punishment of excommunication.

The Kind of Care the Abbot Should Have for the Excommunicated (RBen §27)

1 It is with all solicitude that the Abbot should care for delinquent brothers, for *it is not the healthy who have need of a physician, but those who are sick* (Matt 9:12). 2 And thus he should in every way act as a wise physician,

2 Temerity – nerve.

sending *senpectae*, that is older and wise brothers, 3 who can, as it were in secret, console the wavering brother and convince him to make humble satisfaction, thus comforting him, *lest he be devoured by excessive sorrow* (2 Cor 2:7); 4 rather, as the apostle also says, *Let love towards him be intensified* (2 Cor 2:8) and let all pray for him. 5 With the greatest possible solicitude the Abbot should hasten to employ all wisdom and diligence so as not to lose any one of the sheep entrusted to him. 6 For he should know that he has undertaken to care for weak souls, not to exercise tyranny over the strong; 7 and he ought to fear the threat of the prophet in which God says: *What you saw to be fat you took for yourselves, and what was injured you cast away* (Ezek 34:3–4). 8 And he should imitate the loving example of the good shepherd, who, leaving the ninety-nine sheep on the mountains, went to seek the one which had lost its way: 9 its weakness inspired such compassion that *He* deigned[3] to *place it on His own* sacred *shoulders* and thus carry it back to the flock (Luke 15:5).

Those Who Are Excommunicated— How They Are to Make Satisfaction (RBen §44)

1 He who for more serious faults has been excommunicated from both the oratory[4] and the table is, at the end of the hour for the celebration of the Work of God, to cast himself prostrate before the entrance to the oratory, saying nothing: 2 without asking anything, he is to lie face down, prone on the ground at the feet of all as they leave the oratory; 3 and he is to do this until the Abbot judges that satisfaction

3 Deign – humble oneself.

4 Oratory – the place of prayer; a chapel.

has been made. 4 When he then receives the Abbot's order, he is to prostrate himself first at Abbot's feet, then at the feet of all so that they may pray for him. 5 And then, if the Abbot so orders, he may be received back into choir, but in the rank the Abbot assigns: 6 and he should not presume to lead a psalm, a reading or anything else in the oratory unless the Abbot again commands it: 7 additionally, at every hour that the Work of God is completed he is to prostrate himself on the ground in the place where he stands; 8 and he thus makes satisfaction until the Abbot again commands him to cease from this satisfaction.

9 Those who for lesser faults are excommunicated only from the table are to make satisfaction in the oratory until the Abbot gives the order: 10 they do this until he gives his blessing and says: "It is enough."

Those Who Offend in Other Matters (RBen §46)

1 If someone while laboring at any kind of work, whether in the kitchen, in the cellar, while serving, in the bakery, in the garden, at any craft, or in any place, commits any fault 2 or breaks or loses something, or fails in any way whatever; 3 and if he does not immediately go before the Abbot or the community and of his own accord make satisfaction and admit his fault: 4 if this is made known by means of another, he is to be subjected to more severe correction.

5 If, however, the cause of the sin is hidden in the soul, he is to reveal it only to the Abbot or to spiritual seniors, 6 who know how to heal both their own wounds and those of others without exposing them or making them public.

Attitude of an Abbot toward Those He Rules (RBas §15)

Q: What mind in himself ought the one who presides have towards those who he commands or rules?

R: 1 Before God he should be *as a minister of Christ and steward of the mysteries of God* (1 Cor 4:1), fearing lest he say or prescribe anything apart from the will of God or apart from what is clearly attested in the Scriptures, 2 and be found *bearing false witness to God* (1 Cor 15:15) or sacrilegious, whether by introducing anything foreign to the Lord's teaching, or indeed by allowing to pass or by overlooking anything that is pleasing to God.

3 Towards the brothers, however, he should be *as a nurse cherishing her children* (1 Thess 2:7), being prepared according to the will of the Lord and according to the better good of each, *to share with them not only the Gospel of God, but even his own life* (1 Thess 2:8), 4 mindful of the commandment of our Lord and God (John 20:28), who said: *A new commandment I give to you, that you love one another, even as I have loved you. Greater love has no man than this, that a man lay down his life for his friends* (John 15:12–13).

Changing Work without Permission (RBas §69)

Q: Is it permissible for anyone to excuse himself from the work he is charged to do and to seek something else?

R: 1 Since it is defined that the measure of obedience is *even until death* (Phil 2:8), anyone who avoids what he is charged to do and seeks something else is first of all guilty of disobedience and manifestly shows that he has not yet *denied himself* (Matt 16:24; Mark 8:34; Luke 9:23).

2 Second, he becomes the cause of many more ills both for himself and for others. For he opens the door of contradiction to the many and accustoms himself to contradicting, 3 and since not everyone is able to discern what is better and to choose it, it can happen that with such license someone chooses what is worse.

4 Third, he fosters a suspicion among the brothers that he is motivated by some passion, either for the work he chooses or even in regard to those with whom he must work.

5 And so, not to obey is in every way the cause and root of many evils. 6 But if there is some reason whereby it seems to him he might rightly excuse himself from that task which he is excusing himself, let him put it before the one who presides and leave it to his judgement so that he may examine whether the plea he submits has merit.

Permission Needed (RBas §80)

Q: Ought one go anywhere without a mention from the one who presides?

R: 1 Since the Lord says: *I have not come that I might do anything of myself, but it was he who has sent me* (John 7:28), how much less ought each of us to give himself permission! 2 For whoever does anything by his own authority is manifestly gripped by the disease of pride, and liable to that judgement which says: *That which is exalted among human beings is an abomination in the sight of God* (Luke 16:15). 3 So then, to do anything at all of one's own accord or authority is blameworthy.

Decision to Begin a Craft (RBas §192)

Q: Should those entering the brothers begin to learn crafts immediately?

R: 1 Let those who preside decide.

Discussion Questions

How is the role of an abbot similar or different than the role of leaders in ministry today?

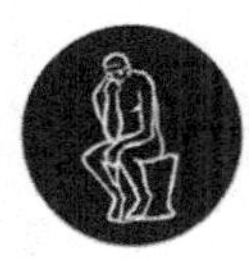

How does an abbot fulfill the role of Christ in the monastery?

How might this chapter's principles about loving those in our community who have fallen away be applied in our ministry contexts today?

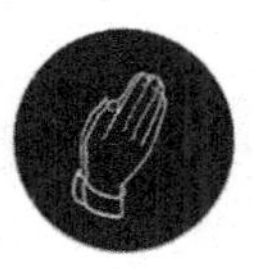

If you were a monk, would you find it easy or difficult to live under the rule of an abbot? To whom have you submitted yourself to "watch for your soul"?

What habits can we develop to guard against "unjustly ruling" or viewing ourselves as superior to those under our care?

THEOLOGY & ETHICS

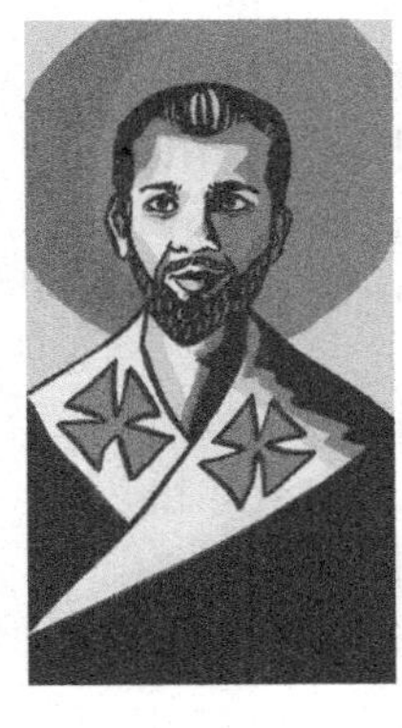

Chapter 3

Legislative Teachings – Other Monastic Offices

All leaders should be assisted by others. In the monastery there is the abbot's assistant called the prior, and then there are "deans" if the community is large enough. This shows that leadership should never be fully vested in one person but in a group. Other leaders provide the main leader with accountability and are a check on her leadership, if necessary. Sometimes congregational leaders isolate themselves, unfortunately. This is not always intentional but it is never a good idea. Isolation can lead to myopia; that is, a leader is too isolated to know what is best for the whole community. Other leaders can ensure that this does not happen. Further, it also gives voice to everyone in the community for sometimes it is the youngest member who has the greatest wisdom in a particular situation. Shared leadership values the input of everyone, helping to ensure that the organization remains a true community, not just a group of people surrounding one charismatic leader.

The Deans of the Monastery (RBen §21)

1 If the community is large, there should be chosen from it brothers of good reputation and a holy way of life to be appointed deans: 2 They are to carefully oversee their deaneries in everything according to the commandments of God and the precepts of their Abbot. 3 The ones chosen deans should be those with whom the Abbot may confidently share his burdens: 4 thus they should not be chosen according to the order of seniority, but rather for the merit of their lives and their wise teaching.

5 Should any of these deans become inflated with pride and be found to have acted reprehensibly; if, having been corrected once, twice, and even a third time, he refuses to amend, let him be deposed 6 and in his place there should be substituted another who is worthy. 7 And concerning the Prior[1] we establish that the same procedure is to be followed.

The Qualities of the Monastery Cellarer (RBen §31)

1 As monastery cellarer there should be chosen from the community one who is wise, of mature character, temperate, not an excessive eater, not haughty, not turbulent, not harmful, not sluggish, not wasteful, 2 but God-fearing; one who can act as a father to the whole community.
3 He is to have charge of everything; 4 he is to do nothing without an order from the Abbot. 5 He is to keep custody over his orders.

6 He is not to sadden the brothers. 7 If one of the brothers happens to request something unreasonably, he is not to treat him with disdain and thus sadden him, rather he

1 Prior – the person in charge of the monastery in the Abbot's absence.

must reasonably and with humility deny the bad request. **8** He is to keep custody over his own soul, remembering always that apostolic saying: *he who has ministered well acquires a good standing for himself* (1 Tim 3:13). **9** He is to care for the sick, for children, for guests, and for the poor with all solicitude[2], knowing without doubt that for all these he will have to give an account on the Day of Judgment (cf. Luke 16:2). **10** He is to look upon all the vessels and goods of the monastery as though they were the sacred vessels of the altar. **11** He is not to neglect anything. **12** He is not to be avaricious[3], not wasteful, not be a squanderer of the monastery's resources; rather he is to do everything in proper measure and according to the order of his Abbot.

13 Above all else he is to have humility: when he has nothing material to give to one who makes a request he is to offer at least a kind word, **14** as it is written: *A kind word is higher than the best gift* (Sir 18:17). **15** All that the Abbot has entrusted to him he is to have in his care, and he is not to presume to do what has been forbidden him. **16** To the brothers he is to offer their allotted ration of food without condescension or delay, so that they are not scandalized, remembering what the Sacred Text says is merited by one who scandalizes one of these little ones (Matt 18:6).

17 If the community is large, helpers are to be given to him, thanks to whose assistance he may retain a peaceful soul while fulfilling the office committed to him. **18** Only at the appropriate hours are items for distribution to be

---

2 Solicitude – attentiveness.

3 Avaricious – greedy.

distributed, or requested items to be requested; so that no one is perturbed or saddened in the house of God.

The Tools and Possessions of the Monastery (RBen §32)

1 The Abbot is to provide for the material goods of the monastery—that is tools, clothes, and any other thing—by means of brothers whose life and character he trusts; 2 and he is to consign to them the different items as he judges best, to be conserved and then collected after use. 3 Of these items the Abbot is to keep a list, so that as the brothers are successively assigned to different tasks, he will know what he gives out and what he receives back. 4 If anyone treats the goods of the monastery improperly or negligently he is to be corrected; 5 if he does not amend, he is to be subjected to the discipline of the Rule.

The Craftsmen of the Monastery (RBen §57)

1 If there are craftsmen in the monastery, they are to practice their crafts in all humility if the Abbot permits it. 2 But if any one of them becomes conceited because of his knowledge of his craft, determining that he thus confers something on the monastery, 3 he is to be taken from that craft and not permitted to exercise it again, unless having humbled himself, the Abbot orders him back to it.

4 If any products of the craftsmen are to be sold, care should be taken that those by whose hands the transaction takes place do not presume to practice any fraud. 5 They are always to remember Ananias and Sapphira (Acts 5:1–11), 6 lest the death which those two incurred in the body be suffered in their souls and those of all who practice any fraud in business of the monastery.

7 In establishing their prices the evil of avarice[4] must not creep in: 8 instead, the goods should always be sold for a little less than those living in the world are able to charge, so that in everything God may be glorified (1 Pet 4:11).

The Prior of the Monastery (RBen §65)

1 Very often it happens that through the appointment of a Prior grave scandals arise in monasteries; 2 for there are some who, inflated by a malignant[5] spirit of pride and esteeming themselves to be second Abbots, assume for themselves tyrannical power, and so feed scandals and create dissensions in the community: 3 and this occurs especially in those places where it is by the same bishop or the same Abbots who ordain the Abbot that the Prior is himself ordained. 4 How absurd this may easily be seen: for as soon as he is ordained he is given an incentive to pride, 5 his thoughts suggesting to him that he is free from the authority of his Abbot 6 since he has been ordained by the very same persons.

7 Thus arise jealousies, quarrels, detractions, competitiveness, dissensions, and depositions from office. 8 And while the Abbot and Prior are opposed to one another it necessarily follows that through this dissension their souls are endangered: 9 and those who are subject to them, being flattered as followers, go to their destruction. 10 The blame for this perilous evil rests on the head of those who were the authors of such disorders.

---

4 Avarice – greed.

5 Malignant – evil.

11 Therefore we regard it expedient for the preservation of peace and charity that the organization of his monastery depend on the will of the Abbot: **12** and, if possible, deans should conduct (as we have already arranged) all the affairs of the monastery according to the disposition of the Abbot; **13** so that, what is committed to several will not cause pride in any single one. **14** But if either the locale requires it or the community reasonably and with humility requests it, and if the Abbot judges it expedient, **15** the Abbot (with the counsel of God-fearing brothers) is to choose whomever he wishes and himself ordain him Prior. **16** But this Prior is to perform with reverence what the Abbot demands of him, doing nothing contrary to the Abbot's will; **17** for the more he is elevated above the rest, the more solicitously he ought to observe the precepts of the Rule.

18 If this Prior proves to have vices, or is deceived by the haughtiness of pride, or proves to have contempt for the holy Rule, he is to be verbally admonished up to four times; **19** if he does not amend, the discipline of the Rule is to be applied to him. **20** But if even then he does not amend, he is to be deposed from the office of Prior and another who is worthy be substituted in his place. **21** But if afterwards he is not quiet and obedient in the community, he is to be expelled from the monastery. **22** Nevertheless, the Abbot is to bear in mind that he must give an account to God of all his judgments, lest the flame of envy or jealousy be kindled in his soul.

Discussion Questions

What would be the equivalent of the dean, cellarer, and prior in our churches and ministries today? What can we learn from their separation of duties?

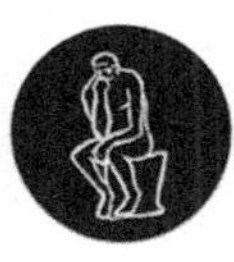

Why is it necessary to have offices or positions within a monastery or church? Why can't we all just do what we feel like doing (Rom 12, 1 Cor 12)?

Why is humility such an important quality of a leader? How does humility make stronger leaders, not weaker ones?

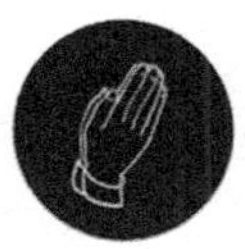

What steps can leaders in ministry take to promote living at peace with one another?

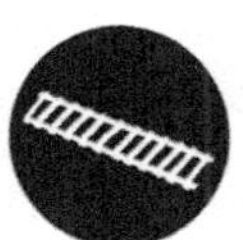

What habits in your life foster humility? What habits would help you develop this character quality?

THEOLOGY & ETHICS

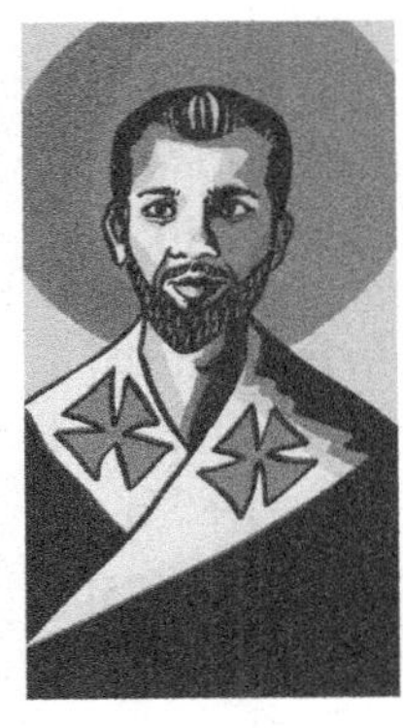

Chapter 4

Spiritual Teachings – The Tools of Good Works

The "tools of good works" are those things that everyone is supposed to be doing, each and every day. In other words, the monastery, as a community, is not just a place where you come and sit but it involves doing things; and these things are called "good works." Modern Christians often do too much for we are always on the move and rarely rest. Modern culture values busyness and productivity. But this is not the right kind of "doing" because "doing" is less about busyness and more about holiness of life. Leaders are doers by nature, and their ability and willingness to "do" is often the reason they are chosen as leaders. But even leaders need to slow down and do a different kind of thing: good works. Communities may be places of feverish activity but this pace can only be maintained with periods of slowing down, sustaining the inner life as well as the outer body.

The Instruments of Good Works (RBen §4)

1 First of all to *love the Lord God with one's whole heart, whole soul, whole strength* (Matt 22:37–39; Mark 12:30–31; Luke 10:47); **2** *then, to love one's neighbor as oneself.* **3** Then, *not to kill,* **4** *not to commit adultery,* **5** *not to engage in theft,* **6** *not to ardently desire* (Rom 13:9), **7** *not to give false testimony* (Matt 19:18; Mark 10:19; Luke 18:20); **8** *to honor all* (1 Pet 2:17), **9** and *not do to another what one does not want done to oneself* (Tob 4:16; Matt 7:12; Luke 6:31).

10 To *deny one's own self in order to follow Christ* (Matt 16:24; Luke 9:23). **11** *To chastise the body* (1 Cor 9:27): **12** not to embrace delicacies; **13** to love fasting. **14** To give new life to the poor; **15** *to clothe the naked,* **16** *to visit the sick* (Matt 25:36), **17** to bury the dead (cf. Tob 1:21, 2:7–9). **18** To help in tribulation, **19** to console the sorrowful.

20 To become a stranger to worldly behavior; **21** to prefer nothing to the love of Christ. **22** Not to carry out anger; **23** not to store up wrath, awaiting a time of revenge. **24** Not to cling to deceit within the heart, **25** not to give a false greeting of peace. **26** Not to turn away from love. **27** Not to swear lest you swear falsely (Matt 5:34); **28** to bring forth the truth from heart and mouth.

29 *Not to return evil for evil* (1 Thess 5:15, 1 Pet 3:9). **30** Not to cause injury, but rather to bear it patiently. **31** *To love one's enemies* (Matt 5:44; Luke 6:27). **32** Not to curse back those who curse one, but rather to bless them (1 Pet 3:9; Luke 6:28). **33** *To endure persecution for justice's sake* (Matt 5:10).

34 *Not to be proud* (Titus 1:7), **35** *not given to wine* (Titus 1:7, 1 Tim 3:3); **36** not to be a glutton (Sir 37:32), **37** nor given to sleeping (Prov 20:13), **38** *nor lazy* (Rom 12:11); **39** not given to murmuring **40** or to speaking ill of others (Wisd 1:11).

41 To place one's hope in God (Ps 72:28). **42** To attribute whatever good one sees in oneself to God, not to oneself; **43** but always to clearly acknowledge and take personal responsibility for the evil one does.

44 To fear the day of judgment, **45** to dread hell; **46** to desire eternal life with all spiritual ardent yearning, **47** to daily keep death before one's eyes. **48** To keep custody at every hour over the actions of one's life, **49** to know with certainty that God sees one in every place. **50** To instantly hurl the evil thoughts of one's heart against Christ (Ps 136:9) and to lay them open to one's spiritual father; **51** to keep custody of one's mouth against depraved speech, **52** not to love excessive speaking, **53** not to speak words that are vain or apt to provoke laughter (cf. 2 Tim 2:16), **54** not to love frequent or raucous laughter (cf. Sir 21:23).

55 To listen willingly to holy readings, **56** to prostrate[1] frequently in prayer; **57** to daily confess one's past faults to God in prayer with tears and sighs, **58** to amend these faults for the future.

59 *Not to gratify the desires of the flesh* (Gal 5:16): **60** to hate one's own will, **61** to obey the precepts of the Abbot in everything, even if he should (may it never happen!)

1 Prostrate – to lie face down.

act otherwise, remembering that precept of the Lord: *What they say, do; but what they do, do not* (Matt 23:3).

62 Not to wish to be called holy before one is so; but first to be holy, so as to be truly called so. 63 To daily fulfill in one's actions the precepts of God; 64 to love chastity; 65 to hate no one; 66 not to have jealousy, 67 not to act out of envy, 68 not to love contention, 69 to flee from conceit. 70 To reverence the seniors 71 and to love the juniors. 72 In the love of Christ to pray for enemies; 73 to make peace with opponents before the setting of the sun.

74 And never to despair of the mercy of God.

75 Behold, these are the instruments of the spiritual art. 76 If we employ them night and day without ceasing and on the Day of Judgement return them, then these will be the wages by which the Lord will recompense us, as he promised: 77 *What eye has not seen, nor ear heard, the Lord has prepared for those who love him* (1 Cor 2:9).

78 For the workshop in which we diligently use all these instruments is the enclosure of the monastery and stability in the community.

Repeated Sin (RBas §22)

Q: What shall they do who have repented of some sin but fall into the same sin again?

R: 1 He who has offended once and incurs this same sin again is seen to indicate this about himself: first that he is not purified of what is prior to the sin, from which, as from a kind of noxious root there sprout the same ills as before. 2 It is as if someone cuts off the branches of a tree but leaves behind the root. As long as the root remains in the ground it will eventually generate shoots from the same stock. So also with sin: **3** since not all who commit an offense take their impulse from the sins themselves—rather the cause of the offense arises from yet other offences—**4** it is necessary for him who wishes to purify himself wholly from sin to cut out from below the very first causes of defect.

5 For example, if there has been something of *strife and envy* (cf. Rom 13:13, et al.), it does not take a beginning from itself, but has a root of arrogance and the love of human glory; **6** for he who seeks glory from men either harries with disputes or envies those who act uprightly, that is, with anyone through whom he appears to be held in less praise or admiration.

7 Therefore, if someone who has been censured[2] once for the vice of envy or contention[3] falls into the same again, **8** let him recognize that the primary cause of which we spoke above from which arises envy or contentiousness is the love of glory which he has lurking in his innermost marrow. **9** He therefore ought to be cured by the contrary and opposite, that is, by exercises of humility. Such exercises of humility are that he submit himself to menial tasks and give himself to lowly acts of service. **10** In this way the vice of arrogance and human glory shall be able to be cured, so that, once he is established in the disposition of humility, he will not fall again into the offense of arrogance and vainglory.

---

2 Censured – corrected.

3 Contention – conflict.

The Practice of Silence (RBas §136)

Q: Is it good to practice complete silence?

R: 1 Silence and taciturnity[4] are good when they befit the time and the person, as we are taught by the holy Scripture, which says on one occasion: *He who understands will keep silent at that time, for it is an evil time* (Amos 5:13), 2 and again on another occasion: *I set a guard over my mouth, when the sinner rose up against me; I was dumb and humbled myself and kept silent even from good things* (Ps 38:1–2), 3 and elsewhere: *If a revelation is made to one seated, let the one who was speaking first keep silent* (1 Cor 14:30) and again: *let the women among you keep silent in the churches* (1 Cor 14:34). 4 And there is also another occasion when it says to those who have an incontinent[5] tongue: *Let no evil speech proceed from your mouth, but only what is good for the upbuilding of the faith* (Eph 4:29). 5 Now taciturnity is necessary at all times until the vices of the tongue and rashness of speech are pruned and one learns to speak appropriately and at the right time and beneficially, 6 as it is written: *Let their speech be seasoned with salt . . . that it may impart grace to the hearers* (Col 4:6; Eph 4:29).

---

4 Taciturnity – shy and reserved.

5 Incontinent – uncontrolled.

Discussion Questions

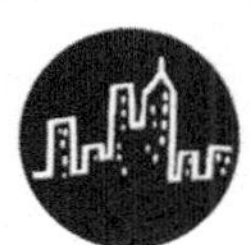

What is your "workshop" in which you need to employ "tools of good works"?

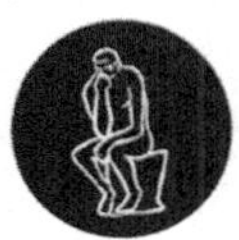

A tool is a device intended to make a task easier. Why do you think Benedict called these good works "tools"?

Is the fact that the two most important tools are to "love the Lord God with one's whole heart, whole soul, whole strength" and "to love one's neighbor as oneself" a practiced reality in your life?

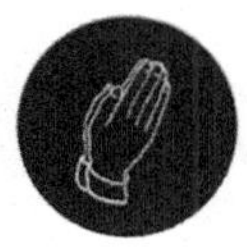

What are situations in your ministry context where censuring a sinner or the practice of silence could be beneficial?

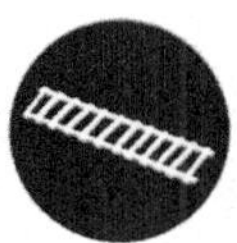

Benedict says we should use these tools "night and day without ceasing." What habits could assist us in doing this more consistently?

THEOLOGY & ETHICS

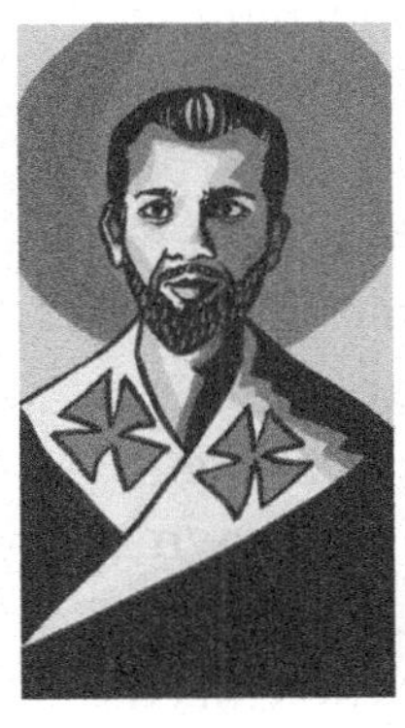

Chapter 5

Spiritual Teachings – Personal Behavior

Though we are all members of some form of community (family, church, etc.), we do not cease to be individuals. While all monks dress alike, they do not lose their individuality. Thus, just as there are guidelines for the whole community, so there are guidelines for individuals within the community. In contemporary culture social media apps tend to give individuals too much sense of self-importance; that is, I can say whatever I want about whomever I want without anyone's permission. Ideally, though, individual behaviors should reflect the communities to which we belong. The reason I treat everyone with dignity is because that is consistent with Christian theology. Leaders should resist the temptation to flatten everything out and treat everyone the same. That might work in military boot camps but it will likely fail in most other communities. Wise leaders encourage individuality but limit its potentially sinful expression through clear community guidelines.

Obedience (RBen §5)

1 The first step of humility is obedience without hesitation. 2 This comes naturally to those who esteem nothing as more beloved to them than Christ. 3 Whether on account of the holy service they have professed or because of the fear of hell and the glory of eternal life, 4 as soon as anything is ordered by the superior it is as if it had been commanded by God himself; and they cannot bear any hesitation in doing it. 5 Of these men the Lord says: on hearing with his ear he has obeyed me (Ps 18:44). 6 And again he says to teachers: he who hears you hears me (Luke 10:16). 7 Such as these, therefore, leaving immediately all that is theirs and forsaking their own wills 8 at once disengage their hands, and leaving unfinished what they were doing, follow by their deeds with the eager step of obedience the voice of him who commands: 9 and as it were in a single moment the master's bidding and the disciple's completed work are both, in the swiftness of the fear of God, instantly achieved.

10 Those whom love impels to advance on the way of eternal life—11 these lay hold of the narrow way of which the Lord says: Narrow is the way which leads to life (Matt 7:14): 12 so that by neither living according to their own wills, nor obeying their own desires and pleasures, they walk instead according to the judgment and command of another, living in community and desiring to have an Abbot govern them. 13 Without doubt such as these embody that saying of the Lord which reads: I did not come do my own will, but that of him who sent me (John 6:38).

14 But this very obedience will be acceptable to God and sweet to men only if what is commanded is not done

fearfully, sluggishly, or lukewarmly,[1] and neither with murmuring, nor with an answer showing unwillingness: **15** for the obedience offered to superiors is given to God, just as He Himself said: He who hears you hears me (Luke 10:16). **16** And this obedience ought to be offered with good will, because God loves a cheerful giver (2 Cor 9:7). **17** For if the disciple obeys with ill will and murmurs not only with his lips but also in his heart, **18** even if he fulfills the command he will not be acceptable to God, who sees the heart of the murmurer: **19** and from this no favor will follow; rather he will incur the punishment due to murmurers, unless he amends by making satisfaction.

Excommunication for Faults (RBen §23)

1 If any brother is found to be contumacious,[2] or disobedient, or proud, or a murmurer, or in any way has contempt for the Holy Rule and the precepts of his seniors, **2** let him, according to Our Lord's precept, be admonished once or twice in private by his seniors (cf. Matt 18:15–16). **3** If he does not amend he should be publicly rebuked in the presence of all. **4** If he still refuses to be corrected, he should (provided he understands what this penalty signifies) be subjected to excommunication: **5** however, if he lacks such understanding he should undergo corporal punishment.

More Serious Faults (RBen §25)

1 But that brother who is guilty of a more serious fault is to be suspended both from the common table and from the oratory. **2** None of the brothers may associate with

---

1 Lukewarmly – halfway.

2 Contumacious – rebellious or stubbornly disobedient to authority.

him or engage him in conversation. 3 Laboring in solitude at the work enjoined on him, persisting in the sorrow of penitence, he is to consider that dreadful sentence of the apostle who says: 4 such a man is handed over for the destruction of the flesh, so that the spirit may be saved on the day of the Lord (1 Cor 5:5). 5 And his meals are to be taken alone, in the measure and at the hour the Abbot considers best for him: 6 he may not be blessed by any who pass by, nor may the food be blessed that is given to him.

Those Who, Despite Frequent Correction, Do Not Amend (RBen §28)

1 If a brother who is frequently corrected for some fault, or even excommunicated, does not amend, he should receive a more severe correction: that is, let the punishment of beatings be administered to him. 2 If he then does not correct himself, or even (may it never happen!), inflamed with pride, he wishes to defend his actions, then the Abbot should act as a wise physician: 3 if he has applied compresses and the ointment of his admonitions, the medicine of the Sacred Scriptures, and ultimately the cautery[3] of excommunication or strokes of the rod; 4 and if he still sees that his labors are unavailing, he should add what is even greater—his prayers and those of all the brothers for him, 5 that the Lord who can do all things may affect the healing of the sick brother. 6 But if even by this means he is not healed, then the Abbot may use the knife for amputation, as the apostle says: Banish the evil one from you (1 Cor 5:13), and again: 7 If the unfaithful one departs, let him depart (1 Cor 7:15), 8 lest one diseased sheep infect the whole flock.

---

3 Cautery – medicine.

Those Who Make Mistakes in the Oratory (RBen §45)

1 If anyone makes a mistake while reciting a psalm, responsory, antiphon[4], or lesson and does not make satisfaction there before all by humbling himself, he is to be subjected to greater punishment, 2 for not correcting through humility what he did wrong through negligence. 3 Children, however, are to be whipped for such faults.

If Impossible Things Are Commanded of a Brother (RBen §68)

1 If a brother is commanded to do hard or impossible things, he should receive the order of his superior with all gentleness and obedience. 2 But if he sees that the measure of his strength is exceeded by the weight of the burden, he is to explain the cause of his incapacity to his superior patiently and at an opportune time, 3 without showing pride, resistance, or contradiction. 4 But if after his explanation the superior persists in his command, the junior must know that this is best for him; 5 and out of love, confident of God's help, he is to obey.

That They Should Obey One Another (RBen §71)

1 Not only is the blessing of obedience to be shown by all to the Abbot; the brothers must also obey one another, 2 knowing that by this path of obedience they go to God. 3 The commands, therefore, of the Abbot or the superiors appointed by him (to which we allow no unofficial orders to be preferred) are to be given precedence. 4 For the rest let all the younger brothers obey their elders with all love and courtesy. 5 Anyone who is found to be quarrelsome is to be corrected.

---

4 Antiphon – a one sentence line that comes before and after the psalm.

6 If anyone is rebuked[5] by the Abbot or by any superior in any way for however small a cause, 7 or if he comes to believe that any superior is angered or perplexed about him, however trivially; 8 he should immediately and without delay cast himself on the ground at his feet, remaining there to do penance until the turmoil is healed by the other's blessing. 9 But if anyone is too haughty to do this, he should be subjected to corporal punishment: if he remains unyielding, he must be expelled from the monastery.

To Whom Obedience Is Given (RBas §13)

Q: Do we owe obedience to everyone and anyone?

R: 1 A difference or diversity among those who give orders ought not hinder the obedience to what is proposed, since, for example, Moses did not refuse to hear his father-in-law Jethro, when he gave useful and just counsel (cf. Exod 18:19).

2 But certainly there is no small diversity in the things commanded, for some are seen to be contrary to the commandments of God, 3 others are seen to dissolve the commandment or adulterate it, while others help to fulfill and to build it up. 4 It is therefore necessary to remember the apostolic precept that says: Do not despise prophesyings, but test all things, hold fast to the good, abstain from every semblance of evil (1 Thess 5:20), 5 and again: Purging or demolishing arguments and every high thing exalted against the knowledge of the Lord, taking every thought captive for obedience to Christ (2 Cor 10:4–5). 6 So therefore, if what we have been ordered to do by someone accords with the commandment

5 Rebuked – corrected.

and is expedient for the soul, **7** then we ought to receive it promptly and willingly as the will of God, fulfilling what is written: obeying one another in the love of Christ (Eph 4:2; 5:21).

8 But if we are ordered to do what is contrary to the commandments of God or what appears to dissolve or to adulterate it, it is time for us to say: We ought to obey God rather than men (Acts 5:29), **9** and to be mindful of the Lord who says: They do not follow the voice of a stranger, but flee from him, because they do not recognize the voice of strangers (John 10:5). **10** And we ought to be mindful of the Apostle, who, for our assurance, dared even not to spare the angels when he said: **11** Even if we ourselves or an angel from heaven should proclaim a gospel to you other than the one we have already announced to you, let him be anathema (Gal 1:8). **12** By which we are taught that even if someone is very dear to us, and even of exalted status and held up for admiration, **13** who hinders us from doing what the Lord has prescribed, or orders us to do what the Lord has forbidden to be done, such a one ought to be execrated[6] by all who love the Lord.

Receiving Service (RBas §37)

Q: With what humility ought one accept a service from the brothers?

R: 1 As a slave from his lord, and such as the apostle Peter showed when the Lord served him (cf. John 13:6–9), in which we also learn the danger of those who do not accept services from the brothers.

6 Execrate – to detest or declare morally wrong.

Obedience (RBas §64)

Q: How ought we to obey one another (cf. Eph 5:21; Phil 2:3; 1 Pet 5:5)?

R: 1 As servants do their masters, just as the Lord prescribed: Whoever wants to be great among you, let him be the last of all and the servant of all (Mark 9:34; 10:43–44). 2 So as to further persuade us to humility he added to this: Just as the Son of Man came not to be served, but to serve (Matt 20:28; cf. Mark 10:45), and there is that saying of the Apostle: serve one another through the love of the Spirit (Gal 5:13).

Receiving Clothing or Footwear (RBas §95)

Q: In what disposition ought one to receive clothing or footwear, whatever it may be?

R: 1 If it is too short or too long for the measure of his size he must make this known, yet with all modesty and gentleness. 2 But if he is upset because it is of poorer or cheaper quality, or because it is not new, let him be mindful of that commandment of the Lord, who says: Worthy is, not anyone at all, but the laborer of his hire (Luke 10:7; cf. Matt 10:10). 3 Let him examine himself, whether he has accomplished the works of God worthily and fulfilled all precepts whatever they may be, and then he will not seek anything else, but rather be anxious about the very thing even now given to him, whether he has received more than he deserves. 4 For what was said about food can be observed as a rule for every other matter concerning the needs of the body.

Discussion Questions

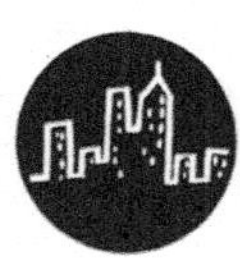

Since many today are taught to question authority, how is "obedience without hesitation" different in twenty-first-century churches and ministries than when Benedict wrote (Matt 23:8; Heb 13:17)?

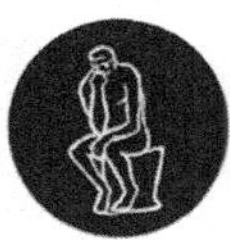

Why do you think Benedict says the first step of humility is obedience without hesitation?

How can excommunication for faults be an act of love in a community?

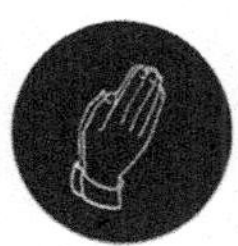

What specifically can we do to develop "humble service" in our church and ministry communities?

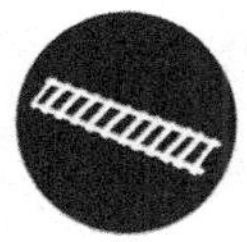

What could you start or stop doing today that would make it easier for you to obey Christ without hesitation tomorrow?

THEOLOGY & ETHICS

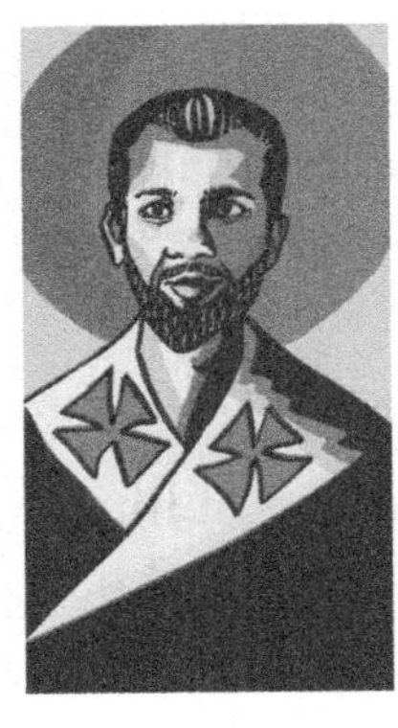

Chapter 6

Spiritual Teachings – Virtues and Discipline

A good life is one where we seek to be virtuous, wherein we treat everyone well and respect the rights of others. This is, in part, made possible when we submit ourselves to others and give those in leadership over us the right to discipline us. As the Bible reminds us, even the Lord disciplines us in love (Hebrews 12). At the same time, discipline can be abused and leaders can use discipline as a form of control and even abuse. Moreover, most of us do not necessarily like discipline. Getting up and exercising each day is hard but the health benefits show that this kind of bodily discipline is good. Thus, discipline is necessary but must be exercised with caution and great wisdom. Leaders who abuse their power will use discipline as a weapon but good congregational leaders will not only use discipline sparingly (and only in accord with the Scriptures) but will also exercise it out of love. Further, strong leaders will submit themselves to discipline too.

Prologue (RBen)

1 Listen, O my son to the precepts of the master, and incline the ear of your heart: willingly receive and faithfully fulfill the admonition of your loving father (cf. Prov 1:8, 4:20, 6:20); 2 that you may return by the labor of obedience to him from whom you had departed through the laziness of disobedience. 3 To you therefore, my words are now addressed, whoever you are, that through renouncing your own will you may fight for the Lord Christ, the true king, by taking up the strong and bright weapons of obedience.

4 First, whenever you begin any good work, beg of him with most earnest prayer to perfect it; 5 so that he who has now granted us the dignity of being counted among the number of his sons may not at any time be grieved by our evil deeds. 6 For we must always so serve him with the good things he has given us, that not only may he never, as an angry father, disinherit his children; 7 but may never as a dread Lord, incensed by our sins, deliver us to everlasting punishment as most wicked servants who would not follow him to glory.

8 Let us then at last arise, since the Scripture arouses us saying: *It is now time for us to rise from sleep* (Rom 13:11). 9 And let us open our eyes to the deifying light;[1] let us attune our ears to what the divine voice admonishes us, daily crying out: 10 *Today if you hear his voice, harden not your hearts* (Ps 95:7–8). 11 And again, *You who have ears to hear, hear what the Spirit says to the churches* (Rev 2:7). 12 And what does he say? *Come my sons, listen to me, I will teach you the fear of the Lord* (Ps 34:12). 13 *Run while*

---

1 Deifying light – the light that makes us be like God in our actions.

you have the light of life, lest the darkness of death seize hold of you (John 12:35).

14 And the Lord, seeking his own workman in the multitude of the people to whom he cries out, says again: **15** *Who is it who desires life, and longs to see good days?* (Ps 34:12). **16** And if you, hearing him, respond, "I am the one!" God says to you: **17** "If you desire true and everlasting life, *keep your tongue from evil and your lips from speaking deceit. Turn aside from evil and do good; seek peace and pursue it* (Ps 34:13–14). **18** And when you have done these things, my *eyes will be upon you, and my ears towards your prayers; and before you call upon me, I will say to you, 'Behold, I am here'* (Isa 58:9). **19** What can be sweeter to us (cf. Ps 34:9) than this voice of the Lord inviting us, dearest brothers? **20** Behold in his loving kindness the Lord shows us the way of life. **21** Having therefore girded our loins with faith and the performance of good works, with the Gospel as guide (Eph 6:14–15) let us walk in his paths, that we may deserve to see him *who has called us into his kingdom* (1 Thess 2:12).

22 Is the tent of this kingdom where we wish to dwell? Unless by our good deeds we run there, we shall never arrive there. **23** But let us with the Prophet inquire of the Lord, saying to him: *Lord, who shall dwell in your tent, or who shall rest upon your holy mountain?* (Ps 15:1). **24** After this question, brothers, let us hear the Lord responding, showing us the way to his tent, **25** saying: *One who walks without stain and works justice;* **26** *one who speaks truth in his heart,* **27** *who has not practiced deceit with his tongue; one who has done no evil to his neighbor, and has not believed false accusations against his neighbor (Ps 15:2–3);* **28** one who has *expelled* the *malignant devil* together with all his advice and persuasiveness *out of the sight* of his heart, casting him to naught; and *has grasped his infantile thoughts, and hurled them against* Christ (Pss 14:4; 136:9). **29** These are they who, fearing the Lord, are not elated over their own good observance; rather, knowing that the good which is in them comes not from themselves but from the Lord, **30** *they magnify* (Ps 15:4) the Lord who works in them, saying with the Prophet: *Not to us, O Lord, not to us, but to your name give the glory* (Ps 115:1). **31** In this way the Apostle Paul imputed nothing of his preaching to himself, but said: *By the grace of God I am what I am* (1 Cor 15:10). **32** And again he says: *He who glories, let him glory in the Lord* (2 Cor 10:17). **33** Hence also the Lord says in the Gospel: *He who hears these words of mine and does them is like a wise man who built his house upon rock:* **34** *the floods came, the winds blew and beat upon that house, and it did not fall; because it was founded upon rock* (Matt 7:24–5).

35 With these admonitions concluded, the Lord is waiting daily for us to respond by our deeds to his holy guidance. **36** Therefore, in order that we may amend our evil ways, the days of our lives have been lengthened as a reprieve, **37** as the apostle says: *Do you not know that the patience of God is leading you to repentance?* (Rom 2:4). **38** For the loving Lord says: *I do not desire the death of a sinner, but that he should be converted and live* (Ezek 33:11).

39 Therefore, brothers, having asked the Lord who is to dwell in his tent, we have heard his commands to those who are to dwell there: it thus remains for us to complete the duties of those who dwell there. **40** Therefore our hearts and bodies must be prepared to fight in holy obedience to his commands. **41** And for that which is hardly possible to us

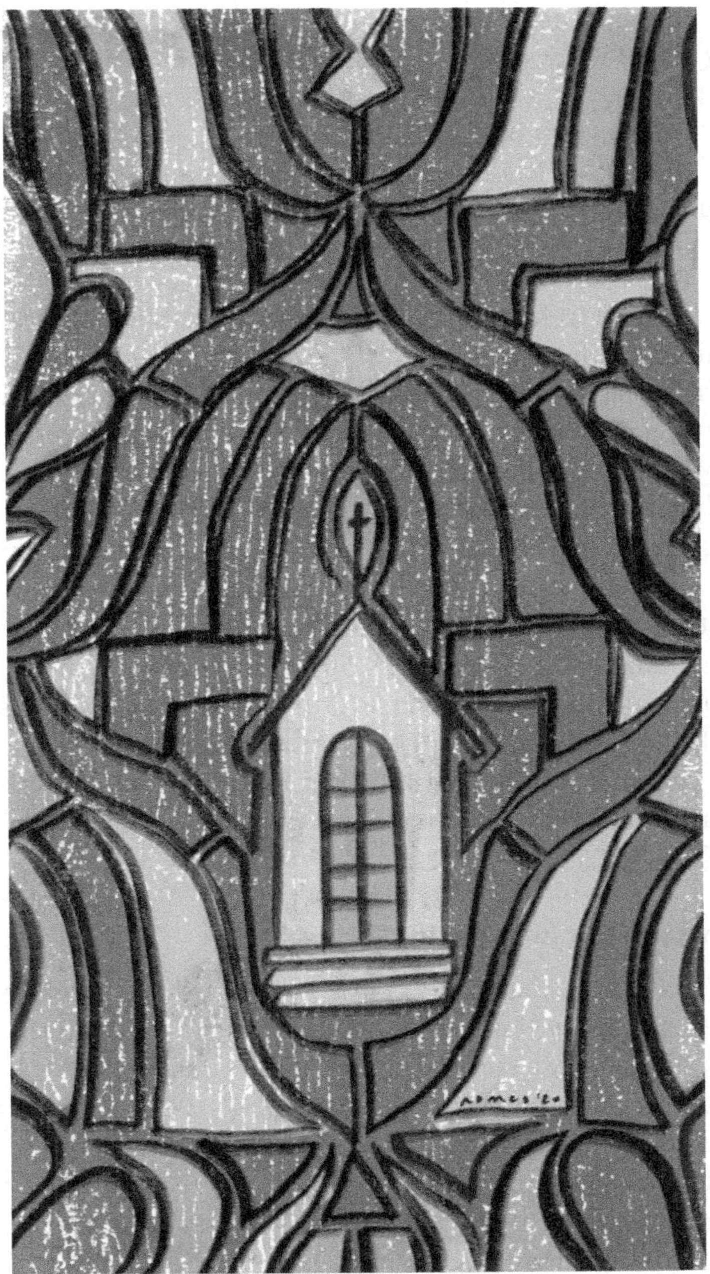

The monastery is "a school of the Lord's service."

by nature, let us ask God to supply by the help of his grace. 42 And if we wish to reach eternal life, escaping the pains of hell, then—43 while there is yet time, while we are still in the flesh and are able to fulfill all these things by this light of life given to us—44 we must run and perform now what will profit us for all eternity.

45 We have therefore, to establish a school of the Lord's service. 46 In instituting it we hope to establish nothing harsh or oppressive. 47 But if anything is somewhat strictly laid down, according to the dictates of equity and for the amendment of vices or for the preservation of love; 48 do not therefore flee in dismay from the way of salvation, which cannot be other than narrow at the beginning (cf. Matt 7:14). 49 Truly as we advance in this way of life and faith, our hearts open wide, and we run with unspeakable sweetness of love on the path of God's commandments (Ps 119:32). 50 So that, never departing from his guidance, but persevering in his teaching (Acts 2:42) in the monastery until death, (Phil 2:8) we may by patience participate in the passion of Christ; that we may deserve also to be partakers of his kingdom. Amen (cf. 1 Pet 4:13; Rom 8:17).

On Restraint in Speaking (RBen §6)

1 Let us do as the prophet says: *I said, I will keep custody over my ways so I do not sin with my tongue: I have kept custody over my mouth. I became speechless, and was humbled, and kept silent concerning good things* (Ps 39:1–3). 2 Here the prophet shows that if we ought to refrain even from good words for the sake of restraining speech, how much more ought we to abstain from evil words, on account of the punishment due to sin! 3 Therefore, on account of

the importance of restraint in speech let permission to speak be seldom granted even to perfect disciples, even when their conversation is good and holy and edifying,
4 for it is written: *In speaking much you cannot avoid sin*
(Prov 10:19); 5 and elsewhere *Death and life are in the hands of the tongue* (Prov 18:21). 6 For speaking and teaching befit the master: remaining silent and listening are proper for the disciple.

7 And therefore, if something is requested of a superior, let it be requested with all humility and reverent submission. 8 But as for ridiculing or otiose[2] words which induce laughter, we permanently ban them in every place; neither do we permit a disciple to open his mouth in such discourse.

Humility (RBen §7)

1 The Holy Scripture cries out to us, brothers, saying: *Everyone who exalts himself shall be humbled, and he who humbles himself shall be exalted* (Luke 14:11; 18:14).
2 Therefore, by saying this it shows us that all exaltation is a kind of pride, 3 against which the prophet indicates that he guards himself, saying: *Lord, my heart is not exalted nor are my eyes lifted up; nor have I walked in great things, nor in wonders above me* (Ps 131:1). 4 And why? *What if I did not think humbly, but instead exalted my soul? Then like a child weaned from its mother—so you would treat my soul* (Ps 131:2).

5 Therefore, brothers, if we wish to arrive at the highest point of humility, and speedily reach that heavenly exaltation to which we can only ascend by the humility

---

2 Otiose – useless.

of this present life, **6** we must by our ever-ascending actions erect a ladder like the one Jacob beheld in his dream, by which the *angels appeared to him descending and ascending* (Gen 28:12). **7** Without doubt this descent and ascent can signify nothing else than that we descend by exaltation and ascend by humility. **8** And the ladder thus erected is our life in the world, which, if the heart is humbled, is lifted up by the Lord to heaven. **9** The sides of the same ladder we assert to be our body and soul, in which the call of God has placed various steps of humility or discipline, which we must ascend.

10 The first step of humility, then, is that one always keeps the *fear of God before his eyes* (Ps 36:2), fleeing every kind of forgetfulness, **11** and that one is ever mindful of all God has commanded, unfolding within his soul that those who despise God will be consumed in hell for their sins, and that eternal life has been prepared for those who fear Him. **12** And keeping custody over himself at every hour from sin and vice of thought, tongue, eyes, hands, feet, of his own will or of fleshly desires, **13** let this man consider that he is regarded from heaven by God at every hour, and that his actions in every place are perceived in the Divine Vision and are reported to God by His angels at every hour.

14 This the prophet demonstrates to us, when he shows that God is always present to our thoughts, saying: *God searches the heart and the loins*[3] (Ps 7:10); **15** and again, *The Lord knows the thoughts of men* (Ps 94:11); **16** and he also says: *You have understood my thoughts from afar* (Ps 139:3); **17** and, *The thought of a man shall confess to you* (Ps 76:11). **18** Therefore, so as to be on guard against

---

3 Loins – that is, the mind.

perverse thoughts let the virtuous brother always say in his heart, *Then shall I be without stain before him, if I have kept myself from my iniquity* (Ps 18:24).

19 For it is truly our own will that we are forbidden to do as Scripture tells us: *and turn away from your own will* (Sir 18:30). **20** And so too we request of God in the [Lord's] Prayer that His will may be done in us. **21** Thus we are rightly taught not to do our will, being warned as Sacred Scripture says that *there are ways which appear right to men, but which at their end plunge into the depths of hell* (Prov 16:25); **22** or again, when we shudder at what is said of the negligent: *They are corrupt and have become abominable in their pleasures* (Ps 14:1).

23 Truly, as regards the desires of the flesh we believe that God is always present to us, as the prophet says to the Lord: *Before you is all my desire* (Ps 38:10). **24** Let us be on our guard then against evil desires, since death has its seat close to the entrance of delight. **25** Hence the precept of Scripture, where it says: *Do not go after your ardent desires* (Sir 18:30).

26 Therefore, *if the eyes of the Lord behold the good and the evil* (Prov 15:3); **27** and *the Lord is always looking down from heaven on the children of men to see whether anyone has understanding or seeks God* (Ps 14:2); **28** and if the angels assigned to us report to the Lord every day, both by day and night, concerning the works we accomplish, **29** then we must be on our guard at every hour, brothers, lest as the prophet says in the psalm, God should see us at any hour *inclining* to evil and *becoming useless* (Ps 14:3); **30** and lest, despite sparing us now because He is loving and expects our conversion and improvement, He should say to us in the future: *This you did and I was silent* (Ps 49:21).

31 The second step of humility is that one does not love his own will, nor delight in satisfying his own desires, **32** but imitates in his deeds that saying of the Lord: *I did not come to do my own will, but that of him who sent me* (John 6:38). **33** And again Scripture says: Gratification deserves punishment, but necessity wins a crown.

34 The third step of humility is that for the love of God one submits himself in all obedience to his superior, imitating the Lord of whom the apostle says: *He was made obedient even unto death* (Phil 2:8).

35 The fourth step of humility is that if in the exercise this very obedience is hard and contrary things, even injustices, are done to one, he embraces patience silently in his conscience, **36** and in enduring does not grow weak or give up, as Scripture says: *He who perseveres to the end will be saved* (Matt 10:22); **37** and again, *Let your heart take comfort, and rely on the Lord* (Ps 27:14). **38** And showing that the faithful ought to bear everything for the Lord, however contrary, this text is placed in the mouth of the one who suffers: *For you we are afflicted with death the whole day; we are esteemed as sheep to be slaughtered* (Rom 8:36; Ps 44:22). **39** And secure in the hope of divine reward they go forward, rejoicing and saying: *But in all these things we are triumphant, because of Him who has loved us* (Rom 8:37). **40** And also in another place Scripture says: *You have tested us, O God; with fire as silver is tested with fire; you have led us into the trap and laid tribulation on our backs* (Ps 66:10–11). **41** And in order to show that we should be under a superior it continues, saying: *You have imposed men over our heads* (Ps 66:12).

42 Indeed, they are fulfilling the precept of the Lord by patience in adversities and injuries who, *when struck on one cheek offer the other; to him who takes away their tunic they give their cloak; and when required to go one mile, they go two* (Matt 5:39–41): **43** with Paul the Apostle they bear *false brothers, bear persecutions, and bless those who curse them* (2 Cor 11:26; 1 Cor 4:12).

44 The fifth step of humility is when through humble confession one does not hide from one's Abbot the evil thoughts that enter one's heart, nor the evils committed in secret. **45** Exhorting us in this regard Scripture says, *Make known to the Lord your way and hope in Him* (Ps 37:5). **46** And again it says: *Confess to the Lord, for He is good; for His mercy is for all ages* (Pss 106:1; 118:1). **47** And again the prophet says: *My offense I have made known to You, and my injustices I have not hidden.* **48** *I said, I will accuse myself before the Lord of my unjust deeds, and You have forgiven the disloyalty of my heart* (Ps 32:5).

49 The sixth step of humility is that a monk should be content with the most common and worst of everything, and in all that is required of him to judge himself a bad and worthless worker, **50** saying of himself with the prophet: *I was reduced to nothing and did not realize it; I have become like a beast before you, yet I am always with you* (Ps 73:22–23).

51 The seventh step of humility is that he should not only pronounce with his tongue that he is inferior to and more common than all, but also believe it in the intimate sensibility of his heart, **52** humbling himself and saying with the prophet: *As for me, I am a worm and no man, shameful among men and an outcast of the people* (Ps 22:7).

53 *I have been exalted, and cast down and confounded* (Ps 88:16). **54** And again: *It is good for me that you have humbled me, that I may learn your commandments* (Ps 119:71, 73).

55 The eighth step of humility is for a monk to do nothing except what is encouraged by the common rule of the monastery or the example of the superiors.

56 The ninth step of humility is that a monk prohibit his tongue from speaking (Ps 34:14), having restraint of speech unless asked a question, **57** for Scripture makes clear that *In speaking much you cannot avoid sin* (Prov 10:19) **58** and, *The talkative man is without direction on earth* (Ps 140:12).

59 The tenth step of humility is that one is not easily or promptly moved to laughter, for it is written: *The fool raises his voice in laughter* (Sir 21:23).

60 The eleventh step of humility is that when speaking the monk does so gently and without laughter, humbly and with gravity, speaking few but reasonable words, and that his voice is not clamorous: **61** as it is written, *A wise man is known by his few words.*

62 The twelfth step of humility is that the monk, not only in his heart, but by means of his own body always indicates his humility to those who see him—**63** that is, at the Work of God[4], in the oratory, in the monastery, in the garden, on the road, in the field, or wherever he may be, whether sitting, walking, or standing—with head always inclined and gaze fixed on the ground, **64** estimating at

4 Work of God – that is, when he prays.

every hour his sins, he should estimate himself as present at the terrible judgment, **65** saying always in his heart what the publican in the Gospel said with eyes fixed on the earth: *Lord, I am not worthy, sinner that I am, to lift my eyes up to heaven* (Luke 18:13); **66** and again, with the prophet: *I am bent down and humbled in every way* (Pss 38:7–9; 119:107).

67 Having therefore ascended all these steps of humility, the monk will soon arrive at that *love* of God which, *being perfect, casts out fear* (1 John 4:18): **68** whereby all that he formerly observed not without dread, he will begin to keep without effort, as if naturally, out of habit; **69** no longer from fear of hell but for the love of Christ, from good habit and delight in virtue. **70** This God through the Holy Spirit will now grant his laborer to manifest, cleansed from vices and sins.

Whether Monks Should Have Anything of Their Own (RBen §33)

1 Above all this vice is to be cut out by the roots from the monastery, **2** no one may presume to give or receive anything without the Abbot's order **3** nor to have anything as their own—not anything—neither book, writing-tablet, pen, nor anything at all **4** since it is not allowed that even their body or their will should remain subject to their own will: **5** rather, for all necessary things let them trust to the father of the monastery, since none of them is allowed to have anything which the Abbot has not given or permitted. **6** *All things are to be held in common by all, as it is written, so that no one may say or presume that anything is his own* (Acts 4:32).

7 But if anyone is found engaging in this most destructive vice he is to be admonished once or twice: 8 if he does not amend he is to be subjected to correction.

The Measure of Food (RBen §39)

1 We believe it will suffice for the daily meal, whether at the sixth or ninth hour, that there be on all tables two dishes of cooked food on account of the variety of illnesses: 2 so that he who is not able to eat one may make his meal of the other. 3 Therefore two cooked dishes will suffice for all the brothers; and if there is any fruit or young vegetables, a third dish is be added. 4 A liberal pound of bread should suffice each day, whether there is only one meal or both lunch and dinner: 5 and if they are to have dinner, a third part of their pound is to be kept back by the cellarer, and returned to them at dinner.

6 If it happens that the work is heavier the Abbot can choose to exercise his power, when expedient, to add something, 7 provided that before all else overindulgence is avoided, and that no monk suffers indigestion. 8 For nothing is more contrary to all things Christian than overindulgence, 9 as Our Lord says: *See that your hearts are not weighed down through overindulgence* (Luke 21:34).

10 To children of immature years the same quantity should not be given: instead, they should receive less than their elders, frugality being observed in all matters. 11 But all are to abstain from eating the flesh of four-footed animals, except the sick who are very weak.

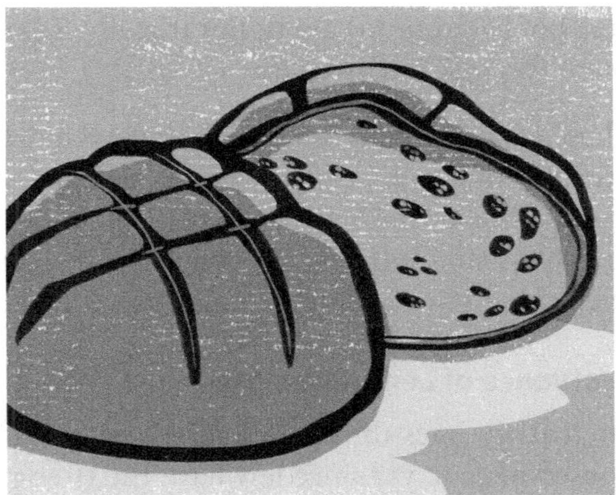

Unhappy monks attempted to poison Benedict's bread.

The Measure of Drink (RBen §40)

1 *Everyone has his proper gift from God: one this, another that* (1 Cor 7:7); 2 and it is therefore with some reluctance that we fix the measure for another. 3 However, taking into account the weakness of some, we believe that a *hemina*[5] of wine for each will suffice each day. 4 But those to whom God gives the strength to abstain should know that they will earn their proper reward.

5 If local necessity, or the work, or the heat of summer suggest that more is advisable, the matter rests with the will of the superior, care being taken in everything that satiety[6] or drunkenness not sneak in. 6 Even though we read that wine is certainly not for monks, yet, since in our days monks cannot be persuaded of this we must at

5 Hemina – a measurement that is equal to about half a bottle.

6 Satiety – being excessively gratified.

least agree not to drink to satiety, but frugally, 7 for wine makes even the wise fall away (Sir 19:2).

8 But where local necessities are such that even the above-mentioned measure cannot be supplied, and instead there is much less or nothing at all, those who dwell there are to bless God and not murmur. 9 This we admonish above everything else: that they refrain from murmuring.

The Observance of Lent (RBen §49)

1 Although at all times the life of a monk ought to be a Lenten observance, 2 yet since few have the strength for this we encourage all during these days of Lent to keep themselves in all purity of life, 3 and to wash away the negligences of other times during these holy days. 4 This we will do worthily if we abstain from all vices and give ourselves to prayer with tears, reading, compunction[7] of heart, and abstinence. 5 Therefore during these days let us augment somewhat our usual quota of service through private prayers and abstinence from food and drink, 6 so that each may offer, above his appointed measure and of his own free will, something to God *in the joy of the Holy Spirit* (1 Thess 1:6): 7 that is, by withholding from his body something of food, drink, sleep, excessive talking, ridiculing; and thus awaiting holy Easter with the joy of spiritual desire (cf. Luke 22:15).

8 Everyone is, however, is to make known to his Abbot what he offers, and do it with his prayer and according to his will, 9 because what is done without permission of the spiritual father will be attributed to presumption and

---

7 Compunction – regret.

vainglory, and will merit no reward. 10 Therefore everything is to be according to the will of the Abbot.

The Clothing and Footwear of the Brothers (RBen §55)

1 Clothing is to be given to the brothers according to the nature of the place where they live and according to its climate; 2 for in cold regions more is required and in warm regions less. 3 This therefore is for the Abbot to consider. 4 We believe, however, that in temperate places a cowl[8] and a tunic[9] will suffice for each monk, 5 the cowl to be of shaggy wool in winter, but in summer thin or worn; 6 also a scapular[10] for work, and to cover their feet stockings and shoes.

7 Concerning the color or coarseness of all these things the monks should not complain; rather, whatever can be easily obtained in the province where they live or can be bought cheaply they should use. 8 The Abbot is to see to the measurements, so that these garments are not too short for those who use them, but rather are properly measured.

9 On receiving new clothes the old should always be returned at once, to be stored in the wardrobe for the poor. 10 For it is sufficient for a monk to have two tunics and two cowls, on account of night wear and on account of laundering these items; 11 anything beyond this is superfluous and is to be cut off. 12 And stockings and whatever else is old are to be returned when they receive new things.

---

8 Cowl – an outer coat.

9 Tunic – a garment like a sweater.

10 Scapular – kind of apron-like garment.

13 Underclothing for those who are sent on a journey is to be received from the wardrobe, which those who return are to wash and replace. **14** Their cowls and tunics should also be somewhat better than their usual wear: those leaving on a journey are to receive these from the wardrobe and those returning are to replace them.

15 For bedding a mat, a heavy and a light blanket, and a pillow suffice. **16** These beds are to be frequently inspected by the Abbot so that personal possessions are not found there; **17** and if anyone is found with something he has not received from the Abbot, he is to be subjected to the most severe discipline. **18** And so as to cut out this vice of personal ownership at the roots, the Abbot is to give out everything that is necessary: **19** that is, cowl, tunic, stockings, shoes, belt, knife, stylus, needle, handkerchief, and writing tablets; so that every excuse based on necessity is removed.

20 However the Abbot must always take into consideration this sentence from the Acts of the Apostles: *They gave to each one according to his need* (Acts 4:35). **21** Therefore the Abbot is also to take into consideration the weaknesses of those in need, not the ill-will of the envious: nevertheless, in all his decisions he is to ponder the retribution of God.

That They May Not Presume to Strike One Another at Will (RBen §70)

1 So as to avoid in the monastery every occasion of presumption, **2** we decree that no one has the right to excommunicate or strike any of his brothers, unless he has received power do to so by the Abbot. **3** For sinners are to be reproved before all, so that the rest may have fear (1 Tim 5:20). **4** Children, however, up to fifteen years of age are to be kept under diligent and watchful discipline by all: 5 yet this too is to be done reasonably and with all measure.

6 For if anyone without precept from the Abbot presumes authority over those who are above that age, or if he acts towards children without discretion, he is to be subjected to the discipline of the Rule; 7 for it is written: *What you do not wish done to you, do not do to another* (Tob 4:16).

The Good Zeal That Monks Ought to Have (RBen §72)

1 Just as there is an evil zeal of bitterness which separates from God and leads to hell, 2 so there is a good zeal which separates from vices and leads to God and to life everlasting. 3 This zeal then, should be practiced by monks with the most fervent love. 4 That is: *they should outdo one another in showing honor* (Rom 12:10). 5 Let them most patiently endure one another's infirmities, whether of body or of character. 6 Let them compete in showing obedience to one another. 7 None should follow what he judges useful for himself, but rather what is better for another: 8 They should practice fraternal charity with a pure love; 9 to God offering loving reverence, 10 loving their Abbot with sincere and humble affection, 11 preferring nothing whatever to Christ, 12 and may he bring us all together to life everlasting. Amen.

The Whole Observance of Justice Is Not Contained in This Rule (RBen §73)

1 We have written this Rule so that, by observing it in monasteries, we may demonstrate that we have somewhat grasped honorable behavior and the beginnings of this way of life. 2 But for those hastening to the perfection of this way of life there are the teachings of the holy Fathers,

the observance of which leads one to the heights of perfection. 3 For what page or what words are there in the divinely-inspired Old and New Testaments that are not a most direct norm for human life? 4 Or what book of the holy Catholic[11] Fathers does not resoundingly proclaim the direct path by which we may reach our Creator? 5 Moreover, the *Conferences* of the Fathers, their *Institutes* and their *Lives*, as well as the Rule of our holy Father Basil—6 what else are these for good-living and obedient monks than instruments of virtue? 7 But to us who are lazy, bad-living, and negligent they bring the blush of shame. 8 Whoever you are, therefore, hastening toward your heavenly homeland; fulfill with the help of Christ this little Rule for beginners we have written: 9 and then at last you will arrive under God's protection at the loftier summits of doctrine and virtue we have spoken of above. Amen.

Relinquishing Property upon Entering the Monastery (RBas §5)

Q: Should one who wishes to join himself to the servants of God relinquish his property to his relatives indifferently?

R: 1 Since the Lord says: *Sell your possessions and give to the poor and you shall have treasure in heaven, and come follow me* (Matt 19:21), and again: *Sell all that you have and give alms* (Luke 12:23), 2 I consider that one who is coming to the service of God ought not to esteem lightly and give up the things that belong to him as he pleases, 3 but should as far as possible assess all things with the utmost diligence, since henceforth they are consecrated to the Lord, and should dispose of them reasonably as far

11 Catholic – universal.

as it can be done, aware that not without peril does one *carry out the work of God negligently* (Jer 48:10).

4 But if his relatives or even his parents should come out against the faith, then he should remember what the Lord says: **5** *There is no one who has left house or brothers or father or mother or wife or children or fields for my sake and for the sake of the gospel, who shall not receive a hundredfold in this present time and in the world to come eternal life* (Mark 10:29–30; Luke 13:26). **6** He must however protest to and denounce those who deny what belongs to him, and resist and take action on behalf of the faith, **7** since they incur a sin of sacrilege (cf. Rom 2:22), according to the commandment of the Lord who says *If your brother sins against you, go and show him his fault and so on* (Matt 18:15).

8 But the sanction of piety forbids us to bring these matters to trial before the secular judges through that saying of the Apostle: *Does any of you, having a grievance against another dare to go to court before the unrighteous instead of before the saints?* (1 Cor 6:1), **9** and again: *it is already an utter defeat for you, that you have litigation among yourselves at all* (1 Cor 6:7).

Necessity of Self-Control (RBas §8)

Q: Is it necessary that one who would give himself to the life of piety and religion also practice *self-control* (cf. Gal 5:22)?

R: 1 That in all things self-control is necessary is clear, first, from the fact that the apostle Paul counts *self-control* among the *fruits of the Holy Spirit* (Gal 5:22–23), **2** and second, he indicates that it is by this means that his *ministry* *is preserved without blame* (cf. 2 Cor 6:3), when he says: *In labors and in vigils, in fasts and in purity* (cf. 2 Cor 6:4–6), 3 and again, *In labor and fatigue, in many vigils, in hunger and thirst, in fasts often* (2 Cor 11:27), and again: *Everyone who contends in the struggle is self-controlled in all things* (1 Cor 9:25), 4 and again: *I treat my body rigorously and bring it into subjection* (1 Cor 9:27), which indeed does not appear to be accomplished in any other way except by self-control.

5 For only through self-control can the ferment of youth and the excitability of that age be restrained and checked as with a bridle, for *soft living is no help to the fool* (Prov 19:10), according to Solomon. 6 *And make no provision for the flesh, says the Apostle, in its cravings* (Rom 13:14), and again: *she who is given over to pleasures is dead even while she lives* (1 Tim 5:6). 7 Yes, and the example of the rich man who lived amidst delicacies shows us that self-control is necessary, lest we too hear what the rich man heard: *You received your good things during your life* (Luke 16:25).

8 Moreover, the Apostle teaches what a perilous thing is self-indulgence when he describes it as a mark of those whom he says withdraw from God, 9 for he says: *In the last days there shall be perilous times, for men will be lovers of self* (2 Tim 3:1–2), and, having listed many kinds of malice, he ends with *the calumniators*[12], *the intemperate, the ungentle* (2 Tim 3:3). 10 And Esau too had intemperance as the tinder[13] of his woes, when he *sold his birthright* for a single meal (Gen 25:33; Heb 12:16); yes, and that

12 Calumniator – slanderer.

13 Tinder – kindling.

primal disobedience happened to man from no other source than through self-indulgence (cf. Gen 3:6).

11 Indeed, the whole life of the saints and of the Lord himself while placed here in the flesh, what else do they put before us than examples of self-control? **12** Moses is said to have persevered without slackening in continual fasting and prayer before God for forty days and to have merited to hand down to the human race the aid of the Law (cf. Deut 25:33). **13** Elijah too is said to have been counted worthy of the vision of God when he himself continued for a like space of time abstaining from food (cf. 1 Kings 19:8). **14** And the merit of Daniel and the three youths before God, when they gained the victory over all their enemies and over the tyrant himself, it came from no other source than self-control (cf. Dan 1:6–16; 3:24–28). **15** Why, John's entire way of life was self-control (cf. Matt 3:4). And it was by this means that the Lord too disclosed the first beginnings of his manifestation (Matt 4:2).**16** Yet by self-control we do not mean complete abstinence from food—this would indeed be the violent dissolution of life—**17** but that self-control which is consistent with the necessary but not superfluous sustenance of life, when we avoid what is gratifying and fulfill solely what necessity requires for the body.

18 In sum then: abstinence from all that is demanded by passionate desire is the virtue of self-control. **19** And so virtue therefore is disclosed not only in regard to the pleasure of food, but also when we abstain from all those things in which we may take delight but by which we are wounded in soul.

20 Accordingly, anyone who is truly self-controlled does not desire human glory, but restrains himself from vices such as wrath and despondency and all those obsessions which untaught and incautious souls are wont[14] to cling to.

21 One might go so far as to say that among all the commandments of God we find that the one is so linked with the other that it is impossible to accomplish one in isolation from another. 22 This is found to be especially the case with self-control itself, in that the humble person is judged to be one who has restrained himself from pride 23 and one who has renounced all his property and, according to the Gospel, sold all his possessions and distributed them to all (cf. Matt 19:21) is without a doubt one who has restrained himself from the desire of money. 24 And the meek too will be one who has mastered his wrath and checked his rage. 25 And the wandering looks of the eye, the listening of the ear and the looseness of the tongue—what else but self-control can subdue and check them?

26 Yes, and self-control also curbs immoderate[15] laughter, just as a mark of intemperance is the kind of laughter that is accompanied by disorderly and unruly gestures. Since the cheerfulness of the mind need only be indicated by smiling, 27 it is unseemly to lift up a cackling laughter in a loud din, which is certainly wont to happen, even involuntarily, through intemperance of mind. 28 Such laughter usually softens and undermines gravity and constancy of mind, whence Solomon says: *Of laughter I have said it is madness* (Eccles 2:2) and, *as the crackle*

---

14 Wont – accustomed.

15 Immoderate – excessive.

of thorns under the cooking pot so is the laughter of fools (Eccles 7:6), **29** and again, *The fool raises his voice in laughter, but the wise man will scarcely smile discreetly* (Sir 21:20). **30** The Lord, too, showed that he had in himself passions of the flesh, that is, those which tend to evidence of virtue, such as weariness and tears and grief. **31** But never is he found to have used laughter, so far as the gospel narrative touches on it. We find there instead that those who laugh shall lament even more when he says: *Woe to you who laugh now, for you shall weep* (Luke 6:25).

32 The ambiguity of "laughter" ought not at all deceive us, for it is often the custom of Scripture to call gladness of soul and a certain more cheerful emotion "laughter" **33** as in: *Sarah said, God has made laughter for me* (Gen 21:6) and again: *Blessed those who weep now for they shall laugh* (cf. Luke 6:21), **34** and in Job it is said: *the* truthful *mouth shall be filled with laughter* (Job 8:21). All these are terms used for the joy of the soul. **35** Therefore one who is superior to every passion and does nothing through the goads of pleasure, but with self-control and sobriety strives against all that can do harm, **36** this is called perfectly self-controlled—and such a one is thereby without a doubt a stranger to every kind of sin. **37** For pleasure is the rat-trap of all evil and through it we are all beguiled into sin. Therefore, anyone who is not undermined or waylaid by it, cuts out from himself every vile germ of sin.

Self-Control (RBas §9)

Q: What is the measure of *self-control* (Gal 5:22)?

R: **1** As far as the vices and passions are concerned, he expects complete abstinence, and never to yield. **2** The extent in regard to food, however: the measure and kind of food shall be proportioned [*sic*] as age and occupation and bodily strength and debility require. **3** For it is impossible that all the brothers should observe the one order or measure or rule, though all those who are healthy can maintain the same measure of abstinence. **4** This however ought to be adapted in individual cases where there is some cause for variation, by the prudence and supervision of those entrusted with the responsibility of this distribution.

5 We cannot of course encompass each individual case in this instruction, but include only what pertains to a common and general framework. **6** Whether there are invalids needing to be built up with food, or those who are fatigued from the work of self-control, or from whatever other tasks they have carried out in the service of piety, let those who preside administer as need and reason require.

7 Since, then, it is therefore impossible to establish the same time for meals for all, or the measure or quality of food, let there be one goal for all: that we do not continue in our eating to satiety.[16] **8** For to fill the stomach and to weigh it down with food renders even the body less useful for any task, since it is then inclined to sleep and more easily susceptible to harm.

9 Indeed, pleasurable tastes must not be followed as the goal of food—the need that serves life is sufficient, with indulgence being shunned. **10** For if we serve pleasure, it is nothing other than to *make a god of our belly* (cf. Phil 3:19). **11** For since our human body is constantly being depleted and dehydrated, and needs replenishment and

16 Satiety – fullness.

refreshment, because of which the appetite for food is natural, **12** therefore the use of food in accord with right reason calls for the replenishment of what has been depleted and the intake of nourishment both solid and liquid.

13 Therefore, whatever in the way of food can fulfill this need of the body quickly and easily should by preference be chosen. **14** And the Lord himself I think showed this, when he refreshed those who *were hungry in the wilderness* (cf. Matt 14:13, 15). Though he could certainly have extended the miracle in the desert and prepared for them a more lavish repast he did nothing of the sort, **15** but furnished for them a simple fare, and served, according to John, *barley bread and small fish* (John 6:9).

16 Of drink he made no mention at all, from which it may no doubt be inferred that the use of water could suffice for all as most necessary **17**—unless perhaps someone appears to be harmed by it because of bodily infirmity, for whom without a doubt is the advice the apostle Paul wrote to Timothy to *avoid what is harmful* (cf. 1 Tim 5:23). **18** But whatever manifestly brings harm to the body should be avoided anyway, for it seems absurd to take food for the sustenance of the body and then again by means of this very food to inflict harm on the body and render it useless for service of the commandments.

19 We ought in every way to use food which is easily and cheaply obtained, so that we are never found running after expensive and extravagant items on a pretext of abstinence **20** while we strive to raise our ordinary, natural food with a flavor of seasonings to a lofty and delicate savor. **21** We ought rather to choose for our own use whatever is easily and cheaply obtained in each locality and available for common use, 22 and bring in from a distance only those things which are really necessary for life, such as oil and the like, or if something is to be used for the relief of the sick.

Personal Property (RBas §29)

Q: Should someone who is among the brothers have anything of his own?

R: 1 This is contrary to the testimony written in the Acts of the Apostles concerning those who first believed, 2 for there it speaks thus: *Not one of them said that any of his possessions was his own, but all things were common to all* (Acts 4:32). 3 If someone therefore says that anything is his own, he without doubt makes himself a stranger to the elect of God and from the love of the Lord who taught in word and completed it in deed and who *laid down his life for his friends* (cf. John 15:13). 4 Now if he himself gave *his life for his friends*, what claim have we on our possessions, which are, after all, external to our life?

Accepting Gifts (RBas §31)

Q: Should one accept anything from relatives in the flesh?

R: 1 It is necessary that relatives render to those coming to the Lord what is their due and subtract nothing, that they may not incur the judgement for sacrilege. 2 But to disburse these things before the eyes of those to whom they appeared to belong often becomes an occasion of inflation and pride for themselves and a cause of grief for the other brothers who came poor to the same way of life, 3 so that there happens what was indicted among the Corinthians by the Apostle where he says: *You put to shame those who have nothing* (1 Cor 11:22).

4 Therefore, if those who preside over the churches in each place are faithful and prudent administrators, let it be brought to them 5 in imitation of those in the Acts of the Apostles who did this, of whom it is said that *bringing the proceeds of their estates they laid it at the feet of the apostles* (Acts 4:35).

6 But inasmuch as it is not everyone's duty to fulfill faithfully administrations of this kind, it is fitting that it be brought to those who have been approved in this office before all. 7 However, the one who presides, through whom all ought to be dispensed, shall exercise discretion even concerning these things.

Brotherly Love (RBas §38)

Q: What kind of love ought we to have for one another?

R: 1 Such as the Lord showed and taught, when he said: *Love one another even as I have loved you; no-one has greater love than to lay down his life for his friends* (John 15:12–13). 2 For if it is necessary to lay down even one's life, then how much more ought we to show devotion and zeal in lesser matters, 3 not of course to accommodate human wishes, but to benefit each towards the goal proposed in common to all of being well pleasing to God.

Loving One's Neighbor (RBas §39)

Q: How shall one be able to fulfill *love for one's neighbor* (cf. Matt 22:36)?

R: 1 In the first place, by fearing the judgement against those who trespass the commandment of the Lord, for he himself said: *Whoever does not believe in the Son shall not have life, but the wrath of God shall stay over him* (John 3:36). 2 Second, by yearning to reach eternal life, for *his commandment is eternal life* (John 12:50).

3 Now *the first and the great commandment is: "You shall love the Lord your God with all your heart and with all your mind and with all your soul," and the second is like it: "You shall love your neighbor as your very self"* (Matt 22:36, 39). 4 Then if one desires to be made like the Lord who said: *A new commandment I give you, that you love one another, even as I have loved you* (John 13:34).

5 But we can appreciate this even from common sense, since if we have received a benefit from a brother for which we love the brother, we have become his debtors and love him deservedly. 6 This is customarily observed even among the Gentiles, as the Lord said in the gospel: *if you love those who love you, what credit is it to you, since even sinners and pagans love those who love them* (Luke 6:32; Matt 5:46–47).

7 If on the other hand a brother ill-treats us in some way or opposes us, then we ought to love him not only on account of the commandment, but on account of that something more which he offers us in the very fact that he harms us, 8—that is, if we believe the Lord who said: *Blessed are you when they reproach you and persecute you and speak all manner of evil against you for my sake:*

9 *Rejoice and leap for joy, for great shall be your reward in heaven* (Matt 5:11–12).

Eating and Drinking (RBas §57)

Q: How does one eat and drink . . . to the glory of God (1 Cor 10:31)?

R: 1 By always keeping in mind God who feeds us, and by bearing witness in every aspect, not only in soul but also in body, that he gives thanks and does not eat carelessly, 2 but rather as God's worker who is being refreshed by him, for which reason let there be sufficient for labor and the fulfillment of the commandments.

Humility (RBas §62)

Q: What is *humility* and how shall we fulfill it (cf. Phil 2:3)?

R: 1 Humility is this: that we *consider* all human beings *better than* us according to the Apostle's definition (cf. Phil 2:3). 2 Now we can accomplish it if we are mindful of the Lord who said: *Learn from me for I am meek and humble in heart* (Matt 11:29), which he often showed and taught in many ways; and we ought to believe him who has promised: *Whoever humbles himself shall be exalted* (Matt 23:12; Luke 14:11). 3 Second, we should strive unremittingly and unceasingly in all our deeds and affairs to be found humbler than others, and by working hard at this practice. 4 For thus we shall be able with difficulty to remove from ourselves the memory of our primal arrogance and to attain the condition of humility, as also usually happens with crafts. 5 The same method applies to accomplishing all the other virtues which come from the commandment of our Lord Jesus Christ.

Our Attitude toward Our Leaders (RBas §84)

Q: With what disposition ought we to obey him who urges us to the work of the commandment?

R: 1 With the same disposition with which a hungry little child obeys the nurse who invites it to her breasts, or with the same disposition with which any human being accepts from anyone the things necessary for life. 2 And indeed, even more so, inasmuch as the future life is more precious than the present life, just as the Lord said: my *commandment is eternal life* (John 12:50). 3 Accordingly, as this present life is secured in the eating of food, so eternal life is secured in the doing of the commandment, just as the Lord himself again says: 4 *My food is to do the will of the Father who sent me* (John 4:34).

Heart Purity (RBas §148)

Q: Who is *pure of heart* (Matt 5:8; Pss 23:4; 50:10)?

R: 1 One who does not have to reprimand himself for transgressing the commandment of God, or overlooking it, or being negligent about it.

Fulfilling the Lord's Commands (RBas §150)

Q: How can one fulfill the commandments of the Lord with inward disposition and with eagerness?

R: 1 We naturally delight in those things which are good and beneficial. 2 If therefore we believe in the things that have been promised, then from the very thing that we hope for there is implanted in our soul the disposition and desire to fulfill everything by which we can attain that which we desire. 3 Therefore if anyone *hates and detests iniquity* (Ps 119:163) and purifies himself from all sin—for just as through infirmity the body loses delight in food, so through the disease of sin the soul loses desire for the commandments of God—4 and if one recalls that *the commandment of God is eternal life* (John 12:50) and that for all who keep it there will be a fulfillment of the promises, 5 then by such means that disposition of soul can arise of which it says: *The judgements of the Lord are true and all of them just, they are more desirable than gold and very precious stone, and sweeter than honey and the honeycomb,* 6 *for indeed your servant keeps them and in keeping them there is great reward* (Ps 18:9–11).

Discussion Questions

In a society where we are encouraged to express our opinions in many forms, including social media, what could we learn from Benedict's virtue of restraint in speaking?

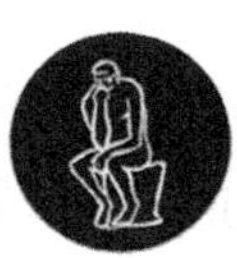

How does Benedict's Prologue guide monks through the process of discerning their call to monastic life? How does it inspire you to want to give your life to following God's call?

Choose one of Benedict's twelve steps of humility and describe how you have either experienced a struggle or victory in that area.

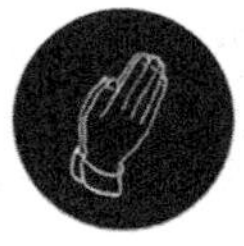

What spiritual benefit do you see in the discipline of simplicity and not owning many possessions?

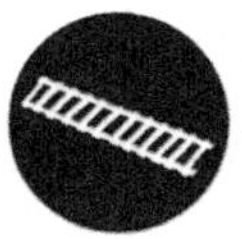

In which area of self-control do you struggle? How could you develop practices in your life that would apply discipline to this area?

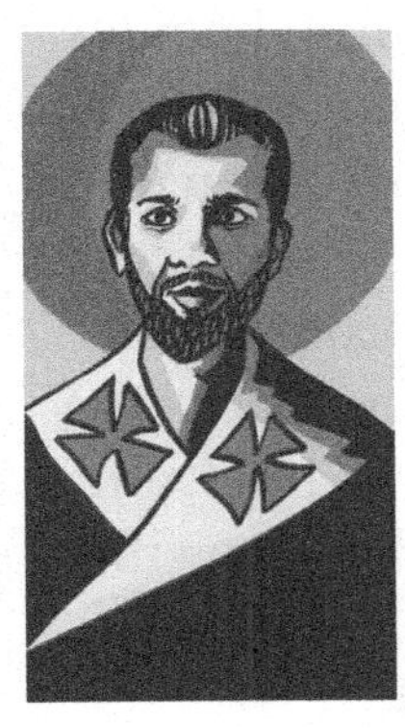

Chapter 7

Spiritual Teachings – Prayer

All Christian believers are expected to pray: "pray without ceasing" (1 Thess 5:17). Jesus often went off alone to pray (e.g., Luke 5:16) but he also prayed with his disciples and followers (e.g., Luke 11). Benedict and Basil value community prayer greatly. Thus, leaders should be people who pray—both individually and with others. In the monastery nearly everything that is done is begun with prayer. One prays before doing the laundry or before and after eating. Thus, how beneficial for Christians to develop the habit of prayer, even if those prayers are short and to the point, if you will. If prayer was important and necessary to the ministry of Jesus Christ, how much more so for the ministry of all leaders. It is easy for competent leaders to assume that they can run an organization in their own strength but this is misguided thinking. Better to entrust the community to God in prayer than to rely only on its human leadership.

Reverence in Prayer (RBen §20)

1 If when we wish to request something of powerful men we do not presume to do so except with humility and reverence, 2 how much more ought we to offer supplications to the universal Lord and God in all humility and purity of devotion? 3 And we know it is not on account of our wordiness that we are heard, but rather through purity of heart and tears of compunction. 4 And therefore prayer ought to be brief and pure, unless it happens to be prolonged by a sentiment inspired by divine grace. 5 In community, however, prayer should always be brief; and at the signal given by the superior all should rise together.

The Oratory of the Monastery (RBen §52)

1 The oratory is to be what it is called, and nothing else should be done or kept there. 2 When the Work of God is finished all should go out in complete silence and with reverence for God, 3 so that a brother who wishes to pray by himself will not be impeded by another's insensitivity. 4 But if he wishes to pray in solitude, he should enter to pray with simplicity, not in a loud voice, but with tears and attentiveness of heart. 5 And therefore one who is not performing this work is not to be permitted to remain in the oratory after the Work of God, so that, as was said, no one else is impeded.

Attending Prayer (RBas §107)

Q: If someone engaged in work in the store-room or the kitchen or a similar task does not hasten to be present at the order of psalmody and of prayer, does his soul suffer no loss?

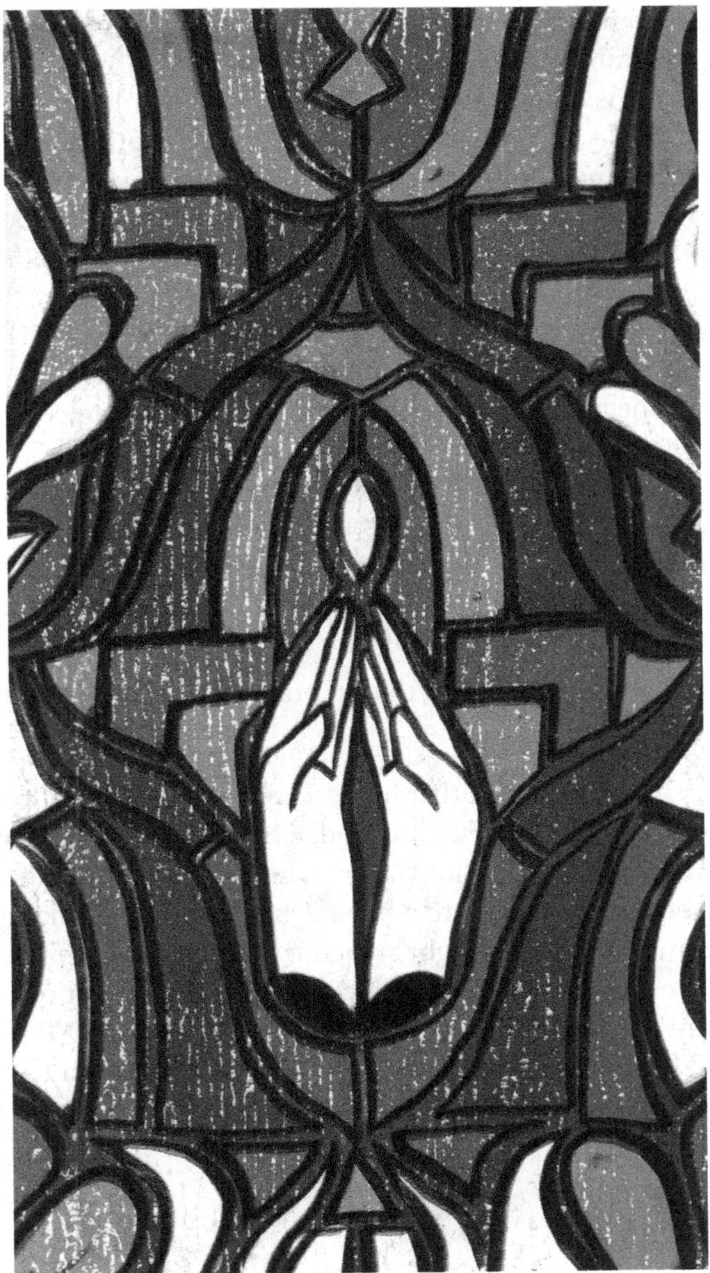

"Chanting and singing psalms in your hearts to the Lord"

R: 1 Each in his own work must keep to his proper rule as a member of the body, and will suffer loss if he neglects what he is enjoined to do, and indeed be in greater peril if he neglects the common purpose of the brothers. 2 So then, he must fulfill with mind and devotion what is written: *chanting and singing psalms in your hearts to the Lord* (Eph 5:19). 3 For if he does not hasten to be bodily present with the others at the place of prayer, let him fulfill what pertains to piety in whatever place he finds himself. 4 Care however ought to be observed lest someone perhaps is able to complete in time what needs to be completed and to hasten, but wants to allege excuses as if he had been detained in a work of service. 5 Anyone who does this answers for a stumbling-block for the others and incurs the penalty of the negligent.

Focused Prayer (RBas §108)

Q: How can one ensure that in prayer his senses do not wander?

R: 1 If he is resolved that he stands before the eyes of God, for if someone who sees his judge or ruler and converses with him does not allow his eye the liberty to roam about or look away elsewhere while he is engaged in speaking, 2 how much more ought someone who approaches God never divert the eyes of his heart but remain intent on him who searches hearts and inward parts (Ps 7:9), 3 so that he fulfills what is written: *Lifting up holy hands without anger and argument* (1 Tim 2:8).

Focused Mind (RBas §109)

Q: Is it possible for a human being to ensure that always and everywhere his mind does not wander, and how can this be done?

R: 1 That it is possible he shows us who said: *My eyes are always on the Lord* (Ps 24:15) and again: *I kept the Lord always in view before me; since he is at my right hand I shall not be shaken* (Ps 15:8). 2 How it may be possible we have already said: that is, if we allow no idleness to the soul, but at all times think on God and his works and benefits and gifts 3 and ponder these things in our mind with *confession* and *thanksgiving* as it is written (cf. Ps 33:1; 1 Tim 2:1).

Singing Wisely

Q: What is it to *sing psalms wisely* (Ps 46:7 LXX)?

R: 1 Just as with all floods, the flavor of each is discerned through taste, so also are prudence and discernment with the words of Holy Scripture. 2 *For the throat*, it says, *tastes food, but the sense discerns words* (cf. Job 12:11; 34:3 LXX). 3 Therefore if one's soul is intent on each word of the psalms, as taste is intent on distinguishing the flavor of foods, such a one fulfills that which is said: *sing psalms wisely* (Ps 46:7).

Remaining Silent During Service (RBas §137)

Q: Should anyone be speaking in the house during the hour of prayers or psalmody?[1]

R: 1 Except for those who have the responsibility of service, or those whom the care of discipline or the arrangement of tasks permits, and they too ought to take great care 2 that they speak only as necessity requires and do so quietly and respectfully, refraining from making any disturbance or even a small annoyance for the others. It is fitting that all the rest maintain silence.

3 For if the Apostle says even to prophets who are teaching in the church: *If there is a revelation to one seated, let the one who was speaking first fall silent* (1 Cor 14:30), then how much more at the time of psalmody or prayers is it fitting that all refrain from speech and observe silence, 4 unless perhaps as we said above, because of the common supervision there is need of speech.

1 Psalmody – singing the Psalms.

Discussion Questions

Regular times of corporate prayer were built into each day in the monastery. What are the barriers and hindrances to recovering rhythms of corporate prayer in our current ministry context?

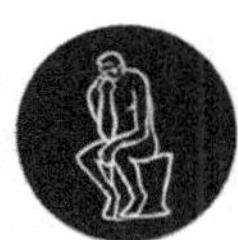

Do you think we give enough time and space for prayer in our places of worship? If not, how can we improve?

How do we approach God when we pray? How might that approach change after reading this chapter?

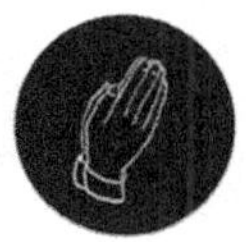

What practical advice can you take from this chapter the next time your mind wanders during prayer?

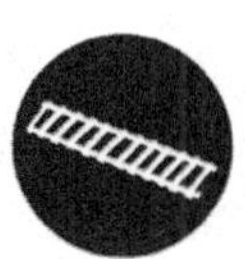

Basil compares singing psalms to tasting food. What habits can improve our appetite and develop a hunger for "eating right" both individually and corporately?

THEOLOGY & ETHICS

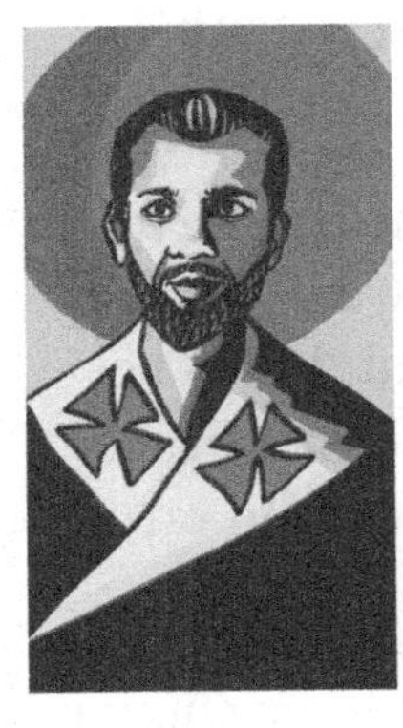

Chapter 8

Spiritual Teachings – Hospitality

Some of us are, by nature, "people persons"; that is, we love to meet new people and/or we love to be around others. Some of us, on the other hand, like to be alone more than we like to be with others. Furthermore, many of us are uncomfortable with meeting others, either because of our own shyness or introversion or because they are too different from me. But the whole point of community is to bring people together, despite their differences, and unite them into one common group. In doing so we are practicing a kind of hospitality in which we welcome others into our lives and voluntarily weave our lives together into a new kind of life. Good leaders will do this by example, not just by word. Congregational leaders need to see themselves as not standing above the community but as members of the community. In the monastic context, the abbot or abbess of a community is still, at the end of the day, just a monk like everyone else. And this should be true of all leaders.

The Reception of Guests (RBen §53)

1 All guests who present themselves are to be received as Christ, for He will say: *I was a stranger and you took me in* (Matt 25:35). 2 And to everyone fitting honor is to be shown, especially to those of the household of faith (Gal 6:10) and to pilgrims.

3 When, therefore, a guest is announced, he is to be met by the superior and the brothers with every ceremony of love: 4 thus first they are to pray together, and thus be united to one another in peace. 5 But this kiss of peace is not to be offered until prayer has first been said on account of the illusions of the devil.

6 And in this very salutation all humility is to be shown to all arriving or departing guests: 7 by bowing the head or prostrating the whole body on the ground Christ is to be adored in them just as he is received in them. 8 And having been received the guests are to be led to prayer, and afterwards the superior or anyone he appoints is to sit with them. 9 The divine law is to be read to the guest for his edification, and afterwards all kindness is to be shown him. 10 The superior is to break his fast for the sake of the guest, unless it happens to be a principal fast-day which cannot be broken: 11 the brothers, however, are to follow their customary fast. 12 Water is to be poured on the hands of the guests by the Abbot, 13 and the feet of all guests are to be washed by the Abbot and the whole community. 14 After the washing they are to say this verse: *We have received your mercy, O God, in the midst of your temple* (Ps 48:10).

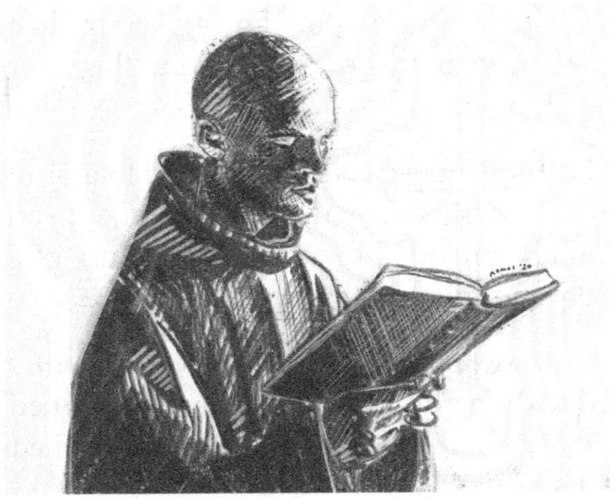

The Abbot of a monastery stands in the place of Christ.

15 In the reception of the poor and of pilgrims the greatest care and solicitude should be shown, because in them Christ is more especially received: For the very awe we have of the rich insures that they receive honor.

16 The kitchen for the Abbot and guests is to be set apart by itself so that guests who arrive at uncertain hours (and who are never lacking in a monastery) may not disturb the brothers. **17** In this kitchen each year two brothers are to be placed who can fulfill this duty properly. **18** These, if they require it, are to be offered help so that they may serve without murmuring; and when, on the other hand, they are occupied with less, they are to go out wherever they are commanded to work. **19** And not only to them, but in all the duties of the monastery this same consideration is to be shown:

20 that is, when help is required it is given to them; and again, when they are free they obey what they are commanded to do.

21 And the guest-house is to be assigned to a brother whose soul is possessed by the fear of God: 22 sufficient beds should be provided there. And the house of God is to be wisely administered by the wise.

23 Guests, however, are not to be associated with or conversed with for any reason by one not assigned to it: 24 instead, if he happens to meet or see them, he is to humbly greet them as we have said; and as he asks their blessing he is to continue on, saying that he is not permitted to converse with a guest.

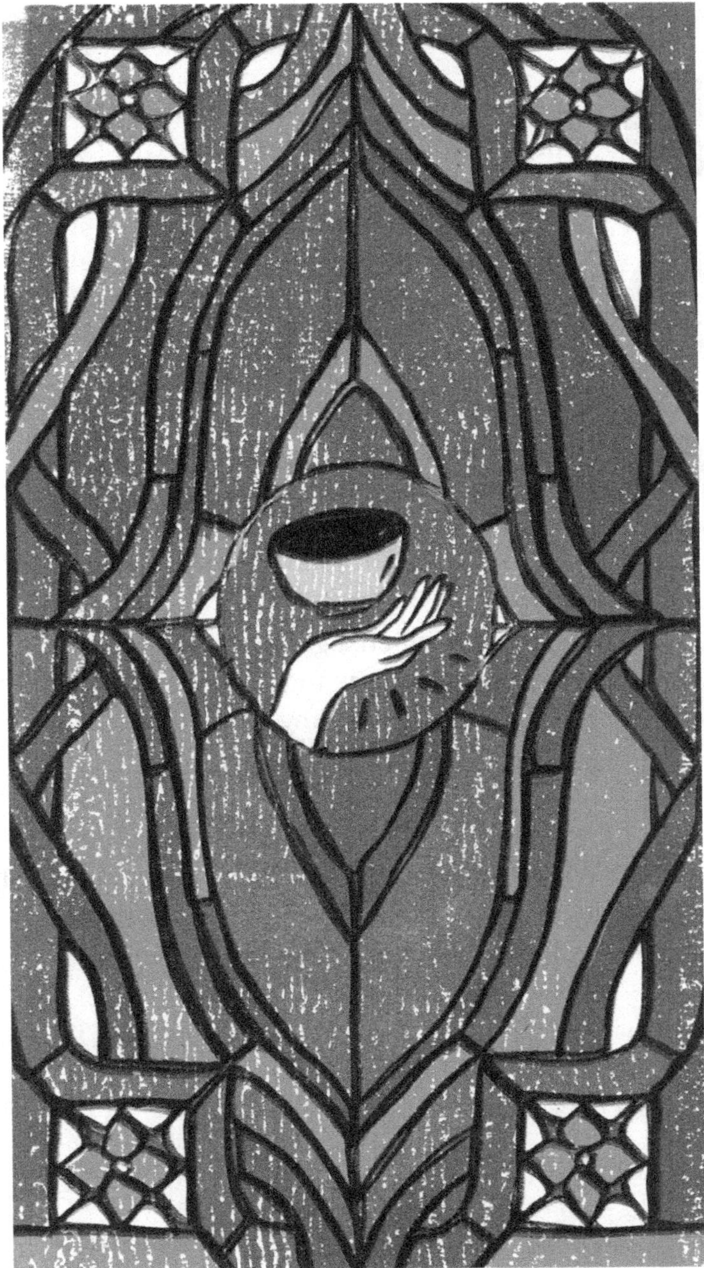

"All guests who present themselves are to be received as Christ."

Discussion Questions

How could these principles of hospitality apply to those visiting our ministries?

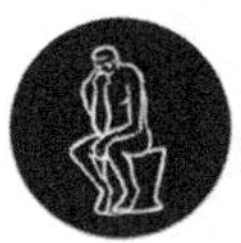

What is Benedict's definition of hospitality? How does it compare to our definition of hospitality?

How does the idea of receiving guests as if they were Christ challenge you as you practice hospitality (Matt 25)?

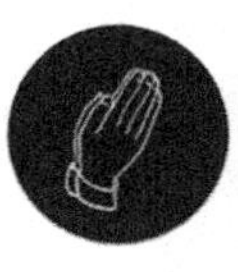

The first act when a guest is announced in a monastery is to pray together. Do you welcome guests in this way? How could it set the tone for their visit?

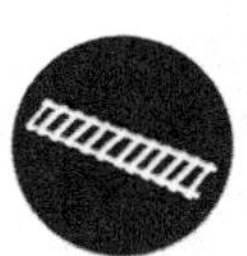

What habits can we begin to develop to assist us in "receiving guests as Christ" instead of seeing them as an inconvenience to our scheduled plans?

Afterword

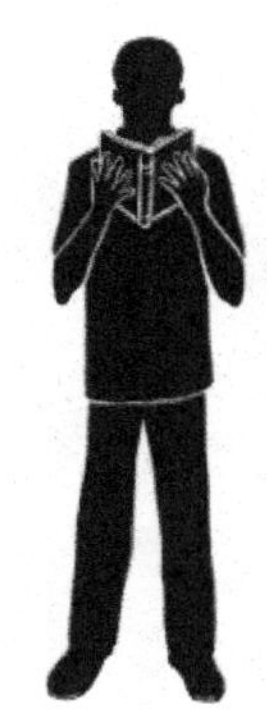

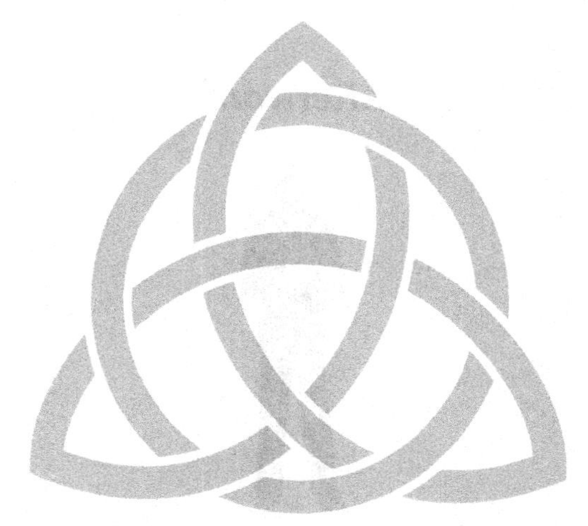

THEOLOGY & ETHICS

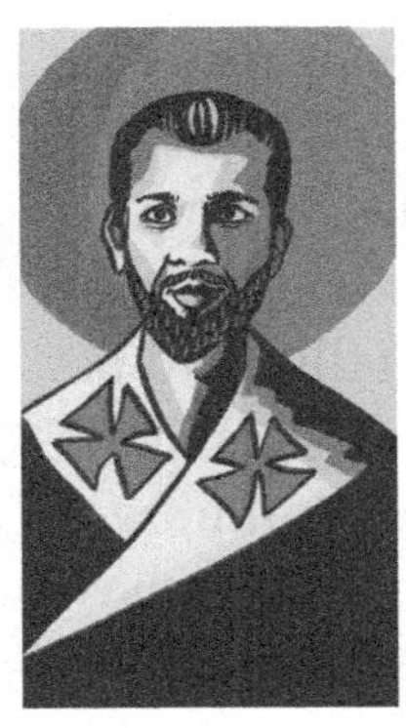

Afterword

As we have seen, the rules of Benedict of Nursia and Basil of Caesarea touch on a lot of areas, though not all, of course. The purpose of these rules is to facilitate the monk's relationship to God; and to organize the life of the monastery/community. Given that most of us are not monks in the traditional sense we come to these rules already having to do a bit of adjustment so that they can "fit" our lives and, as it turns out, they are easily adjusted so as to help the Christian believer in her relationship to God. That is, the spiritual teachings of these documents apply to all Christians, not just monks and nuns. Moreover, many (perhaps even most) people live in some type of community. A married couple without children is still a community of two! Thus, these rules, when they talk about things related to living in community have something to say to all of us as well.

Nonetheless, there is so much information in these rules that one might be overwhelmed! Thus, let me suggest three main takeaways:

1. All Christian believers should try to live their life in accordance with a rule. A rule of life sets out the parameters of one's Christian life. The Bible, of course, is our main rule of life and it tells us many things: to pray, to avoid sin and to love God and our neighbor, for example. But other rules, like the ones by Benedict and Basil, can also help us to see how to live well. For example, the Bible tells us to be humble (James 4:10) but Benedict's rule fleshes out for us the steps that we can ascend to gain humility. Living a ruled life means being intentional about how we cultivate our spiritual lives and these rules can help us.

2. All Christians should live together in community well and that takes organization. Every family has an unwritten set of rules. For example, I have two teenaged sons and they understand that there are rules in our family though we have never written them down. Most basically we have rules like "lock the door when you are the last one coming inside at night" and "put your dirty dishes in the dishwasher." But we also have unwritten rules of greater importance like "when you drive the car you will obey the speed limit" and "you can only have friends over with permission." All of these rules are meant to ensure that our family life runs smoothly and that we do not offend or upset each other. But even if we live in other kinds of community we should still live with others well and, again, that takes effort and some sort of rules and guidelines. To help us do this why not look to those who have gone before us, like Benedict and Basil?

3. While we seek to grow in our own relationship with God and while we strive to live well in community, let us remember the importance of welcoming others into our lives (i.e., practice hospitality). Many of us are happy to spend time with people we like but we are not always eager to get to know strangers. Nonetheless, Benedict in particular encourages us to be hospitable to all people, which, of course, is what the Scriptures also say: "Contribute to the needs of the saints and seek to show hospitality" (Rom. 12:13) and "Show hospitality to one another without grumbling" (1 Pet. 4:9).

So, let us strive as Christian believers to live lives according to a rule that will help us become holy like God is holy; to live well with others; and to be hospitable to all people, especially those who are different than us.

The way to do this, I think, is to develop your own rule of life, using whatever is helpful from the rules of Benedict and Basil. Living according to a rule of life will help you to make the best use of your time and energy as your strive to become a godly Christian and it does not have to be an overly complicated process. One could develop a rule of life in three steps. First, read, reread and meditate on the Bible and the rules of Benedict and Basil, asking yourself, what are the practices and habits from these texts that should be in my own rule of life? Make a list of those things and be specific. For example, do not just say, "I will pray every day" but instead say, "I will pray once every morning for ten minutes and once at night for ten minutes." Second, take an inventory of your daily life, asking yourself, what are my daily commitments? What are the things that I do that I should stop doing or do less? What are things that I do not do that I should start doing? Lastly, take what you learned from the first two steps and devise a daily and/or weekly rule of life. Though more could be said, this is at least a start to living a ruled life akin to that espoused by Benedict and Basil. And it is only by living according to a rule of life that one will experience the blessings of such a life.

Resources for Application

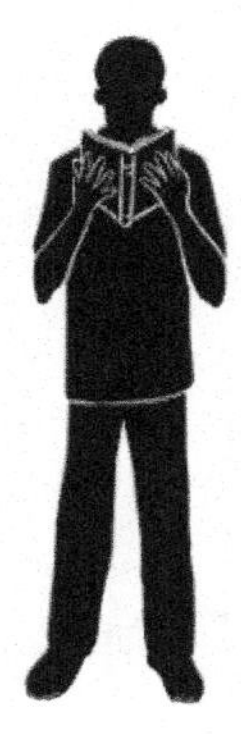

THEOLOGY & ETHICS

Soul Work and Soul Care:
Learning to Be Intentional about Our "Rule of Life"

By Hank Voss

No one presumes to teach an art until he has first carefully studied it. Look how foolish it is for the inexperienced to assume pastoral authority, since the care of souls is the art of arts!

~ Gregory the Great, c. 590

Your leaders . . . keep watch over your souls and will give an account for their work.

~ Hebrews 13:17a

Each *Sacred Roots Spiritual Classic* has a "Soul Work and Soul Care" resource to illustrate how Christian leaders across cultures and generations have found a particular spiritual classic helpful in pastoral ministry. "Soul work" includes the *personal* work of watering, weeding, pruning, and fertilizing the garden of one's own soul. In a similar way, "soul care" involves the *pastoral* work of nurturing growth in another's friendship with God. When Jesus discusses soul work and soul care, he often uses metaphors from the medical and agricultural professions. Like a doctor for souls, or a farmer caring for an orchard of fruit trees, congregational leaders who hope to serve as soul surgeons can learn much from the wisdom of those who have gone before.

Becoming a Community of Disciples: Learning to Be Intentional about Our "Rule of Life"

Every Christian leader must learn the importance of a regular daily time with God. Some call this set time "devotions," "quiet time," "prayer time," or simply "my time with the Lord." Yet as important as this time is, we know that our pursuit of God involves much more than a daily devotional time. What do we call the wider intentional pursuit of God in our lives as individuals and as families of faith? Across the centuries, the most common term for a disciple's plan for pursuing God is a "rule of life."

What is a "rule of life"? In simplest terms, it is an intentional plan for growing in our relationship with God. The word "intentional" in the previous sentence is of great importance. Jesus's brother, James, challenges us to "draw near to God." The best of rewards is promised for those who obey—we discover that God responds by drawing near to us (Jas 4:8). For the lover of God, there is no greater reward than the presence of God (Ps 27:4). For thousands of years saints who know that God is a rewarder of those who diligently seek him have been intentional about how they order their time on a daily, weekly, quarterly, and annual basis in order to better seek the Lord. Consider Daniel, who three times a day spent time in prayer as his "rule of life." Consider other Old Testament saints who paused to make morning and evening sacrifices as part of their daily "rule." Consider the author of Psalm 119 whose rule of life consisted of eight daily "pauses" for prayer: "Seven times a day I praise you" (v. 164) and "at midnight I rise to praise you" (v. 64). In the New Testament we find the disciples pausing at the "hour of prayer" to talk with God as a regular habit. Like many other devout Jews of the first century, the apostle Peter would pause for morning and evening prayer, as well as prayer at noon (Acts 10:9) and at 3:00 p.m. (Acts 3:1; cf. Matt 27:46).

Across the New Testament, disciples of Jesus are encouraged to be intentional about the practical ways in which we pursue our relationship with God. The example of biblical leaders provides a practical vision of what pursuing God looks like. But they do not only set an example of intentional pursuit of God—these leaders also invite us to follow their lead. Consider the texts and commands in Table 1.

Table 1: New Testament Encouragement to Pursue God

Action Believers Are Called to Do	Author/s	Text
1. *Pursue holiness, righteousness and godliness.*	*Paul, Author of Hebrews*	*1 Tim 6:11; Phil 3:12; 2 Tim 2:22; Heb 12:14*
2. *Train yourself to be godly.*	*Paul, Author of Hebrews*	*1 Tim 4:7–8; Tit 2:12; Heb 5:14*
3. *Learn how to show godliness and be like Christ.*	*Paul*	*Eph 4:20; 1 Tim 5:4*
4. *Press on to become more like Christ.*	*Paul*	*Phil 3:12–16*
5. *Cleanse yourself . . . and bring holiness to completion.*	*Paul*	*2 Cor 7:1 cf. Ps 15*
6. *Put to death sinful actions.*	*Paul*	*Rom 8:13; Col 3:5*
7. *Put on or clothe yourself with Christ/new self.*	*Paul*	*Rom 13:14; Gal 3:27; Eph 4:24; Col 3:5–17*

Action Believers Are Called to Do	Author/s	Text
8. *Walk in the good works God prepared for us to do.*	*Paul*	*Eph 2:10; 4:1*
9. *Draw near to God.*	*James*	*Jas 4:8*
10. *Make every effort to increase godliness.*	*Peter*	*2 Pet 1:5–6*
11. *Be(come) Holy!*	*Peter and Paul*	*1 Pet 1:15–16; Rom 12:1 (Lev 11:44–45)*
12. *Be imitators of me, as I am of Christ.*	*Paul*	*1 Cor 11:1*

In *Becoming a Community of Disciples* we have seen that ancient communities of disciples have taken these New Testament commands with a seriousness that often humbles our contemporary claims to be "pursuing God." We have seen that Benedict and Basil led communities of disciples who were highly intentional about their daily, weekly, quarterly, and annual rhythms in imitation of biblical leaders like Moses, David, Daniel, and Peter. In Egypt's desert a Christian leader named Pachomius (d. 346) organized thousands of serious disciples into communities that would gather every morning and evening to pray twelve psalms. They prayed through more than twenty Psalms a day in order to pray through the whole book of Psalms together each week in community. Other leaders, like Augustine (from Africa), also developed "rules of life" that have shaped millions of believers to this day.

Read the four definitions below. As you do, underline or circle the key words. A rule of life is . . .

A holistic description of the Spirit-empowered rhythms and relationships that create, redeem, sustain and transform the life God invites you to humbly fulfill for Christ's glory.

~ Stephen Macchia

An intentional, conscious plan to keep God at the center of everything we do . . . the starting point and foundation of any Rule is a desire to be with God and to love him

~ Peter Scazzero

The regular, rhythmic practice of spiritual disciplines integrated into ordinary life for the purpose of developing and deepening a relationship with God.

~ Klaus Issler

A rule of life seeks to address the interplay between these two questions: How do I want to live so I can be who I want to be?

~ Ruth Haley Barton

In the box below, write your own definition of a "rule of life."

A Rule of Life is . . .

For additional resources on the history of discipleship communities and their use of rules of life, see the following:

Peters, Greg. *Monkhood of All Believers: The Monastic Foundation of Christian Spirituality*. Grand Rapids: Baker Academic, 2018.

———. *Reforming the Monastery: Protestant Theologies of the Religious Life*. Cascade, 2013.

———. "Spiritual Theology: A Historical Overview." In *Reading the Christian Spiritual Classics: A Guide for Evangelicals*, edited by Jamin Goggin and Kyle Strobel, 79–94. Downers Grove, IL: InterVarsity, 2013.

———. *Story of Monasticism: Retrieving an Ancient Tradition for Contemporary Spirituality*. Grand Rapids, Michigan: Baker Academic, 2015.

Intentional about Our Personal and Corporate "Rule of Life"

With a definition for "rule of life," we can explore practical implications. What is your intentional plan for seeking the Lord? What means will you use to bring your vision into reality? What is your personal "rule of life" for practically pursuing the Lord on a daily, weekly, quarterly, and annual basis? What is the community "rule" pursued by your church, network, or family of churches? Our readings in *Becoming a Community of Disciples* provide several powerful examples of how communities in the past have pursued seeking the Lord. Use the sections below to reflect on your own daily, weekly, quarterly, and annual rhythms.

"Rule of Life": Intentional about My Daily Rhythms

"Only that which is done on a daily basis will ever dominate your life." As a young student, I once heard the missionary and scholar Dr. Ralph Winter make this remark, and it still echoes in my mind. If we want our life to be dominated by God's presence and power, we must intentionally pursue a daily strategy. Disciples who follow the Rule of St. Benedict spend an average of four hours a day in prayer, reading, and meditation on Scripture. Is this possible in our modern North American context? The answer may not be as simple as we suppose. Modern researchers report that the average North American spends well over four hours a day on electronic devices watching television, playing games, or scrolling through social media. Could some or all of this time be reinvested in seeking the Lord? We might not be able to change the world, but we can choose how we will spend our own leisure time. What practices would you like to pursue on a daily basis? What spiritual disciplines have you seen modeled in the lives of mentors? What practices have you read about in the lives of great Christian leaders from the past that you would like to imitate in the present?

Consider the following spiritual disciplines or practices. Underline those you already practice on a regular basis. Circle those you are interested in exploring further.

Table 2: Forty-Four Spiritual Disciplines

Bible Reading	Intercessory Prayer	Worship in Song	Mentoring
Bible Study	Thanksgiving and Praise	Lord's Supper	Discipling
Bible Memorization	Lament Prayer	Simplicity	Spiritual Friendship
Bible Meditation	Breath or Arrow Prayers	Unplugging	Hospitality
Praying the Bible	Conversational Prayer	Secrecy	Witness
Lectio Divina	Continual Prayer, the "minute game"	Silence	Justice
Storying Scripture	Fixed-Hour Prayer	Service	Truth-Telling
Speaking Scripture	Prayer Walking	Accountability Partners	Stewardship
Singing Scripture	Fasting	Conversation	Creation Care
Hand Copying Scripture	Journaling Prayer	Chastity	Evangelism
Psalm Work	Examen	Small Group	Almsgiving

If you would like more information about one of the forty-four sample spiritual disciplines above, each receives a solid introduction in one of the following resources:

Augustine of Hippo. *Praying the Psalms with Augustine and Friends*. Edited by Carmen Joy Imes. Sacred Roots Spiritual Classics 1. Wichita, KS: The Urban Ministry Institute, 2021.

Calhoun, Adele Ahlberg. *Spiritual Disciplines Handbook: Practices That Transform Us*. Revised. Downers Grove: InterVarsity, 2015. This resource describes and explains seventy-five spiritual disciplines.

Collins, Phil. Taylor University Center for Scripture Engagement. www.biblegateway.com/resources/scripture-engagement/main/practices. This website provides free articles on spiritual disciplines related to engaging the Bible.

Foster, Richard J. *Celebration of Discipline: The Path to Spiritual Growth*. San Francisco: Harper, 1998. This resource describes twelve spiritual disciplines.

Thurman, Howard. *Deep Is the Hunger; Meditations for Apostles of Sensitiveness*. Richmond, IN: Friends United Press, 1951.

———. *Disciplines of the Spirit*. Richmond, IN: Friends United Press, 1977.

Willard, Dallas. *The Spirit of the Disciplines: Understanding How God Changes Lives*. San Francisco: Harper and Row, 1988.

"Rule of Life": Intentional about My Weekly Rhythms

When God structured his people's week as recorded in the first five books of the Bible, He reserved one day in seven for rest and worship. He gave his people the gift of the

Sabbath to pray and play. Jesus regularly practiced sabbath, as did the disciples and apostles in the book of Acts. There is much wisdom in guarding one day a week for rest. Perhaps keeping a sabbath day is a spiritual discipline you want to explore as part of your weekly rhythm? Perhaps there are other disciplines you want to explore as part of your normal weekly schedule? For example, some may choose a day or a meal each week to try the discipline of fasting. Use the chart below to plan your "ideal week" for practicing your spiritual disciplines. Review the spiritual disciplines in Table 2 for ideas.

Table 3: Weekly Plan for Spiritual Disciplines

Day	Morning	Afternoon	Evening
Sunday			
Monday			
Tuesday			
Wednesday			
Thursday			
Friday			
Saturday			

For more on the Sabbath, consider the following resources:

Dawn, Marva J. *Keeping the Sabbath Wholly: Ceasing, Resting, Embracing, Feasting*. Grand Rapids: Eerdmans, 1989.

———. *The Sense of the Call: A Sabbath Way of Life for Those Who Serve God, the Church, and the World*. Grand Rapids: Eerdmans, 2006.

"Rule of Life": Intentional about My Quarterly Rhythms

In the Old Testament, God's people were directed to adopt rhythms for their monthly or quarterly practices that still serve as examples for us today. Every month, God's people celebrated a new moon feast in which they gathered with family and friends to thank God for his faithfulness. Perhaps you gather monthly with family and friends to celebrate birthdays or remember to pray for a particular missional priority? We see another practical example in the life of Jesus—the practice of regular spiritual retreats. Jesus would regularly go away for solitude retreats in order to prioritize time alone with his Father. On average, he took one "spiritual retreat" every four or five months. Consider Table 4 and the example it provides for our own habit of periodic spiritual retreats.

Table 4: Jesus's Practice of Silence and Solitude

Event	Type	References
Jesus's preparation years were not necessarily solitude, but are worth reflecting on. What was Jesus doing during this time?	*Jesus spent thirty years in quietness. Consider also his weekly sabbath practice during this time. He spent more than four years resting (1,560 sabbath days)!*	*(#27) Luke 3:23*
Desert Month	*Jesus spent forty days in solitude, prayer, and fasting in the wilderness.*	*(#28) Matt 4:1–11 Mark 1:12–13 Luke 4:1–13*
Lonely Hours	*Jesus spent a block of time (3–4 hours?) in solitude and prayer. He had regular places he would go.*	*(#50) Mark 1:35–39 Luke 4:42–44 (compare also Luke 11:1)*
Habitual Half Day	*Jesus would "often slip away to the wilderness and pray."*	*(#52) Luke 5:16*
All Night Vigil	*"He went off to the mountain . . . he spent the whole night in prayer to God" before a major decision.*	*(#63) Luke 6:12–16*
Executive Team Retreat	*"Come away by yourselves to a lonely place, and rest a while."*	*(#104) Mark 6:31–34*

Event	Type	References
Habitual Half Day/Night	*"He went up on the mountain by Himself to pray; and when it was evening, He was there alone."*	*(#106) Matt 14:22–23 Mark 6:45–46 Luke 6:14–15*
Friend Retreat	*"He brought them up to a high mountain by themselves."*	*(#121) Matt 17:1–8 Mark 9:2–8 Luke 9:28–36a*
All Night Vigil	*"And he withdrew from them about a stone's throw, and he knelt down and began to pray."*	*(#226) Matt 26:36–46 Mark 14:32–42 Luke 22: 40b–46 John 18:1*

#xx refer to episode numbers in *A Harmony of the Gospels*, by Gundry and Thomas (1978).

Jesus spent time in "solitude" multiple times during each year of his public ministry (at least eight times in a three-year period). He also participated in the three pilgrim festivals (spiritual retreats in Jerusalem for worship) every year, adding an additional nine corporate retreats during his three years of ministry. Use the table below to create a plan for the personal and corporate retreats you hope to take in the next one to three years.

Table 5: My Rhythm for Personal Retreats

Date	Type of Retreat *(Solitude, Study, Prayer, Planning, Marriage, Parenting, Vision, Review, etc.)*	Place	Notes

"Rule of Life": Intentional about My Annual Rhythms

God has given the gift of rhythms to all humans—even to all creation. Our days consist of morning and evening. Days blend into the seasons of the solar year. Ancient Babylonian and Hebrew calendars were based on the lunar calendar and would reset after a nineteen-year cycle. Our modern calendars are based on the solar year. The earth turns on a regular rhythm around the sun every 365 days to complete one solar year. The sun itself rotates around the center of the Milky Way galaxy in a "cosmic year" lasting some two hundred and fifty million solar years at the sun's current speed. Everything in creation follows rhythms.

Just as disciples are intentional about daily, weekly, and monthly/quarterly rhythms, so we are intentional about annual rhythms. Many forget that the English word "holiday" originates from the combination of "Holy" and "Day." The annual events one commemorates—either with days of fasting or feasting—reveal a great deal about core values and cherished priorities. In the Old Testament, God asked his "Holy Nation," Israel, to plan annual celebrations to remind themselves about God's saving activities. Three times a year the whole community gathered for a family retreat at Jerusalem to celebrate God's great salvation actions (Passover, Pentecost, Tabernacles). There was also a time for the whole community to fast on particular days.

The early church followed the example of ancient Israel when they identified particular days and seasons to focus attention on the great saving activities in the life of Christ. The Christian Year is an annual calendar aimed at keeping the birth, life, death, resurrection, and ascension of Jesus, together with the gift of the Holy Spirit at Pentecost, continually before the eyes of God's people in a repeating rhythm. Using the table below, underline the annual holy days you or your church community currently commemorate. Circle any that you are interested in celebrating in the next year.

Table 6: Commemorating the Life of Jesus on an Annual Basis

Holy Day or Season	Month	Notes
Advent	*December*	
Christmas	*December*	
Epiphany	*January–February*	
Lent	*February–April*	
Holy Week	*March or April*	
Easter	*March or April*	
Pentecost	*April through November*	

In addition to annually commemorating the life of Jesus, many churches celebrate or remember the lives of important leaders from the church, from their culture, or from their national history. The table below lists holidays often celebrated in North America. Are there holidays below that you could use as part of your annual rhythm to intentionally focus on Christ and his mission in the world? If so, which ones? Are there other holidays not on the list you might choose to commemorate? What are they?

Table 7: Other Annual "Holy" Days to Consider for a Rule of Life

"Holy" Day	Month	Notes
New Year's Day	*January*	
Martin Luther King Day	*January*	
Valentine's Day	*February*	
Black History Month	*February*	
Esther's Fast, and International Women's Day	*March*	
Creation or Earth Day	*April*	
Mother's Day	*May*	
Memorial Day	*May*	
Father's Day	*June*	
Fourth of July	*July*	
Labor Day	*September*	
Disability Awareness Sunday	*October*	
Halloween	*October*	
Reformation Day	*October*	
Thanksgiving Day	*November*	
Birthdays		
Marriage Anniversaries		
Death Anniversaries		

The following resources can help you explore further the holidays and commemorations identified above.

Davis, Don. "Living in the Way: Pilgrimage and the Seasons of the Church Year." In *A Sojourner's Quest*, edited by Don L. Davis, 147–79. Wichita, KS: The Urban Ministry Institute, 2010.

———. *Marking Time: Forming Spirituality through the Church Year*. Wichita, KS: The Urban Ministry Institute, 2009.

Larsen, Timothy, ed. *The Oxford Handbook of Christmas*. Oxford: Oxford University Press, 2020.

Metzger, Paul Louis. *Setting the Spiritual Clock: Sacred Time Breaking Through the Secular Eclipse*. Eugene, OR: Cascade, 2020.

Webber, Robert E. *Ancient-Future Time: Forming Spirituality through the Christian Year*. Grand Rapids: Baker, 2004.

A "Rule of Life": Putting It All Together

"And as for all who walk by this rule, peace and mercy be upon them, and upon the Israel of God."

~ Galatians 6:16

"The one who offers thanksgiving as his sacrifice glorifies me; to one who orders his way rightly I will show the salvation of God!"

~ Psalm 50:23

Use the table below to gather onto a single page your plan for intentional pursuit of God. Once you have it summarized, share it with a wise and trusted friend. Remember to have grace with yourself, just as your Father in heaven is full of grace. Meet with a mentor or friend annually to compare notes on your "rule of life." Use that meeting as an opportunity to evaluate and adapt things. Remember that while some disciplines may work in every season of life, others will come and go. Be open to the Holy Spirit's leading and remember that neither our success in keeping a rule nor our failure to follow one will change the amount of love the Father in heaven has for us. Rest in that love (1 John 3:1).

Table 8: My Rule of Life in Summary Form

Daily	Weekly
Monthly	Annually

As you develop your personal or community rule of life, the following resources may prove useful.

Davis, Don. "Fleshing out the Universal Priesthood: Recommended Order for Morning and Evening Sacrifices." In *A Sojourner's Quest*, edited by Don L. Davis, 225–35. Wichita, KS: The Urban Ministry Institute, 2010.

———. "The Laws of Sowing and Reaping." In *A Sojourner's Quest*, edited by Don L. Davis, 239–56. Wichita, KS: The Urban Ministry Institute, 2010.

———. "Spiritual Blueprints: Templates for Spiritual Formation." In *A Sojourner's Quest*, edited by Don L. Davis, 219–24. Wichita, KS: The Urban Ministry Institute, 2010.

———. *Master the Bible Guidebook: Charting Your Course through Scripture Memorization*. Wichita, KS: The Urban Ministry Institute, 2008.

———. *Get Your Pretense On! Living as an Ambassador of the Kingdom of God*. Wichita, KS: The Urban Ministry Institute, 2018.

———. "The Sacred Roots Annual: A Swiss Army Knife of Spiritual Formation." In *Show Me Your Glory: Sacred Roots Annual 2019–2020*, 47–53. Wichita, KS: The Urban Ministry Institute, 2019.

Macchia, Stephen A. *Crafting a Rule of Life: An Invitation to a Well-Ordered Way*. Downers Grove, IL: Intervarsity, 2012.

Scazzero, Peter. *The Emotionally Healthy Leader: How Transforming Your Inner Life Will Deeply Transform Your Church, Team, and the World*. Grand Rapids: Zondervan, 2015.

Willard, Dallas. *Renovation of the Heart: Putting on the Character of Christ*. Colorado Springs, CO: NavPress, 2002.

Continuing the Conversation

There are a lot of books about The Rule of Benedict, and not too many on The Rule of Basil. Many of the books on The Rule of Benedict are not too academic and are meant for everyone, not just scholars. If you are interested in learning more about Christian monasticism in general I would recommend a book that I wrote: Greg Peters, *The Story of Monasticism: Retrieving an Ancient Tradition for Contemporary Spirituality* (Grand Rapids: Baker Academic, 2015). If you do want a more technical study of The Rule of Benedict, the best is Terrence G. Kardong's *Benedict's Rule: A Translation and Commentary* (Collegeville, MN: Liturgical Press, 1996). Of the books that introduce The Rule of Benedict and help to make it practical in one's spiritual life include the following:

Will Derkse, *The Rule of Benedict for Beginners: Spirituality for Daily Life* (Collegeville, MN: Liturgical Press, 2003);

Terrence G. Kardong, *Conversation with Saint Benedict: The Rule in Today's World* (Collegeville, MN: Liturgical Press, 2012);

Rowan Williams, *The Way of St Benedict* (London: Bloomsbury Continuum, 2020); and

Norvene Vest, *Preferring Christ: A Devotional Commentary on the Rule of St. Benedict* (Harrisburg, PA: Morehouse Publishing, 1990).

The life of St. Benedict was written by Gregory the Great (d. 604) and is available in an English translation: Terrence G. Kardong, *The Life of St. Benedict by Gregory the Great: Translation and Commentary* (Collegeville, MN: Liturgical Press, 2009).

Books on The Rule of Basil are academic and include Anna M. Silvas, trans., *The Rule of St. Basil in Latin and English: A Revised Critical Edition* (Collegeville, MN: Liturgical Press, 2013). For an introduction to his life and thought see Stephen M. Hildebrand, *Basil of Caesarea (The Early Church Fathers)* (Abingdon, UK: Routledge, 2018); or, Stephen M. Hildebrand, *Basil of Caesarea (Foundations of Theological Exegesis and Christian Spirituality)* (Grand Rapids: Baker Academic, 2014).

Monastic rules were written for specific monastic communities and The Rule of Benedict is the most well-known. There are books of Christian spirituality that are not technically monastic rules but are like them. The most well-known are probably Jeremy Taylor's *Holy Living and Dying* and John Wesley's *A Plain Account of Christian Perfection*, both of which should be read by those who are spiritually mature.

Map of Important Places: Benedict of Nursia and Basil the Great

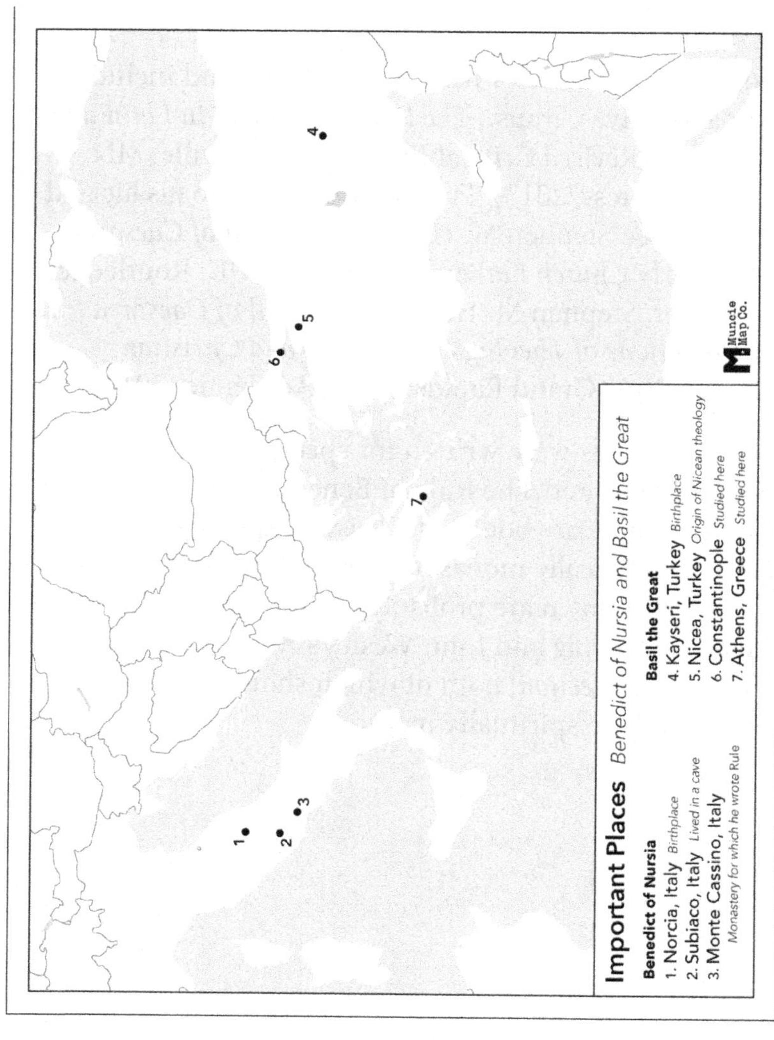

A Letter to God's Friends and Fellow Warriors On Why We Read the Sacred Roots Spiritual Classics Together

Scholars like big books; small books change the world.

~ Rev. Dr. Glen Scorgie

Dear Friends and Fellow Warriors,

Greetings in the strong name of Jesus! What a joy to know that Jesus calls us "Friend" (John 15). What an honor to stand with sisters and brothers from every century and culture to shout, "Worthy is the Lamb!" What a privilege to serve in the Lamb's army, not fighting flesh and blood, but God's *internal* (the flesh), *external* (the world) and *infernal* (the Devil) enemies. In light of this cosmic struggle, we put on a wartime (not peacetime) mindset as we follow Jesus. Moses stated that God is present and at work in every generation (Ps 90:1), and the *Sacred Roots Spiritual Classics* are for those who desire to be used within their sphere of influence like David was used by God in his generation (Ps 57:2; Acts 13:36).

Our Context: A Battle with God's Internal, External, and Infernal Enemies

Scripture teaches our daily need to choose a missional mindset (Matt 6:10). God's kingdom never advances in neutral territory. Every inch in creation, including each inch of our soul, is a contested battlefield. God's enemies are threefold. First, there is an *internal* enemy hiding within the heart of each redeemed child of God. God loves us, even though we often battle a "Judas-heart"—a tendency to betray our Lord (John 12:6). Scripture names this brokenness the "flesh," the old "man" or the "sin nature" (Rom 8; Gal 5–6). We work to kill ("mortify") this sin lest it succeed in killing us (Rom 6:13).

Second, as followers of Jesus, we battle all *external* enemies opposing the Lamb's kingdom. Sickened by sin, polluted by greed, corrupted by self-centeredness, idolatry and oppression; our world is not the way it is supposed to be. What God created good has been twisted and now often grieves the Holy Spirit. We choose to stand with Shadrach, Meshach and Abednego in refusing to bow to the principalities and powers of the age (Dan 3), or to accept the besetting sins of our ethnicities, nations and generations. Scripture and our sacred roots shine painful yet purifying light on our blind spots.

Finally, we are not ignorant of the Devil's schemes. We may not know if a demon's name is "Screwtape" or "Legion," but we do know that an *infernal* enemy opposes God's kingdom *shalom*. He is the Devil, Satan, the Father of Lies, the Accuser, and one day soon he and his demons will be completely crushed. In this time between the times, the Lamb's followers resist and renounce the Devil and all his ways with the sword of the Spirit which is the Word of God.

Our Mission: To Be Faithful Stewards and Wise Servants in Our Generation

Scripture contains a number of "history" psalms (Pss 78, 105, 106, 136; Neh 9:6–38; cf. Heb 11). These songs challenge us to reflect on women and men who chose to serve God in their generation—Abraham and Sarah,

Moses, Phinehas, Rahab, David, Esther and many others. History psalms also warn of those who ignored or refused to participate in God's work (Pharaoh, Dathan, Abiram, Og). Leaders like Rahab the prostitute (Matt 1:5; Heb 11:35; James 2:25) and King David were far from perfect (Ps 51). Yet Scripture declares that leaders like David "served the purposes of God in his own generation" (Acts 13:36).

Do you want God to use you in your generation? Are you willing to be a David or Esther today? God is already at work in our communities, schools and workplaces. Sometimes the neighborhoods with the greatest challenges (those with giants like "Goliath" and armies of Philistine enemies) are the very places God finds servants and stewards he can use (1 Sam 17; 1 Cor 4:1).

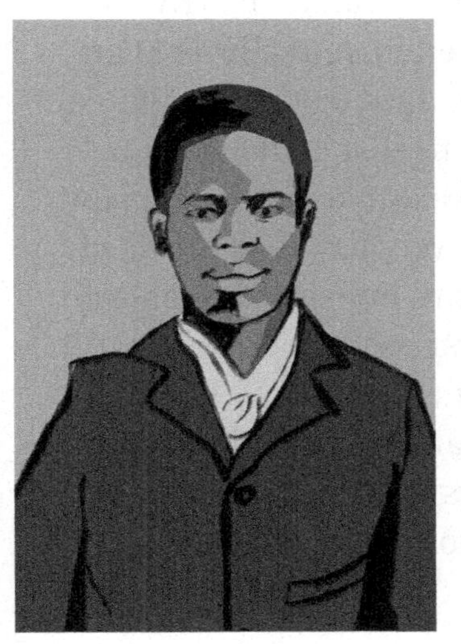

Like King David, Prince Kaboo of the Kru people in Liberia chose to participate in God's work in his generation. As a child, Prince Kaboo (1873–1893) was taken hostage by a rival tribe and was about to be executed when he experienced a supernatural deliverance. After weeks of traveling through the jungle, Kaboo arrived a mission station near Monrovia, Liberia's capital. There, as a fourteen-year-old teenager, he wholeheartedly gave his life to Jesus Christ.

Prince Kaboo took on the name Samuel Kaboo Morris at his baptism, and he spent the next four years working and studying Scripture—especially Jesus' teaching about the Holy Spirit as recorded by his friend John (John 14–17). Kaboo was fascinated with the Holy Spirit, for he had personally experienced the Holy Spirit's powerful deliverance. Eventually, the missionaries told Kaboo they had taught him all they knew and that if he wanted to learn more about the Holy Spirit, he would need to travel to the United States. Kaboo felt the need for more training about the Holy Spirit before being ready to return to the Kru as an evangelist. With no shoes or money, Kaboo walked to Monrovia's harbor to find passage to New York—trusting his Father in Heaven to provide.

Kaboo's story is powerful. The ship that transported Kaboo experienced revival with the captain and many crew coming to Christ. Within a few hours of arriving in New York, Kaboo led seventeen men to Christ at an inner-city rescue mission. On his third day in the United States, the eighteen-year-old evangelist preached at a Sunday school meeting and revival broke out with a new missionary society organized that very day. God provided money for Kaboo's college tuition, housing, books and necessities. By the end of his first week in America, Kaboo had arrived in Fort Wayne, Indiana to begin studying at Taylor University—an evangelical college committed to raising up workers for the harvest fields who walk in the power of the Holy Spirit (Matt 9:36; Acts 1:8).

Prince Kaboo's arrival at Taylor University transformed not only Taylor University's campus, but also the whole city of Fort Wayne. On his first Sunday in town, Kaboo walked to the front of the church and asked for permission to pray. As he prayed, the power and presence of the Holy

Spirit descended on the congregation in a way none had ever experienced before. The pastor reported, "what I said and what Sammy said I do not remember, but I know my soul was on fire as never before. . . . No such visitation of the Holy Spirit had ever been witnessed" by our congregation.[1]

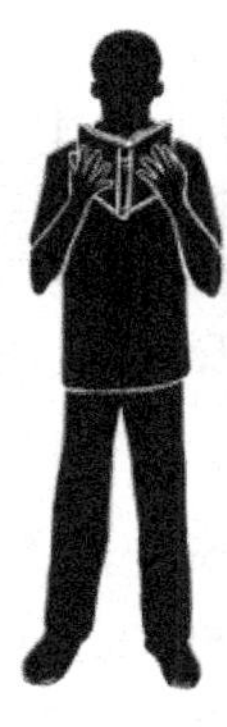

Two years later, on May 12, 1893, at the age of twenty, Prince Samuel Kaboo Morris died from an illness contracted after traveling through a snowstorm to preach. Since his death, Kaboo's story has influenced thousands of students at Taylor University and elsewhere to participate with the Holy Spirit in mission and seek the Spirit's power in witness. John Wengatz was a student at Taylor in 1906, the year he first read Kaboo's story. Some fifty years later, after a lifetime invested as a missionary in Africa, Wengatz remarked "my tears never cease to flow as I read that unrepeatable story."[2] Although Kaboo died at twenty, he was used mightily by God in his generation. Will those who tell the story of your life say the same?

Our Vision: Toward Ten Thousand "Tozers"

If you are pursuing God with the same passion and hunger displayed by Samuel Kaboo Morris, than you will be glad to meet A. W. Tozer (1897–1963). Tozer grew up poor without the opportunity to complete high school. While working in a tire factory he heard the good news

---

1 Lindley Baldwin, *Samuel Morris: The African Boy God Sent to Prepare an American University for Its Mission to the World* (Minneapolis, MN: Bethany House, 1987), 59.

2 John Wengatz, *Sammy Morris: Spirit-Filled Life* (Upland, IN: Taylor University Press, 1954), Preface.

about Jesus, repented and believed. At nineteen, he began to preach, becoming one of the most influential pastors in his generation. His books *The Pursuit of God* and *The Knowledge of the Holy* have helped millions know and love the Triune God revealed in Scripture. When asked how he learned to read Scripture with such clarity and theological depth, Pastor Tozer would often point to his "friends" and "teachers." These teachers were a list of some thirty-five Christian spiritual classics read and reread throughout Tozer's life. *Sacred Roots Spiritual Classics* (*SRSC*) are for those with a hunger for the Holy Spirit like Prince Kaboo and a desire to be used like Pastor Tozer.

The Sacred Roots Project envisions ten thousand Christian leaders, serving in challenging ministry contexts across North America, engaging with spiritual classics in community by the year 2030. Will you join this growing community as we pursue God together by reading and discussing spiritual classics with gospel friends and kingdom co-workers (Matt 9:35)?

A larger dream also informs the Sacred Roots Project—a dream that imagines a million Christian workers equipped to serve among the global poor (Matt 9:36–38). The Center for the Study of Global Christianity reports that in the middle of 2020 there are approximately two and a half billion people living in urban poverty.[3] This number will increase to over four billion by the year 2050. Sacred Roots dreams of equipping one million Christian leaders among this great multitude—women and men like Prince Kaboo—with access to excellent editions of some of the greatest spiritual classics the Christian tradition has

3 For the most current statistics, see www.gordonconwell.edu/center-for-global-christianity/resources/status-of-global-christianity/.

produced. Ultimately, the goal is increased faithfulness as leaders mature in representing Christ in local churches that are centered on Scripture, grounded in Great Tradition truth (Nicene), and engaged in contextually relevant witness to Christ's love in thousands of diverse contexts.[4]

Our Strategy: Scripture, Friendship and Spiritual Classics

Sacred Roots' strategy is simple. We believe fresh readings of Christian spiritual classics can lead Christian leaders into a deeper engagement with the God revealed in Scripture and into deeper friendships with one another.

Christian spiritual classics strengthen and deepen our roots in Scripture and help us produce the Spirit's fruit. One day Jesus asked a serious student of the Bible a simple question, "*How do you read it?*" (Luke 10:26). Of the more than three hundred questions asked by Jesus in the Gospels, few are more relevant today. Faithfulness in our generation demands that we learn to read Scripture in a way consistent with the foundational truths held by followers of Jesus in every culture since the first century. We read Christian spiritual classics to discover faithful and fruitful readings of Scripture. As Dr. Davis has noted, the church's "Great Tradition" perennially opens our eyes to new riches in Scripture's "Authoritative Tradition."[5]

A truth believed by all Christians, in all places, and at all times is that there is one God who exists as Father, Son, and Holy Spirit. From "before to beyond time," an eternal

---

4 Don Davis, *Sacred Roots: A Primer on Retrieving the Great Tradition* (Wichita, KS: The Urban Ministry Institute, 2010), 35–45.

5 Ibid.

friendship between the Trinity's three persons has existed at the center of reality. Spiritual friendship provides the start and heart of truth. Just as spiritual classics can reveal new riches from Scripture, so they help us grow in love for God and neighbors. They can provide practical help in deepening our friendships with the Father, the Son, the Holy Spirit and with other believers—both with believers in this generation and with those surrounding us in the great cloud of witnesses (Heb 12:1; 13:7). Why do Christian leaders desperately need to pursue strong friendships? Start with these three reasons.

1. First, each of us has eyes far too small to see what God wants to show us! No one can begin to grasp the great things God is doing across 100 billion galaxies and throughout the many generations since the universe's creation. Friends, standing in different places provides additional eyes to see from different perspectives what God is doing in the world and across history.

2. Second, each of us battles a sinful nature that distorts our perception of the truth. We need friends who speak truth to us, sharpening us like iron sharpening iron (Prov 27:17).

3. Third, all of us view creation through a particular culture's time and place. Each culture exists with a unique version of virtue and vice. Friends who speak to us from other cultures and centuries often affirm virtues in our culture, but they can also reflect ways our culture's vice habitually offends against kingdom *shalom*.

In sum, *Sacred Roots Spiritual Classics* help us grow in our friendship with God and neighbor (Matt 22:37–40). Neighbors include the living Christian leaders with whom we read and discuss this spiritual classic. However, "neighbor" also includes the author (or authors) of this spiritual classic. These women and men walked faithfully with God and neighbor. Their life and teachings produced good fruit in their generation and then continued to do so in the lives of other Christian leaders—often across many cultures and centuries. As an editorial team, we can personally testify to the fruitfulness of the time we have spent with our "friends," the "ancient witnesses" in the *Sacred Roots Spiritual Classics*. If you choose to invest in careful conversation with these saints of old (Heb 13:7), we are confident you will not only experience practical fruit in the present, but you will also gain new friends for eternity.

Tactical Notes: Christian Leaders Are Christian Readers

Throughout church history, fruitful Christian leaders have been intentional readers. Augustine (d. 430), a pastor and bishop in Africa, was challenged to a new level of ministry by reading a spiritual biography about an Egyptian Christian leader named Anthony (d. 356).[6] Protestant leaders like Martin Luther, John Calvin, John Wesley, Elizabeth Fry, Phoebe Palmer and many others all published editions of spiritual classics for Christian leaders in their generation. Charles Harrison Mason (d. 1961), founder of the largest Pentecostal denomination in North America (Church of God in Christ), was called to ministry through a reading

6 Athanasius, *Renewal in Christ: Athanasius on the Christian Life*, ed. Jeremy Treat, *Sacred Roots Spiritual Classics 6* (Wichita, KS: The Urban Ministry Institute, 2022).

of the autobiography of missionary and evangelist Amanda Smith.[7] More recently, leaders like C. S. Lewis, A. W. Tozer, James Houston, and Rick Warren have encouraged Christian leaders to read wisely, especially choosing Christian spiritual classics.[8]

How to Read the Text

***Plan* your reading.** Reading a spiritual classic is a bit like reading your Bible. You can read it anywhere or anytime, but there are times and places that will position you to better receive insight and truth. *SRSC* readers tend to read each spiritual classic several times, and many will "read" it in both a written version (print or electronic) and in an audible version (audio book). We read to hear what the original author of the text is saying and to understand what the Holy Spirit might be directing our attention to hear or reflect upon. On your day of rest (Sabbath) reserve some time to read or at least set aside some time to plan when you will read from your spiritual classic that week. If you have a daily commute, perhaps use some of the time to listen and reflect on an audible version of the *SRSC*.

***Work* your reading plan.** Once you have planned to read your spiritual classic, begin with the **Introduction.** The introduction is written by a contemporary friend with significant ministry experience. This friend has spent much

---

7 Amanda Smith, *An Autobiography: The Story of the Lord's Dealings with Mrs. Amanda Smith, the Colored Evangelist; Containing an Account of Her Life Work of Faith, and Her Travels in America, England, Ireland, Scotland, India, and Africa, as an Independent Missionary* (Chicago: Meyer, 1893).

8 Explore the essays in Jamin Goggin and Kyle Strobel, eds., *Reading the Christian Spiritual Classics: A Guide for Evangelicals* (Downers Grove, IL: InterVarsity, 2013).

time reading and getting to know the spiritual classic and the author who wrote it. Often, the introduction is written by someone who has read the spiritual classic dozens, if not hundreds, of times. The introduction will help you get the most out of your first several readings of the text.

After reading the Introduction, notice that all *Sacred Roots Spiritual Classics* are divided into eight **Chapters**. These chapters are not always of equal length, but they all are weighty enough to engage your head, heart, and hands as well as your habitat and habits. Following the eight chapters, every *SRSC* includes a short section called **Continuing the Conversation.** If you enjoyed reading the spiritual classic, then Continuing the Conversation will help you discover more resources to engage the author(s) of the spiritual classic.

The *Sacred Roots Spiritual Classics* are divided into ten parts to make it easier to talk about the text with friends and co-workers. The table below provides four (of many) examples of how to read a *SRSC* with a group of friends. When friends commit to read and discuss a *SRSC* together, the group is called a **Sacred Roots Cohort.**

<table>
<tr><th>SRSC Section to Read</th><th>"Sunday School" Class</th><th>"Church-Based Seminary" Module</th><th>Monthly Pastor's Meeting</th><th>Quarterly Retreat Discussion Group</th></tr>
<tr><td></td><td>Ten Weeks</td><td>Eight Weeks</td><td>Monthly</td><td>Quarterly</td></tr>
<tr><td>Introduction</td><td>Week 1</td><td rowspan="2">Week 1</td><td rowspan="3">Month 1</td><td rowspan="10">Read text before retreat and then discuss</td></tr>
<tr><td>Ch. 1</td><td>Week 2</td></tr>
<tr><td>Ch. 2</td><td>Week 3</td><td>Week 2</td></tr>
<tr><td>Ch. 3</td><td>Week 4</td><td>Week 3</td><td rowspan="4">Month 2</td></tr>
<tr><td>Ch. 4</td><td>Week 5</td><td>Week 4</td></tr>
<tr><td>Ch. 5</td><td>Week 6</td><td>Week 5</td></tr>
<tr><td>Ch. 6</td><td>Week 7</td><td>Week 6</td></tr>
<tr><td>Ch. 7</td><td>Week 8</td><td>Week 7</td><td rowspan="3">Month 3</td></tr>
<tr><td>Ch. 8</td><td>Week 9</td><td rowspan="2">Week 8</td></tr>
<tr><td>Continuing the Conversation</td><td>Week 10</td></tr>
</table>

***Review* your reading.** The best readers, like the best leaders, do more than make a plan and work it. They also pause to take time to review their work—or in this case—their reading.[9] Robert Clinton has noted that only around 25% of leaders in the Bible finished well.[10] If we hope to finish well in our generation we must learn to *attend* to our habitat, our head, our heart, our hands, and our habits. To *attend* means to pay attention, to apply our self, to prioritize and to value something enough to give it our time and our energy. Each chapter concludes with five types of questions aimed at helping you review your progress toward finishing well and hearing Jesus say, "Well done, good and faithful servant" (Matt 25:23).

Habitat? Habitat questions ask us to pause and look around at our environment, our culture, our generation, our nationality, and the things that make up the *Zeitgeist* (spirit of the times). Questions may ask about the author's habitat or our own. Since the *SRSC* were written across many centuries and cultures, they often help us notice aspects of our culture needing attention.

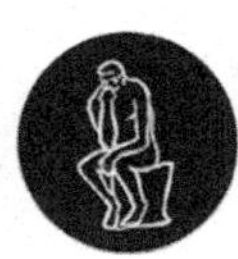

Head? Auguste Rodin's sculpture known as *The Thinker* sits before an 18-foot-tall sculpture called *The Gates of Hell*. The massive sculptural group reflects Rodin's engagement with a spiritual classic by Dante, *The Divine Comedy*. *Head questions* require serious intellectual

---

9 The PWR (Plan, Work, Review) process is explained further by Don Allsman, *The Heroic Venture: A Parable of Project Leadership* (Wichita, KS: The Urban Ministry Institute, 2006).

10 Robert Clinton, *The Making of a Leader: Recognizing the Lessons and Stages of Leadership Development*, Rev. ed. (Colorado Springs, CO: NavPress, 2012), 185–87.

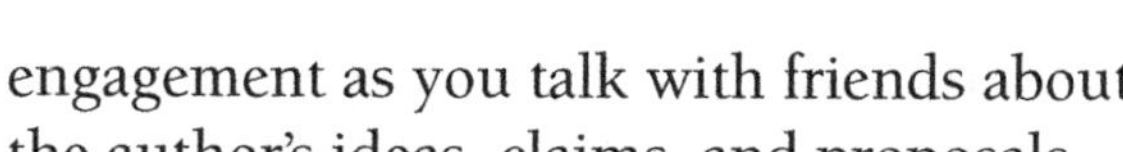

engagement as you talk with friends about the author's ideas, claims, and proposals.

Heart? In August of 1541 John Calvin wrote a letter to a friend with this promise: "When I remember that I am not my own, I offer up my heart presented as a sacrifice to God." Calvin's personal seal expressed this sincere desire. God not only owns our mind, but also our will and emotions. *Heart questions* will help you attend to the people and things to which you give your loves.

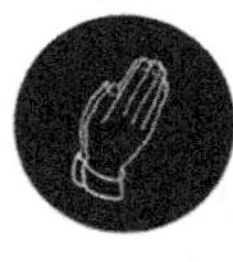

Hands? Albrecht Dürer sketched a drawing called *Study of the Hands of an Apostle* in the year 1508. The apostles were men of action, yet Dürer portrays the apostle's hands in prayer. The action to which *SRSC* call us are often surprising. *Hands questions* will challenge you to evaluate carefully what action you are to take after a particular reading.

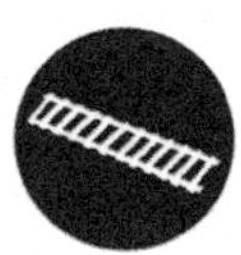

Habits? Charlotte Mason (d. 1923) was a master teacher. She believed Christian formation must carefully attend to habit formation. Like laying railroad tracks, habit formation is hard work. But once laid, great work requires little effort just as railroad cars run smoothly on tracks. *Habit questions* challenge you to reflect on small daily or weekly actions that form your character and the character of those around you.

Reading with Friends

The *Sacred Roots Spiritual Classics* are not meant to be read alone; indeed, it is impossible to do so. Every time we open a *SRSC* we read a book that *has been read* by thousands of Christian leaders in previous generations, *is being read* by thousands of Christian leaders in our generation, and *will be read* (if the return of Christ tarries) by thousands of Christian leaders in generations after us. The readers before us have already finished their race. These thousands of Christian leaders read the text in hundreds of different cultures and across dozens of different generations. All these "friends" read this text with you now. As you read the *SRSC*, imagine yourself talking about *Benedict's Rule* (*SRSC* 2) with the reformer Martin Luther; or picture yourself discussing Madam Guyon's *A Short and Easy Method of Prayer* with the missionary Amy Carmichael. Remember you never read a *Sacred Roots Spiritual Classic* alone.

However, it is not just leaders who have gone before, it is also leaders in the present with whom you must imagine reading this *SRSC*. Whatever benefit you find in reading will be doubled when you share it with a friend. Whatever trouble or difficulty you find in reading the text will be halved when you share it with a friend. Resolve to never read a *Sacred Roots Spiritual Classic* alone.

Perhaps you have noticed that the word "generation" has already appeared in this preface more than fifteen times? The *SRSC* represent the work of many generations working together. Five generations of evangelicals have worked and prayed together on this project since its public commencement in 2018. But these five generations of living evangelicals represent only a small sample of the many generations who have tested the faithfulness and fruitfulness of the *SRSC*. Why does this matter? In part, it matters because these texts are treasures to use and then pass on to the next generation of leaders. Recognize the emerging leaders God has called you to serve and steward—share the *Sacred Roots Spiritual Classics* with them.

Careful readers of Scripture know that the most influential leaders among God's people have always worked in teams. King David's teams became legends—"the three," "the thirty." The list of Paul's missionary and ministry team members whose first name we know from the New Testament runs to nearly one hundred. Our Sacred Roots team of teams prays that this text will be a blessing and a reliable resource for you and your gospel friends as you pursue kingdom business together.

Grace and Peace,

Don, Uche, Greg, May, Ryan, Isaiah, and Hank

The Nicene Creed with Scriptural Support

The Urban Ministry Institute

We believe in one God,
Deut 6:4–5; Mark 12:29; 1 Cor 8:6

the Father Almighty,
Gen 17:1; Dan 4:35; Matt 6:9; Eph 4:6; Rev 1:8

Maker of heaven and earth
Gen 1:1; Isa 40:28; Rev 10:6

and of all things visible and invisible.
Ps 148; Rom 11:36; Rev 4:11

We believe in one Lord Jesus Christ, the only Begotten Son of God, begotten of the Father before all ages, God from God, Light from Light, True God from True God, begotten not created, of the same essence as the Father,
John 1:1–2; 3:18; 8:58; 14:9–10; 20:28; Col 1:15, 17; Heb 1:3–6

through whom all things were made.
John 1:3; Col 1:16

Who for us men and for our salvation came down from heaven and was incarnate by the Holy Spirit and the Virgin Mary and became human.
Matt 1:20–23; Luke 19:10; John 1:14; 6:38

Who for us too, was crucified under Pontius Pilate, suffered and was buried.
Matt 27:1–2; Mark 15:24–39, 43–47; Acts 13:29; Rom 5:8; Heb 2:10; 13:12

The third day he rose again according to the Scriptures,

Mark 16:5–7; Luke 24:6–8; Acts 1:3; Rom 6:9; 10:9; 2 Tim 2:8

ascended into heaven, and is seated at the right hand of the Father.

Mark 16:19; Eph 1:19–20

He will come again in glory to judge the living and the dead, and his Kingdom will have no end.

Isa 9:7; Matt 24:30; John 5:22; Acts 1:11; 17:31; Rom 14:9; 2 Cor 5:10; 2 Tim 4:1

We believe in the Holy Spirit, the Lord and life-giver,

Gen 1:1–2; Job 33:4; Pss 104:30; 139:7–8; Luke 4:18–19; John 3:5–6; Acts 1:1–2; 1 Cor 2:11; Rev 3:22

who proceeds from the Father and the Son,

John 14:16–18, 26; 15:26; 20:22

who together with the Father and Son is worshiped and glorified,

Isa 6:3; Matt 28:19; 2 Cor 13:14; Rev 4:8

who spoke by the prophets.

Num 11:29; Mic 3:8; Acts 2:17–18; 2 Pet 1:21

We believe in one holy, catholic, and apostolic Church.

Matt 16:18; 1 Cor 1:2; 10:17; Eph 5:25–28; 1 Tim 3:15; Rev 7:9

We acknowledge one baptism for the forgiveness of sin,

Acts 22:16; Eph 4:4–5; 1 Pet 3:21

And we look for the resurrection of the dead and the life of the age to come.

Isa 11:6–10; Mic 4:1–7; Luke 18:29–30; Rev 21:1–5; 21:22–22:5

Amen.

Memory Verses

Below are suggested memory verses, one for each section of the Creed.

The Father

Rev 4:11 (ESV) — Worthy are you, our Lord and God, to receive glory and honor and power, for you created all things, and by your will they existed and were created.

The Son

John 1:1 (ESV) — In the beginning was the Word, and the Word was with God, and the Word was God.

The Son's Mission

1 Cor 15:3–5 (ESV) — For what I received I passed on to you as of first importance: that Christ died for our sins according to the Scriptures, that he was buried, that he was raised on the third day according to the Scriptures, and that he appeared to Peter, and then to the Twelve.

The Holy Spirit

Rom 8:11 (ESV) — If the Spirit of him who raised Jesus from the dead dwells in you, he who raised Christ Jesus from the dead will also give life to your mortal bodies through his Spirit who dwells in you.

The Church

1 Pet 2:9 (ESV) — But you are a chosen race, a royal priesthood, a holy nation, a people for his own possession, that you may proclaim the excellencies of him who called you out of darkness into his marvelous light.

Our Hope

1 Thess 4:16–17 (ESV) — For the Lord himself will descend from heaven with a cry of command, with the voice of an archangel, and with the sound of the trumpet of God. And the dead in Christ will rise first. Then we who are alive, who are left, will be caught up together with them in the clouds to meet the Lord in the air, and so we will always be with the Lord.

From Before to Beyond Time:
The Plan of God and Human History

Adapted from Suzanne de Dietrich. *God's Unfolding Purpose.* Philadelphia: Westminster Press, 1976.

I. Before Time (Eternity Past)

1 Cor. 2:7 (ESV) – But we impart a secret and hidden wisdom of God, which God decreed before the ages for our glory (cf. Titus 1:2).

A. The Eternal Triune God
B. God's Eternal Purpose
C. The Mystery of Iniquity
D. The Principalities and Powers

II. Beginning of Time (Creation and Fall)

Gen. 1:1 (ESV) – In the beginning, God created the heavens and the earth.

A. Creative Word
B. Humanity
C. Fall
D. Reign of Death and First Signs of Grace

III. Unfolding of Time (God's Plan Revealed through Israel)

Gal. 3:8 (ESV) – And the Scripture, foreseeing that God would justify the Gentiles by faith, preached the Gospel beforehand to Abraham, saying, "In you shall all the nations be blessed" (cf. Rom. 9:4-5).

A. Promise (Patriarchs)
B. Exodus and Covenant at Sinai
C. Promised Land
D. The City, the Temple, and the Throne (Prophet, Priest, and King)
E. Exile
F. Remnant

IV. Fullness of Time (Incarnation of the Messiah)

Gal. 4:4-5 (ESV) – But when the fullness of time had come, God sent forth his Son, born of woman, born under the law, to redeem those who were under the law, so that we might receive adoption as sons.

A. The King Comes to His Kingdom
B. The Present Reality of His Reign
C. The Secret of the Kingdom: the Already and the Not Yet
D. The Crucified King
E. The Risen Lord

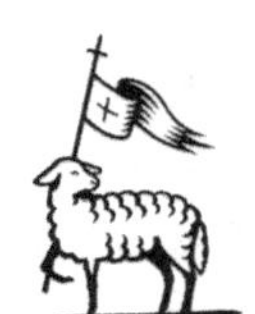

V. The Last Times (The Descent of the Holy Spirit)

Acts 2:16-18 (ESV) – But this is what was uttered through the prophet Joel: "'And in the last days it shall be,' God declares, 'that I will pour out my Spirit on all flesh, and your sons and your daughters shall prophesy, and your young men shall see visions, and your old men shall dream dreams; even on my male servants and female servants in those days I will pour out my Spirit, and they shall prophesy.'"

A. Between the Times: the Church as Foretaste of the Kingdom
B. The Church as Agent of the Kingdom
C. The Conflict Between the Kingdoms of Darkness and Light

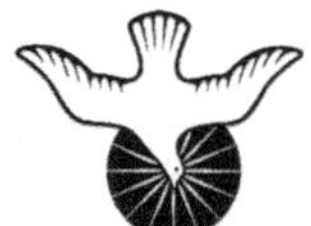

VI. The Fulfillment of Time (The Second Coming)

Matt. 13:40-43 (ESV) – Just as the weeds are gathered and burned with fire, so will it be at the close of the age. The Son of Man will send his angels, and they will gather out of his Kingdom all causes of sin and all lawbreakers, and throw them into the fiery furnace. In that place there will be weeping and gnashing of teeth. Then the righteous will shine like the sun in the Kingdom of their Father. He who has ears, let him hear.

A. The Return of Christ
B. Judgment
C. The Consummation of His Kingdom

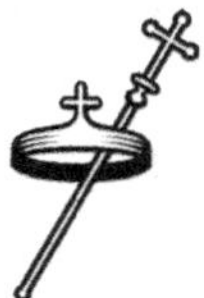

VII. Beyond Time (Eternity Future)

1 Cor. 15:24-28 (ESV) – Then comes the end, when he delivers the Kingdom to God the Father after destroying every rule and every authority and power. For he must reign until he has put all his enemies under his feet. The last enemy to be destroyed is death. For "God has put all things in subjection under his feet." But when it says, "all things are put in subjection," it is plain that he is excepted who put all things in subjection under him. When all things are subjected to him, then the Son himself will also be subjected to him who put all things in subjection under him, that God may be all in all.

A. Kingdom Handed Over to God the Father

B. God as All in All

About the Sacred Roots Project

The Sacred Roots Thriving in Ministry Project seeks to equip and empower under-resourced congregational leaders in urban, rural, and incarcerated communities. One avenue for accomplishing this goal is the *Sacred Roots Spiritual Classics*, a series of abridged Christian spiritual classics that equip congregational leaders to engage the wealth of the Great Tradition.

Other *Sacred Roots Spiritual Classics* include:

Praying the Psalms with Augustine and Friends
Edited by Dr. Carmen Joy Imes

Spiritual Friendship:
Learning How to Be Friends with God and One Another
Edited by Rev. Dr. Hank Voss

Christian Mission and Poverty:
Wisdom from 2,000 Years of Church History
Edited by Rev. Dr. Andrew Draper

Books Jesus Read: Learning from the Apocrypha
Edited by Dr. Robert F. Lay

Renewal in Christ: Athanasius on the Christian Life
Edited by Rev. Dr. Jeremy Treat

Social Justice and Scripture: The Witness of Las Casas
Edited by Rev. Dr. Robert Chao Romero and Rev. Marcos Canales

The Senior Editorial Team of the *Sacred Roots Spiritual Classics* includes:

Rev. Dr. Don Davis
Publisher
The Urban Ministry Institute

Rev. Dr. Hank Voss
Executive Editor
Taylor University

Dr. Uche Anizor
Senior Editor
Biola University, Talbot School of Theology

Rev. Dr. Greg Peters
Senior Editor
Biola University, Torrey Honors College

Dr. May Young
Senior Editor
Taylor University

Rev. Ryan Carter
Managing Editor
The Urban Ministry Institute

Isaiah Swain
Managing Editor
Taylor University

The Senior Editorial Team acknowledges and appreciates Dr. Gwenfair Adams (Gordon-Conwell Theological Seminary), Dr. Betsy Barber (Biola University), Rev. Dr.

Nigel Black (Winslow Baptist Church), Dr. Jonathan Calvillo (Boston University School of Divinity), Dr. Laura Edwards (Taylor University), Rev. Nathan Esla (Lutheran Bible Translators), Dr. Nancy Frazier (Dallas Theological Seminary), Dr. Jeff Greenman (Regent College), Dr. Kevin Hector (University of Chicago Divinity School), Rev. Dr. Wil Hernandez (Centerquest), Dr. James Houston (Regent College), Dr. Evan B. Howard (Spirituality Shoppe), Rev. Susie Krehbiel (Missionary, Retired), Rev. Dr. Tim Larsen (Wheaton College), Dr. Stephanie Lowery (Africa International University), Dr. Daniel Owens (Hanoi Bible College), Rev. Dr. Oscar Owens (West Angeles Church of God), Dr. Bob Priest (Taylor University), Rev. Dr. Robert Romero (University of California, Los Angeles), Rev. Dr. Jerry Root (Wheaton College), Dr. Fred Sanders (Biola University), Dr. Glen Scorgie (Bethel University), Dr. Kyle Strobel (Biola University), Dr. Daniel Treier (Wheaton College), and Dr. Kevin Vanhoozer (Trinity Evangelical Divinity School) for their support and encouragement. Illustrations throughout the *Sacred Roots* volumes are done by Naomi Noyes.

The *Sacred Roots Spiritual Classics* are dedicated to all Christian leaders who have loved the poor and have recognized the importance of Christian spiritual classics for nurturing the next generation. We especially recognize these fourteen:

John Wesley (1703–1791)

Rebecca Protten (1718–1780)

Elizabeth Fry (1780–1845)

Phoebe Palmer (1807–1874)

Dora Yu (1873–1931)

A. W. Tozer (1897–1963)

Howard Thurman (1899–1981)

Watchman Nee (1903–1972)

James Houston (1922–)

J. I. Packer (1926–2020)

Tom Oden (1931–2016)

René Padilla (1932–)

Dallas Willard (1935–2013)

Bruce Demarest (1935–)

Remember your leaders,
those who spoke to you the word of God.
Consider the outcome of their way of life,
and imitate their faith.

~ Hebrews 13:7

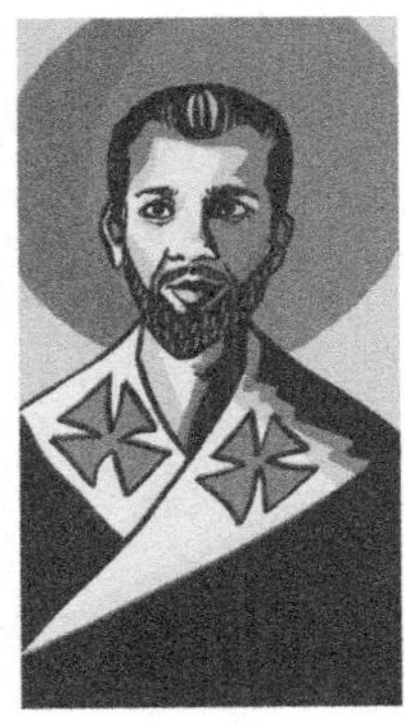

Scripture Index

Genesis

1:1, 161, 165
1:1–2, 162
3:6, 87
17:1, 161
21:6, 89
25:33, 86
28:12, 72

Exodus

18:19, 60

Leviticus

11:44–45, 124

Numbers

11:29, 162

Deuteronomy

6:4–5, 161
25:33, 87

Judges

17:6, 13

1 Samuel

2:11–4:18, 30
3, 21
17, 147

1 Kings

19:8, 87

Nehemiah

9:6–38, 146

Job

8:21, 89
12:11, 103
33:4, 162
34:3, 103

Psalms

7:9, 102
7:10, 72
14:1, 73
14:2, 73
14:3, 73
14:4, 68
15, 123
15:1, 67
15:2–3, 67
15:4, 68
15:8, 103
18:9–11, 97
18:24, 73
18:44, 56
22:7, 75
23:4, 96
24:15, 103
27:4, 122
27:14, 74
32:5, 75
33:1, 103
34:9, 31, 67
34:12, 66, 67
34:13–14, 67
34:14, 76
36:2, 72
37:5, 75
38:1–2, 52
38:7–9, 77
38:10, 73
39:1–3, 70
40:11, 28
44:22, 74
46:7, 103
48:10, 108
49:21, 74
50:1–17, 29
50:10, 96
50:23, 138
51, 147
57:2, 145
66:10–11, 74
66:12, 74
72:28, 49
73:22–23, 75
76:11, 72
78, 146
88:16, 76
90:1, 145
93:20, 24
94:11, 72
95:7–8, 66
104:30, 162
105, 146
106, 146
106:1, 75
115:1, 68

118:1, 75
119:32, 70
119:64, 122
119:71, 76
119:73, 76
119:107, 77
119:163, 97
119:164, 122
131:1, 71
131:2, 71
136, 146
136:9, 49, 68
139:3, 72
139:7–8, 162
140:12, 76
148, 161

Proverbs

1:8, 66
4:20, 66
6:20, 66
10:19, 71, 76
15:3, 73
16:25, 73
18:21, 71
19:10, 86
20:13, 49
23:14, 30
27:17, 152
27:21, 14
29:19, 30

Ecclesiastes

2:2, 88
7:6, 89

Isaiah

1:2, 28
6:3, 162
9:7, 162
11:6–10, 162
40:28, 161
58:9, 67

Jeremiah

48:10, 85

Ezekiel

20:27, 28
33:11, 68
34:3–4, 33

Daniel

1:6–16, 87
3, 146
4:35, 161
13:44–62, 21

Amos

5:13, 52

Micah

3:8, 162
4:1–7, 162

Matthew

1:5, 147
1:20–23, 161
3:4, 87
4:1–11, 132
4:2, 87
5:8, 96
5:10, 48
5:11–12, 95
5:34, 48
5:39–41, 75
5:44, 48
5:46–47, 94
6:9, 161
6:10, 145
6:33, 31
7:3, 29
7:12, 48
7:14, 56, 70
7:24–25, 68
9:12, 32
9:35, 150
9:36, 148
9:36–38, 150
10:10, 62
10:22, 74
11:29, 95
13:40–43, 166
14:13, 91
14:15, 91
14:22–23, 133
16:18, 162
16:24, 35, 48
17:1–8, 133
18:6, 41
18:15, 85
18:15–16, 57
19:18, 48
19:21, 84, 88
20:28, 62
22:36, 94
22:37–39, 48
22:37–40, 153
22:39, 94
23:3, 50
23:6, 22
23:8, 63
23:12, 95
24:30, 162
25, 112
25:23, 157
25:35, 108
25:36, 16, 48
25:40, 16, 23
26:36–46, 133
27:1–2, 161
27:46, 123
28:19, 162

Mark

1:12–13, 132
1:35–39, 132
6:31–34, 132
6:45–46, 133
8:34, 35
9:2–8, 133

9:34, 62
10:19, 48
10:29–30, 85
10:43–44, 62
10:45, 62
12:29, 161
12:30–31, 48
14:32–42, 133
15:24–39, 161
15:43–47, 161
16:5–7, 162
16:19, 162

Luke

3:23, 132
4:1–13, 132
4:18–19, 162
4:42–44, 132
5:16, 99, 132
6:12–16, 132
6:14–15, 133
6:21, 89
6:25, 89
6:27, 48
6:28, 48
6:31, 48
6:32, 94
9:23, 35, 48
9:28–36a, 133
10:7, 62
10:16, 56, 57
10:26, 151
10:47, 48
11, 99
11:1, 132
12:23, 84
12:48, 30
13:26, 85
14:7–8, 22
14:8–10, 23
14:11, 71, 95
15:5, 33
16:2, 21, 30, 41
16:15, 36
16:25, 86
18:13, 77
18:14, 71
18:20, 48
18:29–30, 162
19:10, 161
21:34, 78
22:15, 80
22:40b–46, 133
24:6–8, 162

John

1:1, 163
1:1–2, 161
1:3, 161
1:14, 161
3:5–6, 162
3:18, 161
3:36, 94
4:34, 96
5:22, 162
6:9, 91

6:38, 56, 74, 161
7:28, 36
8:58, 161
10:5, 61
12:6, 146
12:35, 67
12:50, 94, 96, 97
13:6–9, 61
13:34, 94
14–17, 148
14:9–10, 161
14:16–18, 162
14:26, 162
15, 145
15:12–13, 35, 93
15:13, 92
15:26, 162
18:1, 133
20:22, 162
20:28, 35, 161

Acts

1:1–2, 162
1:3, 162
1:8, 148
1:11, 162
2:16–18, 166
2:17–18, 162
2:42, 4, 70
2:44–45, 4
3:1, 123
4:32, 77, 92
4:35, 15, 82, 93
5:1–11, 42
5:29, 61
10:9, 123
13:29, 161
13:36, 145, 147
17:31, 162
22:16, 162

Romans

2:4, 68
2:11, 29
2:22, 85
5:8, 161
6:9, 162
6:13, 146
8, 146
8:11, 163
8:13, 123
8:15, 28
8:17, 70
8:36, 74
8:37, 74
9:4–5, 165
10:9, 162
11:36, 161
12, 45
12:1, 124
12:10, 22, 83
12:11, 49
12:13, 117
13:9, 48

13:11, 66
13:13, 51
13:14, 86, 123
14:9, 162

1 Corinthians

1:2, 162
1:10, 4
2:7, 165
2:9, 50
2:11, 162
4:1, 35, 147
4:12, 75
5:5, 58
5:13, 58
6:1, 85
6:7, 85
7:7, 79
7:15, 58
8:6, 161
9:25, 86
9:27, 29, 48, 86
10:17, 162
10:31, 95
11:1, 124
11:22, 93
12, 45
14:30, 52, 104
14:34, 52
14:40, 23
15:3–5, 163
15:10, 68
15:15, 35
15:24–28, 167

2 Corinthians

2:7, 33
2:8, 33
5:10, 162
6:3, 86
6:4–6, 86
7:1, 123
9:7, 57
10:4–5, 60
10:17, 68
11:26, 75
11:27, 86
13:14, 162

Galatians

1:8, 61
3:8, 165
3:27, 123
3:28, 29
4:4–5, 166
4:4–7, 4
5–6, 146
5:13, 62
5:16, 49
5:22, 85, 89
5:22–23, 85
6:10, 108
6:16, 138

Ephesians

1:19–20, 162
2:10, 124
4:1, 124
4:1–7, 4
4:2, 61
4:4–5, 162
4:6, 161
4:20, 123
4:24, 123
4:29, 52
4:32, 4
5:19, 102
5:21, 61, 62
5:25–28, 162
6:8, 29
6:14–15, 67

Philippians

2:3, 62, 95
2:8, 24, 35, 70, 74
3:12, 123
3:12–16, 123
3:19, 90

Colossians

1:15, 161
1:16, 161
1:17, 161
3:5, 123
3:5–17, 123
4:6, 52

1 Thessalonians

1:6, 80
2:7, 35
2:8, 35
2:12, 67
4:16–17, 164
5:15, 48
5:17, 99
5:20, 60

1 Timothy

2:1, 103
2:8, 102
3:3, 49
3:13, 41
3:15, 162
4:7–8, 123
5:4, 123
5:6, 86
5:20, 82
5:23, 91
6:11, 123

2 Timothy

2:8, 162
2:16, 49
2:22, 123
3:1–2, 86
3:3, 86
4:1, 162
4:2, 29

Titus

1:2, 165
1:7, 49
2:12, 123

Hebrews

1:3–6, 161
2:10, 161
5:14, 123
11, 146
11:35, 147
12, 65
12:1, 152
12:14, 123
12:16, 86
13:7, 152, 153, 171
13:12, 161
13:17a, 121
13:17, 63

James

2:25, 147
4:8, 122, 124
4:10, 116

1 Peter

1:15–16, 124
2:9, 163
2:17, 48
3:9, 48
3:21, 162
4:9, 117
4:11, 43
4:13, 70
5:5, 62

2 Peter

1:5–6, 124
1:21, 162

1 John

3:1, 139
4:18, 77

Revelation

1:8, 161
2:7, 66
3:22, 162
4:8, 162
4:11, 161, 163
7:9, 162
10:6, 161
21:1–5, 162
21:22–22:5, 162

Made in the USA
Middletown, DE
21 July 2023

35458651R00109